Unbroken

Unbroken

FRANK STANFIELD

Kingstone Publishing

Unbroken

Copyright © 2011
Frank Stanfield

Cover illustration by Mona Gambetta
Interior Design by BookMasters

Scripture taken from *The Message*. Copyright 1993, 1994, 1995, 1996, 2000, 2001, 2002. Used by permission of NavPress Publishing Group.

Scripture taken from the New King James Version. Copyright © 1982 by Thomas Nelson, Inc. Used by permission. All rights reserved.

Published by Kingstone Publishing
Kingstone Media Group
P.O. Box 491600
Leesburg, FL 34749-1600

www.KingstoneMedia.com

Printed in the United States of America by
Kingstone Media Group

Library of Congress Cataloguing-in-Publication information is on file.

ISBN 978-1-61328-017-1

Dedicated

...to the memory of Jamilya and Jasmine

Foreword

Dorothy Lewis made a huge impression on me before I ever met her. She had been mercilessly carjacked, raped, shot and left for dead and her two young daughters shot to death in a highly publicized homicide case. But it wasn't just the fact that she survived the brutal attack by two young men that impressed me. It was the fact that she remained strong—her faith in God unbroken—that really set her apart.

I was a longtime newspaper editor and reporter when Dorothy and her children were attacked in 1993. At the time, I was mostly covering local government and some police news for *The Orlando Sentinel,* but I would soon become a court reporter in the paper's Lake County bureau, just north of Orlando. Over the years I would see two kinds of crime victims and their families: Those who were angry and bitter and those who were not. It is easy to understand why someone would be bitter. After all, they have lost a loved one or seen one suffer, and the court system can be a confusing, frustrating place, seemingly loaded up on the side of the defendant's scale of justice. But that bitterness can eat a hole in the soul and attack a person's physical and mental health. I have seen it many times.

But even in cases where there was Christian forgiveness and calm, Dorothy stood out. She seemed to possess an unreal kind of peace—not from tranquilizers (I've seen pharmaceutical calmness)—but the kind of peace that can only come from the Holy Spirit.

"How can you do this?" people would ask her. "You must be so strong."

But Dorothy would set them straight. "I'm not a strong person," she would tell them. "God has given me strength."

No false humility here. She's just being honest. She talks in this book about the struggles, including whether to ask God the "why?" question, kicking herself for not doing more (in her mind) to protect her children, and the fight to overcome her wounds, both mental and physical.

Her faith, already strong, has been strengthened, and she has since shared it with many others. That is the reason that now, after all this time, she wants to tell her story in this book. It is an amazing story, and it doesn't end with merely surviving a hell-on-earth ordeal.

How else could you characterize the crime? As Dorothy was being abducted at gunpoint with her two children, she was praying aloud when she heard the most blood-curdling words imaginable.

"I was just …. calling Jesus' name and the guy that was driving, he said: 'Well, you can stop calling Jesus, 'cause Jesus isn't doing this. This is Satan doing this.'"

Before ending my career in newspapers I used to say, "You can't make this stuff up," usually after trying to guess what would cause someone to unleash a torrent of murder and mayhem on innocent victims. Even as a somewhat creative thinker and a man who also embraces Christianity, it was hard for me to comprehend what happened to Dorothy and how God has healed her and led her to minister to others. In the end, it's an uplifting, miraculous story about how to continually seek the light, as Jesus put it, in a time of darkness.

Methodology

This is an unusual book in some respects, so it only stands to reason that it has taken some unusual preparation. This book is part biographical, part historical, part true-crime, part theological and part devotional.

I have spent many hours interviewing Dorothy and her family. I have also interviewed many of the law enforcement officers, the trial lawyers and the judge who presided over both trials. I have spent countless hours poring through court records, depositions and press accounts.

Because so many people have compared her to Job in the Bible, I have also studied the great book in the Bible, looked at the writings of others and interviewed a renown Old Testament scholar.

Eric Mitchell, Ph.D., is assistant professor of Old Testament and Archaeology at Southwestern Baptist Theological Seminary in Fort Worth, Texas, acting director of the Charles C. Tandy Archaeology Museum and coauthor of *Old Testament Survey,* with Paul House.

Some readers might be tempted to skip this chapter, thinking that it is just some dry discourse on an ancient, mystifying book in the Old Testament. First, it would be a grave misunderstanding about the Book of Job, because it addresses the often asked question of why bad things happen to good people. Secondly, some very prominent modern writers have also chimed in on the question that everyone asks sooner or later: "Why me?" And lastly, it gives us yet another glimpse into the spiritual journey that Dorothy has embarked upon since this horrible crime took place.

This book also shows the vast contrast between the killers' upbringing and that of Dorothy's family. They all had one thing in common: They didn't have much money. But the difference was that Dorothy's family was relying on the Lord, not mean streets pop culture to get by.

Of course, the greatest treat for readers will be hearing Dorothy, in her own words, describe what it has been like to overcome the horrific results of a forced ride with pure evil. Dorothy takes us beyond the hospital and the counselors to God's prayer-filled throne room and the miraculous "spiritual surgery," as she calls it, that saved her life.

Chapters are packed with her quotes, and three of the chapters are strictly in her own words. First, she talks about "Why I Want to Tell My Story." Second, she writes a chapter called "What the Enemy Meant for Evil, God Meant for Good." And finally, she writes a chapter simply called "On Peace."

Her words, of course, soar through all the chapters, including one of the most enlightening ones of all: "Forgiveness."

Dorothy recently told me that it has been therapeutic for her to write about her journey. Hopefully, it also will be therapeutic for you, the reader, but most of all, it will provide an enlightening glimpse into the love of God.

Acknowledgments

I am deeply indebted to many people for their assistance in turning this dream project into a reality.

One of my key helpers was Eric Mitchell, Ph.D., at Southwestern Baptist Theological Seminary. He not only gave me keen insight into the Book of Job, but took the time to make key editing suggestions.

I would like to thank Circuit Judge Mark Hill for talking about the case, and for allowing me to have access to the court files. Thanks also go to Circuit Judge G. Richard Singletary. Thanks are also in order for the clerks in the Lake County Clerk of the Circuit Court office, who do a wonderful job, as usual.

I appreciate the valuable time given by Assistant State Attorney Bill Gross and Circuit Judge T. Michael Johnson, Chief Assistant Public Defender Bill Stone, Jeffery Pfister, and Circuit Judge Mark Nacke.

Greta Snitkin deserves a special note of thanks for telling it like it is. Eustis Deputy Chief of Police Anthony Robinson also merits special praise for his kindness and insights.

At the risk of forgetting someone, I am also in debt to Pat Kicklighter, former State Attorney investigator, his daughter, Cindy Brown, Florida Department of Law Enforcement investigators Bud Hart, Robert A. O'Connor and David West.

I can never forget the kindness and support of Dorothy's family: her mother, Elsie Thomas, brothers James and Arthur Gene, sisters Margaret, Ozietta, Denese, godmother Emma, Rosalyn Lewis, and Dorothy and Brock's son, Joshua, a kind-hearted future leader, if ever there was one. Special thanks also go out to Hugh III, Nikia and Kristopher for sharing their experiences.

Brock deserves special mention because it was his vision that led this dynamic co-pastor team to Art Ayris at Kingstone Media. I can never say enough about Art's encouragement and kindness in the publication of this book.

Of course, what can you say about my co-author Dorothy? Her courage, faith and witness speak for themselves.

A special thanks also goes to my wife, Jackie, for her patience and encouragement. I could not have completed this book without her.

The greatest praise, of course, goes to our Lord and Savior, Jesus Christ. Or, as Dorothy would say, "To God be the glory."

Why I Want to Tell My Story

I have been asked, "Why do you want to tell your story?"

It's a fair question. After all, not many people have gone through what I have experienced, and if they had, they understandably might not want to recall such a horrible experience, let alone talk about it.

But I would like to tell my story because I know it will help others, and I want God to be glorified.

I was carjacked, raped, shot four times (head, mouth, and leg) and left for dead. When I came to in the hospital, I found out that my two daughters had been shot in the head and were dead.

I wondered what good could come from such a horrific crime. Surprisingly, there were a lot of good things.

The best thing is that many souls were saved, including members of my own family. Unbelievers became believers, and the power of God was manifested in me.

My faith in God is so much stronger. I became a better spokesperson about the love and power of God.

A tall, handsome man found me, and I became his good thing (Proverbs 18:22).

I immediately became a stepmother to three wonderful children. A few years later, I gave birth to an amazing son who has given me so much joy.

Satan meant evil against me, but God meant it for my good. When I look back over my life and think things over, I can truly say that the good things in my life outweigh the bad.

"And we know that all things work together for good to those who love God, to those who are the called according to His purpose" (Romans 8:28 NKJV).

Whenever I give my testimony about the power of God, many people are in awe. People have said to me: "After hearing about all that you have been through, I don't have anything to complain about."

I want people to know that God is good, and He will help you get through any situation, any challenge.

God is not evil and does not cause evil things to happen.

I have been asked the question: "If God is so good, why did He let this happen to you?"

There may be various reasons why God did not stop it. He could have, but He has reasons that we cannot possibly understand. Maybe He was sparing my daughters from something in the future. Maybe the trauma they experienced that night would have affected them very adversely in the future. Maybe He needed them more.

Perhaps the best way that I can answer this question is to refer to Job in the Bible.

In Job, Satan is looking for ways to test man's loyalty to God when God says, "Have you considered my servant Job?"

God then allows Satan to inflict physical injuries on Job, kill his family and destroy his property. Job doesn't know why all this is happening. All he knows is that he hasn't done anything to bring it all on himself.

For years people kept saying, "You're like Job!" And I kept saying, "I'm not Job. I don't want to be Job."

But, like Job, I may have been "considered" for this trial. God obviously saw something in me that I didn't see in myself. He knew what I could bear. I'll talk more about this later.

This story may seem hard to believe at certain points, even to those who are aware of the kind of evil that we hear about on TV and in the newspapers. Ironically, one of the two young men who were committing this horrible crime put it into perspective in his own words when I was repeating the name of Jesus in prayer and he said, "This is Satan doing this."

The trial judge would later remark that he was saying it to terrorize his victims.

How can you stand up against this kind of evil?

I'm reminded of the scripture from the Message Bible in 1 Corinthians 10:13, which reads: "No test or temptation that comes your way is beyond the course of what others have had to face. All you need to remember is that God will never let you down; he'll never let you be pushed past your limit; he'll always be there to help you come through it."

Even though I was faced with a mother's worst nightmare, He never left me, and God is still carrying me through it. The word of God says, "We often suffer, but we are never crushed. Even when we don't know what to do, we never give up. In times of trouble, God is with us, and when we are knocked down, we get up again" (2 Corinthians 4:8-9 CEV).

God is faithful. He has proven Himself in my life so many times.

I want to tell my story to show that God is real and that God is loving. And I want to share with you the fact that He will change your life and bring hope and purpose to you, if you let Him.

CHAPTER 1

Not a Dream

Dorothy Lewis, lying perfectly still in her hospital bed, could hear a man's voice as she struggled to regain consciousness.

"I work with your sister, Margaret," said the doctor.

"My sister doesn't work in Eustis."

"You're not in Eustis, you're in Orlando," the physician replied.

She could then hear the voice of her sister, Margaret Reid. Without opening her eyes she asked the question she had been dreading to ask: "Is this a dream?"

"No," she said.

"Did the girls make it?"

"No."

"They didn't have to hurt my babies," Dorothy said. She then turned her head away from Margaret and didn't say anything else for about four hours. When she did speak again, she asked another question. "Where are my babies? Margaret, where are my babies?"

"Dorothy!" exclaimed Margaret, afraid that Dorothy had forgotten what she had told her earlier.

"I know you said that they didn't make it. I want to know who has their bodies," Dorothy replied.

"Cunningham," Margaret said, referring to a local funeral home.

Too grief stricken to even reply in words, Dorothy made a kind of mournful clucking sound.

It was then that Margaret asked a silent, prayerful question: "God, how much can this girl take?"

It was a tough but fair question. Dorothy wasn't in a "dream" but in a horrible situation worse than any nightmare imaginable.

The 35-year-old widow had gone to the grocery store on Saturday night to pick up a few things she needed to make a salad for a church luncheon the next day. It was late and normally she liked to be home before dark.

Accompanying her on this seemingly routine mission were her daughters, Jamilya, 7, and Jasmine, 3.

Eustis, Florida, on January 30, 1993, was and still is a small town north of Orlando. Most people were thinking about going to church the next day, or watching the Super Bowl XXVII game between the Dallas Cowboys and Buffalo Bills—anything but murder.

But when Dorothy and her daughters walked out of the store that night, they were walking into a deadly trap.

They would be carjacked by 18-year-old Richard Henyard and 14-year-old Alfonza Smalls, Jr., and taken to an isolated dirt road where Dorothy would be raped, shot and left for dead and her children murdered in one of the most heinous crimes in the history of Central Florida.

Dorothy's close-knit family, reeling from the shock of losing the two little girls, worried about Dorothy. She had been shot four times at close range, including a round that knocked out teeth when it burrowed its way to the back of her mouth, and a shot so close to the middle of her forehead that it left a powder burn.

Would there be brain injury, permanent disfigurement or psychological damage, the family wondered? And what about the psychological horror of losing her children? She was so close to her daughters that people often remarked that it seemed she never went anywhere without them.

Dorothy's family came from humble surroundings but her five siblings had grown up harboring lofty dreams of wanting to be famous and making a lot of money. Dorothy had just one goal, however. "I wanted to be a good wife for my husband and a good mother."

It wasn't just something that Dorothy casually mentioned, said her sister, Margaret Reid-Lewis.

"Dorothy had always told me, 'If something happens to my babies you might as well lock me up.'"

"I told her God will not let that happen."

Yet, on a cold night, on a desolate dirt road, the unthinkable did happen.

The blow came just three years after Dorothy's 31-year-old husband died unexpectedly of meningitis. As an engineer with a defense contractor, Lewis had been a good provider and a good father to his daughters when he suddenly succumbed to the fatal illness.

And now, this.

"Dorothy was just beginning to be happy again," said her mother, Elsie Thomas.

No Hint of Trouble

No one could have imagined the tragedy in the hours leading up to the attack, certainly not Dorothy.

"I was naive about a lot of things," she said later. "I didn't look for the worst in people."

Lake County had long been rural, and even its towns were small. Before being clobbered by devastating freezes in the 1980s, the county was known for its thousands of acres of orange and grapefruit trees, and its many lakes. The cold weather destroyed the trees, turning once paradise-looking groves into miles of dead sticks.

Later, many groves were bulldozed and transformed into housing developments, turning large portions of the county into a bedroom community for Orlando or retirement neighborhoods.

But after being attacked at random, it would be the last time Dorothy would take people at face value, and a lot of residents would remark that it would also change the way they viewed their community.

"That morning I tried my hands at making homemade biscuits," Dorothy recalls. "They were kind of hard, but the girls and I put syrup on them and we ate them like they were good."

A neighbor, whose son had borrowed her late husband's small pickup truck, brought it back around 8:30 a.m.

"After breakfast, Jasmine's babysitter stopped by and the girls took a few minutes to show off their new bikes. Then we got dressed to go to a funeral service which was being held in the small town of Summerfield."

There was a series of phone calls to the busy household that morning. Margaret had talked to Dorothy three times on the phone by 10:30 a.m.

"We were laughing about silly things," said Margaret, who would spend the rest of the day studying for her registered nurse boards scheduled for that coming Tuesday.

Dorothy and the girls left for the drive to Summerfield in neighboring Marion County. Her goal was to get to the funeral home around "twoish," she said.

"At the end of the service, Jamilya and Jasmine wanted to go to my mom's house in Ocklawaha. When I told them they could ride with my mom, Jasmine quickly took off running across the street without looking. She knew better than that. It scared me so bad! I told her not to ever do that again. The girls rode home with mom, and I stayed behind to visit with some of the elderly members of the church who lived in Summerfield and Weirsdale.

"It was getting late in the evening so I went to my mom's house to get the girls and to exchange cars. My mom was getting ready to drive to Tennessee early the next morning to attend the funeral of her brother's wife, and I wanted her to take my 1990 Toyota Camry because it had just been serviced and she wouldn't have any mechanical problems on the road. As mom was helping me get my items out of my car and putting them into her 1989 Chrysler Fifth Avenue, I asked her to give me the lyrics to 'God Will Take Care of You.'"

Elsie Thomas, an accomplished singer, pulled the song out of her memory for Dorothy and the two sang:

"Be not dismayed what e'er be tide
God will take care of you
Beneath His wings of love abide
God will take care of you."

"For some reason I could not get that song out of my mind. I sang that song all the way back to Eustis. It was that song that helped me get through what was about to happen later on."

"The girls kept playing in the house," Thomas said. "Dorothy said, 'Give Granny a hug,' and they put all their hugs on me. Nobody had a clue it would be the last time."

"When the girls and I got home, it was dark, it was around 7:40 p.m. As a single parent, I tried to get home before dark, and not leave my house after dark."

She sat down to do some homework. She was studying to earn a bachelor's degree in education so she could become a teacher. She talked for about an hour on the phone with a friend.

"The girls got their showers and put on their pajamas. Later, I remembered that the next day was the fifth Sunday of the month and I had to bring in a covered dish. I knew everyone enjoyed my strawberry pretzel salad, but I was missing a couple of ingredients.

"I told the girls to find clothes to put on so that we could go to the store while I called Emmalene March, my godmom, who lives in Ocala."

5

It was around 9:30 p.m.

"I told Emma where I was going, and I told her that Jamilya was imitating the way she sticks out her lips. Then Jamilya started talking with Emma. We were all laughing and Emma said, 'I'm not going to talk to you anymore.'"

It turned out to be true. The next time Emma would see the girls would be in the morgue.

CHAPTER 2

"This Is Satan Doing This"

It only took Dorothy about five minutes to drive to the Winn-Dixie in Eustis. The parking lot was dimly lit in some areas but it seemed to her to be OK where she parked her car, close to the front.

Later, a wrongful death suit she filed against the store and the property owners on February 22, 1994, stated that "the Winn-Dixie parking lot was open to the public and was dark, inadequately lit, unguarded, and without any security whatsoever."

Winn-Dixie insisted in its answer that it was not responsible for the parking lot. It was the property owner's fault.

But Dorothy's lawyers cited remarks by a Winn-Dixie co-store manager saying that he "patrols the parking lot at night at least every 30 minutes," and that he was looking out for people who appeared to be "up to no good." If requested, courtesy clerks will accompany customers to the parking lot, he said.

There was an ongoing security issue, and the store didn't tell the property owner about it, the suit said.

"The evidence discloses without controversy, that over 83 percent of the lights at the northern entrance of Winn-Dixie were out on the night in question. Winn-Dixie was aware of this problem, but instead of simply fixing the lights, engaged in a letter-writing campaign with the landlord about who was going to replace 10 burned out fluorescent bulbs," the suit said.

Even more alarming, the suit alleged, two young men, Richard Henyard and Alfonza Smalls, had entered the store around 9:30 p.m.

"The presence of Henyard and Smalls in the store was so menacing that one of the Winn-Dixie employees … was so nervous that she asked the co-manager … to come to her station and be there because she was concerned for her own safety…."

The co-manager "obliged" the employee, the suit said, "but took no steps to protect Ms. Lewis."

The employee that had felt threatened didn't even know about a policy of escorting customers to their cars, the suit added.

Henyard and Smalls took up a position at the front of the door within view of the Winn-Dixie employees, the suit said.

The suit said that Smalls had previously been arrested in the store on a shoplifting charge and a trespass warning had been issued against him. The assistant manager who had been on duty when that occurred was working the night of January 30 "and never did anything to cause Smalls to be removed from the premises…. Neither did anyone else."

The co-manager who stood by the frightened clerk would say in a sworn statement that he had not seen the two outside the store at 10 p.m. In fact, he said the ones he had seen were not Henyard and Smalls.

There were other problems, the suit said, including a spike in shoplifting after dark, which is why the store reportedly locked its doors on the south end of the building.

"This forced customers to use the dimly lit north entrance where Henyard and Smalls were waiting."

The suit quoted the co-manager, who described the lighting as "not real good," "noticeably dark," and "nowhere near what it ought to be."

It alleged that only two out of 12 bulbs were burning.

"This lighting had been out anywhere from one to several weeks. Even though Winn-Dixie knew the bulbs were out, Winn-Dixie took no steps to change them."

Then, in an unusual display of emotion for a lawsuit, Dorothy's lawyer L. Edward McClellan, Jr., of Ocala, again quoted the co-manager saying he would have hired security for the parking lot "only if events were bad enough."

"Upon being asked if the Lewis incident had occurred six months previously whether he would have ordered outside security, he testified that it would have to be continuous—it would have to happen all the time before he would order outside security. One such incident is not enough, it needs to be continuous and, in fact, '… if [a Lewis type incident] happened five times, yes, I would know that I would need to get some security in that parking lot.'"

"Five times!" McClellan wrote. "Four more ladies will be raped and shot and eight more children would have to die before Winn-Dixie does anything. In the face of all this… he states, 'We take care of our customers.' They sure do."

The suit would later be settled out of court. Typically, defendants in such settlements do not admit to liability, and terms are not disclosed.

Winn-Dixie later moved out of the shopping center and built a new store.

Dorothy knew nothing about any alleged security issues when she went to the store that night. Nor did she know a customer by the name of Lynnette Tschida, who just missed being a victim herself.

Tschida, a regular customer, had been warned by a store employee never to go into the parking lot without an escort, according to the suit. "Bad things happen in this parking lot," the unnamed worker said.

But on January 30, just minutes before Henyard and Smalls struck, Tschida, ignoring the warning, narrowly avoided being the victim of the horror that awaited Dorothy and the girls.

Tschida said in her sworn deposition that she had clocked out at her job at a nearby Elks Lodge at 9:56 p.m., after calling her husband and telling him she was going to the Winn-Dixie.

She said she drove her 1985 Pontiac station wagon up near the front door and watched as a couple with a baby tried to get into the store through a door on the south end of the store near a drugstore. It was the door that was locked after dark.

"When I parked the car, I noticed two people sitting on the bench beside the open door," she said, referring to the other end of the store.

"They didn't say anything. They just stared at everybody going in."

The two had their legs stretched out.

"You almost had to step over them to get in."

Asked if there was anything disconcerting about their behavior, she thought for a moment, then said: "They never spoke to each other."

She followed the couple with the baby into the store, went to the deli section and picked up a container of macaroni salad, a slice of cheesecake and some popcorn that her husband had asked her to pick up.

The clerks opened an express lane. She went through and waved at the manager. She knew him because she shopped at the store each week.

Something was bothering her, however.

"It hadn't felt right going in," she said.

"…I put my bag over my arm so that it wouldn't be in my hand. I put my purse over my arm so that nobody could take it. They would have to jerk my arm off. And I had an alarm that my husband bought me, I took that and had it in both hands ready to use it if I needed to," she said.

Lawyers questioning her for her deposition were curious. What was it that made the hackles go up on the back of her neck, they wondered?

"Woman's intu...I mean, it just didn't feel right. It did not feel right. But there wasn't anything, I mean, it didn't feel right to me."

She said the two young men stood up as soon she walked out the door. One walked in front of her, the other fell back.

"I was afraid to turn around and turn my back on the person in front of me, and I still kept trying to think, 'Oh, this is nothing. They're looking for their ride. You're paranoid.'"

Despite avoiding eye contact, she noticed what the younger of the two was wearing: baggy green, long shorts, and a darker, solid color jacket.

He walked past her car to a pickup truck that was parked next to her car.

He had his hands in his pockets. He didn't say anything. Meantime, she was keenly aware that the other menacing figure was behind her.

She put the alarm over her shoulder and showed it. "They knew I had something in my hand," she said.

"I walked around my car, opened my door, threw everything on the seat, jumped in on top of it and shut the door and locked them [doors]."

She had to lock the driver's side door manually because the lock mechanism was broken, but when she flipped the door lock switch, the sound was audible outside the car, she said.

The one who had stood near her car began walking back toward the store.

Relieved that the imminent threat seemed to be over, she opened the cheesecake container and nervously took a few bites. She drove up to another storefront, removed the packages from beneath her and left.

She said she did not call police.

"I didn't because I thought the worst that was going to happen was they would have taken my purse had they gotten a chance."

Dorothy would not be as fortunate as Tschida.

She had scarcely noticed the shadowy figures on the bench.

"I didn't pay that much attention. I got the girls out of the car and went in the store," she told a prosecutor in a taped statement three months after the incident.

Within 15 minutes she found what she was looking for: pretzels, strawberries, gelatin and whipped topping. She wrote a check for $12.17 and walked out the door. It was 10:15 p.m.

She unlocked and opened the passenger door, put the girls in the front seat and lifted the grocery bag over the seat and put it on the backseat. Since it was her mother's car, there were no child restraint seats in the vehicle.

"When I got the girls in the car and locked and closed their door I looked up and saw this guy just sort of standing off and he was looking in my direction," she said.

"Why is that guy looking at me?" she wondered.

"He started to walk toward me as I was walking around the trunk to get in on my side of the car. As I was up to about to the rear of the driver's door [it had not yet been unlocked] he showed me the gun [by lifting his shirt] and said, 'Get in the car and don't say a word.'

"There's another guy that was over on the sidewalk and he looked at that guy and said, 'Hey man, this is the one.'

"So, I asked the guy, 'Well, can I get my babies out of the front seat? Can they sit back with me? And he said, 'Yes.'"

She described the one with the gun as "the younger one," a man she would later identify in a police lineup as Smalls, who went by the nickname "Junior," and sometimes was called "Alfonso." He was only 14, though very large for his age. The other carjacker would turn out to be Richard Henyard, 18, who would be the driver.

"I asked him if they would just take the car and let us go and the younger one said, 'No, we can't do that, but if you just do what we tell you to do, you won't get hurt.'"

Dorothy has replayed this scene in her mind many, many times. At first, she blamed herself for not doing more. Today, she still wishes she could have done something different, though she has come to understand that such thinking is not only counterproductive, but self-destructive. Still, she is sensitive about the topic, in part, because some people have had the gall to question her judgment.

"I know what you're probably thinking," she said recently. "If all he did was show you the gun, why didn't you just run away or scream, or push him or something? Trust me, I have asked myself all of those questions and more. I didn't do any of those things because my babies were in the car. I thought that I could protect them better if I was with them. I thought if I ran away, the girls would get out of the car, and those guys would hurt them. I was told, 'Just do what I tell you to do and no one will get hurt.'"

As the car pulled out of the parking lot, Dorothy said Henyard asked her, "Where you turn the headlights on?"

"I'm not sure, this isn't my car," she replied, and told him approximately where the controls were. "And he turned on the wipers instead."

The two kidnappers began arguing about which direction they should go, with Smalls at one point saying, "Well, man, if you go that way it's a dead end."

Dorothy was sitting in the middle of the backseat, with the girls on either side of her.

"They started crying and Smalls began cursing and telling the girls to 'shut up.'

"I said, 'Well, they're scared.' And he said, 'I don't care, you make them shut … up,' cursing again.

"I was able to get the girls quiet by holding them and saying, 'It's OK.'"

She also said, "Girls, you know, just be quiet. Try to be quiet." "And I just, you know, tried to comfort them."

She then came up with a desperate plan.

"As we were being driven out of the parking lot, I was hoping the car would stop or slow down enough so that the girls and I could jump out. Since we were sitting so close together, I thought that we could all jump together. I told Jamilya, 'When I tell you to jump, you jump, OK?' She said, 'OK.'"

When the car suddenly swerved to make a corner Dorothy's hand flew off the door handle, making a loud noise as it happened.

"Get your hand off that door," he said.

"My hand's not on the door," she replied.

"Doing that kind of stuff, that's going to make me hurt you," the gunman said.

"Of course I said my hand wasn't on the door, because at that particular point, it wasn't. So I wasn't lying about that. When that plan failed, I began to pay attention to the street signs so we could find our way back home. I remember seeing Wall Street; there were other streets but I don't remember them."

It was then that she recalled the most chilling statement made by the abductors on that terrifying night.

"I was just … just saying, 'Jesus, Jesus, Jesus, Jesus, Jesus,' you know, just calling Jesus' name, and the guy that was driving, he said, 'Well, you can stop calling Jesus, 'cause Jesus isn't doing this. This is Satan doing this.'"

The two kidnappers continued to talk about where they were going. At one point, Dorothy thought she heard one of them say something about a park. Soon, she noticed the car was headed down a dark, unpaved country road called Hicks Ditch Road. The road, which is paved now, eventually joined a paved road called Getford Road. It seemed to her that the driver had stopped in the middle of the unpaved road, but in fact, he had pulled off to one side onto an area of the pastureland near a fence where a gate would later be installed.

There were no other cars in sight.

The prosecutor asked: "During this time frame, you must have been anxious to know what these guys intended. Did you ask them at any point, as you're driving along, 'What do you intend to do to us, are you going to hurt us?' Anything along those lines?"

"No… I… I… didn't ask," she said.

"They both got out of the car. The older guy opened my door," she said. He ordered her to get out of the car, so she crawled over Jamilya and got out.

"At this point my emotions seem to be numb, as though I had no feelings at all, like, 'this is so not happening.'"

Both of them took her to the rear of the car where Henyard leaned her up against the trunk of the car, removed her undergarments, called her "a b…" as Dorothy put it, and ordered her to pretend like she was enjoying being raped. Instead, she begged him to stop, adding: "Please don't do this in front of the girls."

"He said, 'Shut up b— and act like you like it.' I didn't know how to act like I liked it, so I said: 'Well it has been a long time for me.'

"The younger guy, he had taken the gun out and put it on the trunk of the car, OK, 'cause he was getting himself ready to do his thing, and he was telling the older guy, 'Hurry up, man, hurry up so I can do it.' When I could see out of the corner of my eye that the gun was on the trunk, I reached for it and the younger guy grabbed it and he says, 'You're not getting this gun b….' That's when he called… started calling me names."

Smalls put the gun down on the ground. "He didn't put it back on the car," she said.

Henyard then picked up the gun. "He was holding the gun while the younger guy raped me."

Smalls then finished his assault.

"The older guy pulls me off the car and he says, 'Go sit on the grass,' (about 3 or 4 feet away) and I said, 'You promised you wouldn't hurt us if … if I did what you wanted me to do.' And then he pushed me on the grass and shot me in the left leg."

The .22-caliber shell went into her knee and came out a few inches away from the entrance wound.

"And then he started coming like closer toward me aiming the gun and that's when I started fighting back and I just remember just fighting, look like all three of us you know, was fighting and I don't remember any more shots," she said, later describing her battle as "swinging like a wildcat."

She remembers thinking, "Somebody is going to get hurt."

"Those are the last words I remember thinking before being shot again."

Henyard and Smalls rolled her into some high grass, got in the car and drove off.

"My next recollection is walking on a dark dirt road with my bare feet," Dorothy said. "At this point I don't know the time of day or how long I've been walking. I'm not even aware of the extent of my injuries. When I realized that I was up and walking, I felt it very important to hide from the headlights of any type of vehicle because I thought those guys were coming back to get me.

"I'm still not sure as to why I was thinking that way. I now know that if I had not hidden, I would have received help much sooner," she said.

She believes she hid three times after seeing headlights. As it turns out, Dorothy may have had a good reason to hide every time a car passed.

Henyard would later claim in a statement to investigators that he and Smalls returned to the site after the children were taken from the car a short distance away and shot to death.

Q: "After … after he [Smalls] shot the kids and dumped them over the fence, did you pass by where you had shot her again?"

A: "Uh-huh."

Q: "Did you see her?"

A: "He asked me was she dead. Yes, sir, I knew she was alive. The lady was not dead."

Because Henyard's statement was riddled with lies, it is impossible to tell if he was telling the truth in this instance. However, the fact that he even thought about it gives credence to Dorothy's fearful idea that the pair might have wanted to return to finish her off.

Of course, it is nothing short of a miracle that she was alive, let alone walking, and that she could have any coherent thoughts at all. Despite being in shock, losing a great deal of blood and suffering gunshot wounds to her head, she was still thinking things through.

"I was looking for a house with an outside light on, and a car because I thought it would be a safe place," she said.

Later, she would think about her search for light and say: "I'm reminded of a passage in the scriptures, in John 9:5, that says 'Jesus is the light of the world.' Maybe I thought Jesus wasn't with me, and I had to find Him to be safe.

"I can remember seeing houses and I was looking for a home that had a light on the outside and a light on in the inside. And I can remember going to one house, knocking on the door and I didn't get an answer, so I kept walking…"

If anyone was in the first home they may have been too frightened to come to the door. Not too long before Dorothy and her family was attacked, there had been another homicide in the low-income neighborhood.

"I saw another house that had a light on the outside and a light on in the inside and I can remember trying to pay close attention to the cars that was under the carport to make sure it wasn't my mom's car, 'cause at this point I don't know where I am, just walking, so I go to the second house and I knock on the door……

"A man's voice from the other side of the door said, 'Yes?' I said, 'My name is Dorothy Lewis. I've been shot and raped; and those boys still have my babies. I need help.'

"Then I leaned up against the wall and let my body slide down to the floor where the hedges were hiding me. The man's voice from the other side of the door said, 'Dorothy, are you still there?' I said, 'Yes.'

"He said, 'Help is on the way.' Shortly after that, I saw blue lights coming toward me."

CHAPTER 3

"Why Can't I Cry?"

Shy, quiet, unassuming, meek Dorothy, battered, bruised, shot and left for dead, had cheated death. Described by her muscular, fierce-looking brother, Arthur Gene Reid, as "a tough little girl," Dorothy was indeed a fighter, though not just for her own life. She struggled to find help for her children in case they were still alive, walking for hours (no one is sure how long she was unconscious) along the darkened road and jumping behind trees when cars drove by.

One of the cars was a police car, dispatched to the desolate area at 1:23 a.m. after an anonymous caller reported seeing a bloody woman in a white dress staggering along the road. Officer John McKimmey never found her, and would kick himself later for not flashing the car's blue lights, said Assistant State Attorney Bill Gross.

But he did something else, Gross noted, something "very astute." After his shift ended at 2 a.m., McKimmey hung around the police department for awhile. And when it became clear just how serious the case was, he remembered seeing a child's dark jacket along the side of the road. He was looking for an injured woman, so he didn't pick it up, but he would remember where he found it and it would lead to the discovery of the children's bodies.

Police started receiving calls around 4:30 a.m. about a badly injured woman knocking on doors and asking for help.

Police and rescue workers who talked to Dorothy as she was being taken to an area where she could be airlifted to a hospital at 5 a.m., were puzzled when they realized she had been with her two young daughters during the attack. They asked her where the girls were.

"They're with their father," she said.

"Their father?" officers wondered. Anthony Robinson, now deputy chief of police in Eustis, didn't know Dorothy or her family at that time and wondered if she was a single parent or if there was a custody issue. Contact with her family soon cleared up the mystery: The girls' father had been dead for three years.

"She must've known, subconsciously," Robinson said.

She also gave a description of her attackers, saying they still had the girls, and gave officers information about her mother, so that they could contact her.

Dorothy was too weak from her wounds to know it, but she would soon be in the arms of one of the finest air rescue teams in the country.

Air Care, of Orlando Regional Medical Center, often makes the difference between life and death in the "golden hour" of trauma.

At least one of their pilots had flown into Hamburger Hill under fire in Vietnam. Now, that pilot or another experienced pilot was headed for the ball field at a nearby middle school where an ambulance, firefighters and police officers were shining their vehicle's headlights onto the makeshift landing zone.

The pilot calls out for the crew, including an onboard trauma flight nurse, to look out for power lines and tree limbs as the chopper begins its descent.

Sometimes it's a "hot" landing, where the pilot keeps the rotors turning for a quick takeoff. Other times, the air crew stabilizes the patient in various ways before loading up and taking off.

It would take awhile for it all to sink in with Dorothy's family. For one thing, the story they were getting was garbled, either intentionally or accidentally, which did not help matters.

Dorothy's mother, Elsie, called Margaret between 4 and 5 a.m., saying that she had received a call from police saying that Dorothy had been "in an accident." Margaret, who had gone to bed with a migraine-like headache, couldn't make sense of it.

"Dorothy wouldn't go to the store this time of morning," she told her mother.

"And Margaret, the girls were not with her," Elsie said.

Both women wondered if the girls had spent the night at godmother Emma's house. Elsie said she would check.

"They've taken her to Orlando," Elsie said of Dorothy, then added the words Margaret did not want to hear: "They think Dorothy is in bad shape."

Margaret jumped into action, driving to ORMC, and calling Dr. Owen Fraser, a physician she worked with at the hospital.

Instead of being allowed to see her sister, Margaret—described by Dorothy as a "strong black woman"—found frustrating roadblocks and misinformation.

"You'd better get over here and take me to her before I start acting up," she told Fraser.

Not only was Margaret fortunate enough to have Fraser on her side, but another doctor she also knew, Dr. Lou Harold II.

Dorothy and her family were lucky in another regard, too. A sex crimes detective from Orange County happened to be in the emergency room when Dorothy came in and realized Dorothy would need a victim advocate.

"I don't think Lake County has anybody here, can you come?" she asked Greta Snitkin.

Snitkin later worked for the U.S. State Department, notifying foreign consulates when one of their citizens runs afoul of the law, suffers serious injury or dies while visiting one of Central Florida's many tourist attractions. But in 1993, she had been working for the

Orange County Sheriff's Office for four years, had already seen a life-time of trauma, and was used to late-night calls for help.

A hospital chaplain had already repeated the accident story to a skeptical Margaret by the time Snitkin arrived. The former court clerk and daughter of a cop, who was in her 40s, was having no part of anyone telling fairy tales to a distraught family member.

"Dorothy's been carjacked, raped, shot and they don't know where the babies are," Snitkin frankly told Margaret.

Snitkin then diplomatically told Margaret that she didn't know why the chaplain was telling her that Dorothy had been in an accident. But she took the chaplain aside and told him: "Don't you ever lie to a victim of a crime—ever, ever, ever." The chaplain is no longer working at the hospital, Snitkin said.

Snitkin also remembers that a 23-year-old police officer was assigned to guard Dorothy at the hospital.

"He was out of his element," Snitkin said. "I think the whole world was out of its element in that case."

Actually, not everyone was out of place.

Dr. Fraser, besides being an excellent doctor for Dorothy, was also able to calm Margaret down.

"They know what they're doing," he said of the team at the Level One trauma center. "Let them do their job."

The family, meanwhile, was learning of the crime in bits and pieces.

Her sister Ozietta Reid practiced a daily ritual in those days, by making a series of phone calls, first to her mother, then Dorothy and Margaret. But she could not reach anyone that morning.

"There were no cell phones back then," she said.

Eventually she began learning details of the crime from Margaret's husband, Al, and her sister, Denese Reid-Ferguson, including the fact that the girls were missing.

"I was thinking the girls had been left somewhere and it was just a matter of time before they would be found and that they would be OK," Ozietta said.

"Never in my wildest imagination did I think that they would be taken from us," she said.

It was unthinkable for another reason, too. In 1989, Ozietta was pregnant with her son, A.J., Margaret was pregnant with her daughter, Aljahra, and Dorothy was pregnant with Jasmine—all at the same time. Her brother James Reid's wife was pregnant with a daughter, too.

Denese fell apart.

"I was crying and falling out, I thought, maybe it's a mistake."

She left her home in the Shores area of Ocala, got into her car and drove to Margaret's house to get the latest details from Margaret's husband. Margaret was getting the inside story and passing details along to Al.

When she started grasping the full horror, she said, "I basically just fell down. I thought, 'No way is this happening to us.'"

It didn't get much better once she arrived at the hospital.

"It was awful, I just had to digest everything."

Even though Denese had made it to the hospital, she was not up to seeing her sister.

"You had to get yourself up mentally to see her. You had to be strong. You couldn't go in wild or with a look on your face."

The fact that the girls had been slain was especially crushing.

Denese's son, Arsenio, and Jamilya were very close. She had last seen Jamilya right before Christmas at her son's birthday party. The two always celebrated each other's birthdays together.

Because Dorothy always kept the girls by her side, "I just had to beg her to let her stay with me," Denese said.

"She could shout, dance, do anything," she said of Jamilya. For some reason she didn't want to dance this time—at first.

"I said, 'I'll love you forever if you dance with me.' It was so cute."

The murders changed everything.

"After that, I was unable to have a birthday party for him. They were so close. I deprived him all those years because I just couldn't deal with it."

Rosalyn Lewis, the mother of Dorothy's late husband, scrambled to gather her family together in New Jersey and hurry to Florida as soon as she heard the news.

"All I knew was that Dorothy was shot and the girls had passed away," she said.

And in her limited experience with such things, she said she had only one thought: "If anyone gets shot, they're not expected to live."

She was relieved when she saw Dorothy in the hospital, however.

"As horrible as it was I was glad to see her."

Her first thought was wondering about what she thought was a giant pimple in the middle of her forehead, not realizing initially that it was a bullet hole.

"How do you get shot in the head and not die?" Rosalyn wondered.

"The first thing she said was, 'I'm sorry about the girls,'" Lewis said.

"I said, 'Honey, you can't do nothing about that. I'm just glad you're here.'"

Injuries

Harold, as the general surgeon attending on call for trauma, knows a lot about gunshot wounds, but even he probably had to wonder how Dorothy was not only still alive but conscious.

One bullet had pierced her upper lip a little to the left and entered her mouth where it slammed into her left central incisor, knocking out teeth in its path. The bullet came out of the hard pallet of her mouth and went down the tongue, apparently a downward shot, he surmised. It went into the base of the tongue. From there it hit the back of her throat near the base of her spine, though not injuring that crucial part of the body.

One bullet went in and out of her leg near her knee. Another grazed the left side of her neck.

But the most fearsome wound was the one just above the bridge of her nose between her eyes. "I've said, if you got a measuring tape or calipers or whatever you want to use, you couldn't have been any closer to the middle of her forehead," Henyard's defense attorney, T. Michael Johnson, remarked years later about her miraculous recovery.

Somehow the bullet, probably because it was a small, high-velocity bullet prone to ricochet, went through the frontal sinus and then under the base of the skull.

The bullet, Harold said, "went obviously outside the cranium and we could see that on X-ray, it just scooted under the base of the skull about halfway back."

After quickly assessing her injuries, he knew that he would not have to perform immediate surgery to save her life.

"After not having to immediately take her into surgery, the next priority was not interfering with investigators," Harold said. "I knew that the clothing had a large amount of blood on it. I did not want to destroy that evidence. I decided we could clearly clean up so investigators could see her and gather evidence."

Realizing that there was not a police photographer immediately available, he scrambled to find a camera and began taking evidence pictures and gave the film to the FDLE.

Pictures taken in the hospital and used as exhibits in the trials appear, at first glance, to be autopsy pictures, and because of the swelling, Dorothy is practically unrecognizable.

Harold especially did not want to do anything to destroy rape evidence, but was frustrated things were taking so long because, "there was some kind of jurisdictional squabble between the Orange and Lake [counties] Medical Examiner's Office."

Despite the fact that Dorothy would not need immediate life-saving surgery, she would have two operations in the week-and-a-half she would first be hospitalized there, including one to repair the protective dura layer around the brain to stop the leakage of spinal fluid. Surgeons "probably obliterated the sinus to make sure she did not get any infection there," he said in a deposition. She would have bullet fragments removed from her mouth and her sinuses, and would have to come back later to have her sinuses reopened. Surgeons also removed bullet fragments from her jaw.

Doctors downgraded her level of consciousness on her chart slightly after noting that one eye was drooping. That was likely because the bullet that hit her between the eyes tracked down the medial wall or the orbit, he said. "In other words, on the right side of the eye socket next to the nose, and caused some fractures in these and some swelling of the eye," he said.

There was also stippling on her face from the gun blasts, indicating the bullets had been fired at point-blank range.

"We also had to worry about what we call compartment syndrome, or bleeding and pressure cutting off circulation in the leg," he told the trial lawyers in a sworn statement.

He said she told him she had been shot in the leg trying to wrestle the gun away from the shooter.

There would be many consultations with many specialists, antibiotics pumped in and evidence collected.

"The first three or four days in the hospital were kind of hazy," she said.

"I thought she was a very large 200-pound black lady," Snitkin said. "It wasn't until a week-and-a-half later that I learned she was 110 pounds. That's how swollen she was."

When Ozietta arrived at the hospital, she found an overflow crowd in the waiting room, including people from other churches that Dorothy knew. People were praying, she said, and doing their best to be supportive.

"I was able to see her," Ozietta said. "It was heart-wrenching, very heart-wrenching to see her laying there. It wasn't Dorothy. I mean, it was Dorothy, but she was swollen, bandages were wrapped around her head. I touched her head and she grimaced, letting me know it was painful."

"It's always something, isn't it Ozie?" Dorothy said.

She couldn't stay long. "It was about all I could take," she said.

Dorothy would later write about some of the continuous painful, physical side effects in a required victim statement for the State Attorney's Office.

"Besides the emotional pain that my family and I endure, I must also bear the physical reminders of this event, reminders which are with me on a daily basis. I now have muscle spasms down the middle of my back, which the doctor does not yet know the cause. For about a month-and-a-half after the abduction, I had to take shots once a week; they have now been reduced to once every two weeks.

"I lost a lot of blood during the time that I was left in the woods. I have numbness in my fingers and neck, which the doctor attributes to the blood loss," she wrote.

"Every time I look into the mirror, I see the bullet mark where I was shot in my forehead, a constant reminder of what happened to my children and me. My entire forehead had to be reconstructed during a partial craniotomy with the placement of metal plates and screws in my head. This required that the top of my head be opened and the skin on the top of my head and forehead be pulled down. Because of the damage to my forehead, some exposed brain tissue had to be reinserted into my skull. It is likely that I will now have arthritis from this. The bullet also damaged one of the nerves in my right eye, damaging the vision in that eye."

Dr. Harold described the process of the frontal craniotomy in matter-of-fact terms in his deposition as repair of the dura tears with grafting.

"The neurosurgeon, you know, goes into the skull and fixes the leak in the membrane and seals the brain off, and then he puts the bone on, and then the ENT [ear, nose and throat] surgeon pulls all the lining out of it and takes a piece of fat and sticks it in there and this thing scars down."

Dorothy also wrote about the loss of teeth, requiring her to wear a partial dental plate, and a wound to her mouth which left a knot on her tongue. She also wrote that she would also have a permanent scar on the left side of her neck from a bullet that grazed her neck.

She also wrote about the loss of taste and smell.

"This exposes me to danger, for example, I am unable to smell fire. It also diminishes a simple pleasure in life that other people take for granted: eating food. I can no longer eat food which I enjoy for the taste; I eat food solely for nourishment. I eat food that I recall enjoying before the abduction. The doctors disagree about the long-term prognosis...."

All of these statements were written for the record seven months after the shootings.

Snitkin was assigned full-time to Dorothy and given unusual authority.

"You tell me when we can interview Dorothy," a detective said. It would be over a week before that interview took place.

On the other hand, it wouldn't be long—mere hours—before the family learned what had happened to the girls.

Even after being told the girls were dead Dorothy had a hard time accepting the fact at first, Emma said.

"They wouldn't let me see Dorothy at first," Emma said. Family members feared that Dorothy would react poorly to seeing her god-mother without the children.

Finally, however, she made the trip from Ocala to Orlando and walked into Dorothy's hospital room.

Dorothy, bandaged, and with one eye covered, started looking around, Emma said.

"I don't see the girls," Dorothy said. "Oh, Jesus, I guess I have to face it now. I don't have the girls."

"We're Going to Fix It"

Defense attorneys would later ask Dr. Harold if Dorothy would have died without treatment of her physical wounds. He said that the in-fection would have been deadly.

Among other issues, Dorothy was told that bullet fragments in her head would have to be removed in the very near future.

"If it ain't broke don't fix it," she said, thinking it would be preferable to leave the fragments inside her body than have to undergo surgery.

"Well, you're broke, and we're going to fix it," the doctor replied.

"After the funerals," she said.

Because she was hospitalized, arrangements for the February 13 funerals were left up to Margaret and other family members. Margaret picked out the Christmas dresses she had bought for the girls for their open casket service. Emma, a hairdresser, did the girls' hair and washed the blood out of Dorothy's.

Family members anxious to see how Dorothy would react wouldn't have to wait long, and she shocked them.

"Blah, Ornery"

The normally easy-going, compliant Dorothy suddenly became "ornery."

"I'm not wearing that," Dorothy said of the dress Margaret had picked out for her, and the family had to call a neighbor to borrow a dress.

"I don't know what to do with you," her mother said.

She was upset when there was a miscommunication about the pickup time for the funeral home limousine, and insisted that she wasn't going to go to the funeral.

And when they did get to the church she saw a gaggle of reporters down the street. After Dorothy vetoed the idea of having reporters inside during the service ("No, just leave me alone!"), the family had asked that no reporters be allowed to attend the service. There was already an overflow crowd. News stories had not only fired up the curious onlookers, but on a positive note, sparked fund drives among teachers, civic clubs and churches to help offset her massive expenses.

"I'm not going in there," Dorothy said after seeing the TV news trucks parked on the street.

The family convinced her to go inside, and Snitkin, after discovering one reporter had gone inside, had that person kicked out. She would end up taking charge of keeping the press at arm's length at the cemetery, too.

"I told the biggest man I could find to get some others and surround the grave site so nobody gets a picture. Nobody got a picture," she said.

"Margaret is a pit bull," Snitkin said. "I'm a Rottweiler. Really, I'm a pussy cat. In my personal life I'm such a patsy. When it comes to victims, I am a Rottweiler."

It wasn't Dorothy's unusual flash of anger—seen by just a handful of close family members—that was the most important barometer of Dorothy's mental health that day.

"I was just kind of blah," Dorothy said, describing a mixture of shock and depression.

But if she was calm on the outside, the inner Dorothy was in turmoil.

"The day of the funeral would be the first time that I had seen Jamilya and Jasmine since that dreadful night. I didn't know how I was going to respond when I saw them. I couldn't see my life going on without them. I thought that I might just drop dead...."

Dorothy, who wrote not only about her physical scars in her victim statement to prosecutors, also wrote about the emotional ones and the sadness she felt.

"These were my children, who had never done anything in life to deserve the horrible deaths which they endured, who did not deserve to be put through the torment and pain that they endured. These were *just children* (her emphasis)," she wrote.

"Even though I am physically young and can have other children, that fact does not lessen the loss that I have suffered. These children were real, live human beings to me, who brought joy into my life and my family's lives. Upon the death of their father several years ago, at least I had the two children that he and I had together. Now, not only is my husband dead, but the two children that he gave me and left with me are also dead. My entire family has been taken away from me and I am left alone," she wrote.

But when the time finally arrived, she was able to walk down the aisle and see her beautiful children for the last time.

"I touched them," she said.

The overflow crowd marveled at her outward composure, but she wasn't comforted by that. In fact, it distressed her even more.

"Why can't I cry?" she asked Snitkin.

"She was so stoic," Snitkin noted.

"I told her, 'When the time comes God will let you cry.'"

"What do I know? I'm just a Jewish grandmother, but it seemed to work."

Snitkin's words, in fact, would eventually come true.

Snitkin was already aware of Dorothy's belief in God and the value that that belief has for healing.

"People who have a good, faith-based life seem to reconstruct quicker," she said.

Even at this moment of indescribable grief, there was still a brightly burning flame of faith for Dorothy as she listened to the comforting words and the music being played at the service, including one song entitled "Jesus, Keep Me Near the Cross."

Some of the music was too slow and too sorrowful for her tastes, however. She motioned an usher to come over and she whispered a request.

"No sad stuff," she said.

CHAPTER 4

Satan's Playhouse

Witnesses would later testify that Henyard had been working up to committing the crime a few days before it occurred. His lawyers would argue that he was destined for it from birth.

One girl said in a sworn statement that she saw Henyard with the gun earlier that weekend.

Ursula Lynette Gathers, a 19-year-old, would say that she had grown up with Henyard and called him "cousin," "because my mom and his godmom are like sisters."

She had seen Henyard that Saturday morning. She was riding in a car with two other girls, including the driver, a young woman by the name of Mona Lisa. One of the girls had a baby in foster care, and they were going to visit the child at the state child protective agency in Tavares. They had brought along a camera. When they stopped, Henyard went inside with the girl. Ursula reached beneath the seat to get the camera, but came up with a gun that Henyard had stashed.

She said he came out of the building, snatched the .22 out of her hand and called her a "dummy" because the gun was loaded. She told him she thought it was a BB gun.

She said he unloaded the weapon, taking out about four or six bullets. And then, in a conversation that boggles the mind but says a lot about the popular culture of the day, she asked if she could get the gun back so she could take some pictures of the handgun, using it as a prop.

"I had it to my head and I had it to Mona's head. I just...."

Henyard's lawyer, T. Michael Johnson, interrupted the deposition questioning by asking: "Why were you all doing that?"

A: "I don't know, because I guess I just wanted some guns in it to make it seem hard."

Q: "I'm sorry?"

A: "To make me seem hard. I wanted to take some with the gun."

Q: "Why do you want to seem hard?"

A: "I don't know, that's how we do now these days."

Q: "What do you mean?"

A: "You know, take a picture with a gun just to make the picture seem right, look right."

Q: "The picture wouldn't be right unless it had a gun in it?"

A: "Or something serious."

Another girl had seen Henyard with another gun.

"He said he wanted to go to a club in Orlando called New Attitude, so he was going to get somebody's car and kill them and put them in the trunk," Shenise Hayes testified.

At one point, the .22-caliber pistol had been kept at Smalls' house. Alfonza told his sister, Tamara, that he was letting Henyard store the gun at their home.

"You can get into trouble holding things for people," she warned.

Once, Henyard pointed the gun at Smalls. "It wasn't serious," said witness Terry Washington. "He was just playing."

Another man, Wilbert Pew, said Henyard had asked him if he wanted him to "go on a little [car] jack with him."

Pew allegedly suggested robbing "a [free] baser" cocaine addict. Henyard nixed that idea, however. "Fiends and rock [cocaine] heads," have little or no money, Henyard remarked.

Anyway, Henyard said, he needed a car so he could drive down to Pahokee in South Florida to see his father. He said he would go "downtown," possibly to the area near a local hospital or the Winn-Dixie to look for a robbery victim.

Plans were a little bit on the fly. Pew said he might go with him to a nearby local club. He agreed to lend Henyard his blue jacket that had a hood on it. The clothing worn that night would later become a key, identifiable piece of evidence linking Henyard to the shootings and implicate a third person as an accessory after the fact.

If one word could sum up the crimes it would be "senseless," Dorothy said. "You want a car? Take the car, don't take us," she said, paraphrasing her remarks to the killers.

And why was a car so important? He said he wanted to drive to South Florida to see his father. He had seen enough of his mother—for a lifetime.

It was because of his mother, Hattie Mae Gamble, that Henyard was an expert on addicts.

His mother was a heavy-duty drinker and marijuana smoker when she was pregnant with him, Henyard's godmother, Jackie Turner, told authorities.

Gamble herself admitted that she had a "very ugly" drinking habit. Gamble drank seven days a week and would drink until she "fell out," Turner said in a sworn statement.

The behavior continued after his birth.

"The house would be full of people and it would be all smoked up," Turner said of Gamble's home. "I asked her why she let people come in her house and do this in front of her kids."

Once, a man came to her house to tell her that Gamble had passed out in a house and men were lined up to have sex with her while she was unconscious. "You're the only one that seems to care about her," the man said. Turner went to the house and rescued her friend.

"Aunt Jackie, I wish you was my mom," Henyard would tell her when he was about 8 or 9.

Apparently he had the same wish when he was 3, said Turner's daughter, Nyoka Wiley, because Ric once walked across town from Hattie's to be with her.

Henyard could never escape Gamble's shadow, however, and would get into fights at school when other kids teased him about his mother having affairs with both men and women. They called her a "bull-dagger," Turner said.

Turner first took Henyard in when he was 10 months old in what would be a back-and-forth existence for the child between her, his father and his mother.

At 15, he was skipping school, was jailed as a juvenile while acting as a lookout in a robbery, refused to go back to school or live with his father, so she said she "put him out," and he went to live with his mother.

He would eventually go back to his father, but his dad's wife of 10 years accused him of stealing.

Henyard called Turner from Pahokee and said he was living in a vacant house and was hungry. Turner told him to go see her ex-husband in that area and ask for money.

The ex-husband refused to give him any money, however, and Henyard ended up being picked up by juvenile authorities.

Turner said in her deposition that her husband left her because of him.

"He [Henyard] was bringing wild boys to the house, drinking...." she said.

Hattie was in jail, so he went to live with his "grandfather," Luther Reed, for a month.

"But he would come to the house every day and I would feed him. He would come to the house, because I told him, you know, I couldn't stand to know that, you know, he be out there on the street, be hungry and have to eat to different people's houses begging for food and things, so I fed him."

It was shortly after this that he came to her house one day and stole her car.

She said that day, he had been drinking. "And I smelled reefer on his breath and I told him, I told him he didn't have to live the pattern of the life that his mother had lived, you know, make something out of his life, go into the service, do anything, just don't start out like that."

He listened quietly, she said, he cried and never talked back to her.

He had his good side, said Wiley, who called him her "godbrother."

"Ric was always doing things to help others," she said in her sworn testimony.

"He's nice, I mean, if you really know Ric, he is a very nice person. He's good, very good with kids. He babysat my kids, my sister's kids. I mean, if you go to my mom's house right now, there is probably like 12 of her grandkids there. It's just his attitude changes, it varies."

She thought that the attitude change might be the result of drinking, though she said she never witnessed it.

After Turner's car was stolen, she took out a warrant for his arrest because she wanted her car back.

In the weeks leading up to the shootings, Wiley said, Henyard stole her young nephew's piggy bank from Turner's home and snuck it out the rear window.

The weekend of the crime, he snuck into Turner's home and stole some food.

Turner didn't just have a soft spot for Ric. She also helped Henyard's older sister, and when she later showed up with a 6-week-old baby, Turner began the unenviable task of helping raise that child until he was between a year and 2 years old. "... and she come and stole him and she carried him back and she kept him a year and she brought him back and I been having him ever since," she said.

Henyard's defense team would describe his father as a hard-working, law-abiding man, but the lawyers said he worked long hours and his wife had no bond with him. Gamble, who never married Henyard's father, had virtually no relationship with Henyard's father.

"He never had a chance," Johnson said of Henyard.

Prosecutor Bill Gross took a much different view. Turner took him to church, provided for his physical needs and taught him right from wrong, she conceded in her answers to the assistant state attorney's questions. During Turner's deposition, Gross asked her how he was acting in jail while awaiting trial.

"The only thing I can say now, the way he is, when I go to visit him, the only thing he talks to me about, is about God.

"I said, 'Now you'll see it.' Because when the pastor was preaching, a lot of times when he was in the church, Ric would be sleeping, or Ric would be playing with the kids or teasing the kids. I told him, I said, 'Sit down and listen to what the preacher is saying. You're going to learn something.'

"And he wouldn't do it. And when I went to the jailhouse and he is talking to me about God, you know, then it's surprising to me. You know, but anyway it's just jailhouse talk."

Ric had a habit of lying to her, Turner said, and she would automatically say, "now tell me the truth."

Gross couldn't resist asking her in her deposition if he had talked about his involvement in the carjacking and shootings.

"Aunt Jackie," he said, "the things that I have been accused of, now, to Miss Lewis, me shooting her, me raping her and everything… I did that. But the children, I didn't shoot those children."

"Do you believe him?" Gross asked.

"I believe he didn't shoot the children."

Gross would get an eyeful of both Henyard's and Smalls' environment while preparing his case against them, but before he even had an inkling of who had committed the crimes, or that it was for sure a double homicide, he would be called by police to come to the narrow, little, red clay Hicks Ditch Road, bordered by pastures, brush and sorrow.

"What Animal Did This?"

Police, at least, had a place to start searching for Jasmine and Jamilya, especially once they determined the spot where Dorothy had been attacked. They also had McKimmey's recollection of where he found the child's jacket. But it was dark and foggy. A small army of searchers walking up and down the road and a pack of tracking dogs were coming up empty.

It wasn't until the sun came up and began burning through the fog that police could see droplets of blood leading off into brush several feet off the road. And it was there, near a barbed wire fence, that police found the bodies. They had been tossed over shrubs about five feet high, Gross said.

Anthony Robinson arrived in time to see a sight unlike any he had ever witnessed among police officers.

"There were guys running down the road, some laying in the road, pounding the dirt, crying, some were just absolutely gone."

Detective Robert "Bud" Hart fell to his knees and became sick.

"[Capt.] Carmine [Aurigemma] had said, 'We've got a double homicide. Go take a look and see what you think,'" Hart recalls.

"We were not used to that level of violence at that time," Robinson said of his small department.

Robinson, who would later say the girls looked like "dressed up dolls," thought about his own daughters, about the same age.

"My thought was, 'What animal did this?'"

The normally good-natured cop also had a flash of anger, and not just at the killers.

"It was a defining moment of why I am in this business," he said. "I wanted to know what kind of God I serve. I thought, 'If God allows this kind of thing, I want no part of it.'"

He said he was especially upset when he later learned of Henyard's "Satan" remark.

"I couldn't deal with that," he said.

It was as if the forces of evil were winning and God was either powerless or didn't care enough to step in and make it right.

As one of the ranking officers however, he had to regain his composure quickly.

"We became more focused, to find out exactly who did this. Those that needed help, we got them out of there. There was no time for us to think about that. We focused on who did it."

Hart was of the same mind.

"I thought, 'They took two beautiful little angels and threw them in the woods like garbage. We'll find these guys by the end of the day.'"

Robinson would fall back on his life's experiences, including that of being raised by a minister.

"If you don't have anything spiritual in your life this job is especially difficult," he said. "This is Satan's playhouse and you've got to learn to deal with this."

But Robinson found that his experience growing up in a church was not enough for this case. The crime would end up being a launching pad for a two-year spiritual journey in search of a God he thought he knew but didn't.

Robinson was 6 when he lost his mother and was moved from Jacksonville to Eustis to be with family.

"I was the most streetwise 6-year-old you would have ever met," he said. At 6, he didn't stray far from home, but he still spent his time on the streets in front of the family home.

When his mother died in 1968 he came to live with an aunt and uncle. The uncle was a pastor.

"All these people going to church all the time… I thought I had stepped off the 'Hee Haw' bus," he said, laughing at the customs and the Southern slow-pace in the rural town in the middle of Florida.

From that point on, he grew up learning about God.

"I believed in God. You don't grow up in a church without believing in God," he said, but adds that he did not have a personal relationship with the Lord.

Things like the concept of being "born again" and "praying in the spirit," as he puts it, were foreign to him.

"I didn't know there was a protocol for prayer," he said.

He said he knew that it was important to pray but didn't know that you could pray for certain things.

As for seeking the Lord, he found out, "the only way is to pray and to seek Him," he said, and refers to the phrase "knocking on the door," which is found in Luke 11:10. That verse says: "For everyone who asks receives; he who seeks finds; and to him who knocks, the door will be opened" (NIV).

In his search for answers, he looked back on his law enforcement cases. As a police officer, of course, he was familiar with fatal accidents and crimes that resulted in the loss of life. But in his observations, the victims usually played a big role in their demise. Not so with Dorothy and the girls.

Eventually, he realized he had been asking the wrong question.

"This was not a case where God allowed this happen," he said. "God is not the author of confusion."

It is, however, a case of God creating opportunities for people to exercise their free will, he realized.

"This was an opportunity for the criminals because the doors were locked [at one end of the store]," he said.

Although Robinson didn't cite the verse, Proverbs 11:27 seems like the perfect scripture for the situation: "He who seeks good finds goodwill, but evil comes to him who searches for it" (NIV).

Robinson's journey eventually led to a different church with a different style of worship.

In the end, it was a case of "right church, wrong pew," he laughed.

And in a twist of fate, or as Robinson refers to it, "God has a sense of humor," Dorothy and his wife became teachers at the same school, and the families have become good friends.

"We don't sit around and talk about gloom and doom stuff," he said. But in their own subtle ways they know the spiritual journey each has taken.

"No way, if she did not know God that she would have gotten through this," he said.

Robinson wasn't the only one affected by the lasting effect of the shock that came with the violent crime.

"I remember one grizzled 20- to 25-year cop with gray hair during the grand jury," said Gross. "I asked a question and there was silence for about 10 minutes. I thought, 'You couldn't have forgotten, we just talked about this 10 minutes ago,' and then I realized he was choked up with emotion."

Dorothy's family also had to come to grips with the horror.

Godmother Emma, who credits Dorothy's influence for bringing her closer to the Lord, admits that when Margaret was a child, she tended to dote on her.

"I thought she was a lot like me," she said.

There is a lot in what she says. If Margaret is "a strong black woman," in Dorothy's words, and "the family spokesman," she learned some of it from her godmother.

While Margaret was trying to break down barriers at the hospital to get to her sister, Emma had badgered a police officer until she found out where the crime scene was and immediately headed for the site.

When she overheard a young officer speculating that Dorothy might have been injured doing something seamy with a man, Emma immediately defended her.

"She wouldn't do that. She's a young minister and she wouldn't do that," she said.

Accompanied by Elsie's pastor, Emma got as close to the crime scene as she could, and not knowing what else to do, began calling the girls' names.

"They were looking at me like I was crazy," she said of the police officers.

"We were just hoping that they had dropped the girls off someplace," Margaret said, summing up the family's thinking. "We couldn't fathom someone doing something like this. We're logical people."

Emma was surprised when an officer came over and said, "They want to talk to you down at the station."

"Why? They didn't want to talk to me before," she said.

At the police station, officers told the two women to wait in a small room, but the tension began taking its toll on the pastor.

"You don't pass out on me and leave me by myself," Emma told the pastor.

Soon, they learned that officers had discovered the girls' bodies.

People react differently to tragic news. Some crumble. Others, driven by adrenalin and raw emotion, charge ahead, even if they don't know where they're going, like a bronco charging out of a chute at a rodeo. For others, it is suddenly as if they have a laser beam of focus. Emma was riding the laser beam.

"I want to go see them," Emma said.

"You can't see them now. They've gone to the morgue."

Emma, now on a different kind of mission but still driven to see them, would end up going to the morgue to make the official identification.

When she finally saw them, she remained strong but it was suddenly very difficult.

"Lord, that was hard," she said.

"Can She Identify Anybody?"

There was a flurry of activity that Sunday morning, and not just along the country road. Police were also at the shopping center where Dorothy and her family had been abducted, searching for clues and asking people at a popular coin-operated laundry if they had heard anything.

One of those doing the asking was Eustis Officer Murnas Colston Jr., and one of the ones doing the talking was a friend and sometime confidential informant, Annie Neal Musibau.

Musibau, or Neal, as she was more commonly known, said her ears perked up when Henyard seemed to know something about the crime. She had been with Henyard and his "Auntie" Linda Miller at the laundry.

"Rick asked us did we hear about a preacher lady being dead. That's all he asked," she said. She asked a police officer at the shopping center what had happened. ".... and so when we came back to the car and told Rick that the two kids were dead and the mother was still alive, Rick got very nervous."

Henyard's question had raised eyebrows because news of the crime was not yet public knowledge. It wasn't on TV, he had not talked to any police officers, and no one had said she was dead.

Neal became very excited.

"I told him, 'Let's go out and investigate because they got a $1,000 reward, you know, they have a reward.' That's what I told him."

Miller would later testify about Henyard's reaction to the news that Dorothy was still alive.

"She didn't even die?" he exclaimed. "Can she identify anybody?"

Miller suggested that if he knew anything about the crime he should go to the police station and tell investigators.

Before he made it to the police station, however, he had a talk with Smalls. Smalls' sister, Colinda, said she couldn't overhear what was said but could see Henyard shaking his finger at her brother.

The most dramatic moment for Officer Colston that day occurred when he was approached by Smalls' sister, Tamara, and a youth named Emanuel Yon Jr., Colston said in his deposition.

Told that her mother wanted to see him, Colston went to the family's home, thinking she might have some information about the victims. Once he arrived, however, he learned that Smalls' mother, Annette, had something much more important to disclose.

"She ... began crying and telling us that he was there at the ... at the crime scene ...."

Smalls said he had witnessed Henyard "killing some little girls," Colston said, so he read him his Miranda rights and took him to the police station.

"Why Did You Shoot Them?"

Detective Hart, who had recovered from being sick at the crime scene, was determined to help in any way he could, and his professional curiosity was heightened by the arrival of FBI agents who wanted to see if the carjacking was under their federal jurisdiction.

"I had only been a detective six months and to work with the FBI was the cat's meow to me."

At the police station he ran into Henyard, a man he knew as a quiet individual who hung out at the Eustis Manors apartments with other young men.

Concerned that Henyard might be wasting the agents' time with some tip that would lead nowhere, Hart said: "Don't be jacking anybody around. Tell people the whole truth," he said.

"I will," Henyard promised.

Hart, as it turned out, was familiar with Smalls, too. He had arrested Smalls on a grand theft auto charge earlier. His impression of him was that, "he was just a silly kid."

Hart had no inkling that he would soon play a dramatic role in the case, though later it almost seemed to him that he would be destined to be drawn into it.

Hart, who had been on vacation, had driven past the desolate road the night before, around midnight.

"It was a bright moon and it was foggy," he said. Because the moon was so bright, even though it was in the first quarter, it looked as if it had been split by the fog.

"I remember thinking it looked like the evilest place in the world."

He was familiar with the area. Because it was on the edge of town and was remote, crack dealers liked to try to slip into Eustis that way.

He was up early that Sunday, washing his unmarked detective's car and thinking about a planned Super Bowl party. When he realized that the battery was dead, he called the station to see if anyone could come by to give him a jump start. Instead, a supervisor gave him a jump start to his day, asking if he could go to Hicks Ditch Road.

The Liar

Henyard began talking to the FBI agents at about 11:30 a.m. Sunday, portraying himself as an innocent bystander who was picked up by two friends in a car. The questioning was bizarre, at first. Either the agents weren't paying attention, pretending not to be paying attention, or were playing a game to get under his skin or to test the consistency of his story.

Q: "What time did you meet them?"
A: "It was about 1 o'clock."
Q: "One o'clock yesterday afternoon or 1 p.m.—1 a.m. this morning?"
A: "1 p.m., yeah, this morning."
Q: "1 a.m. this morning, OK."
A: "And so ...."
Q: "You were at somebody's apartment there?"
A: "Yes, I was just, we, we just stayed out there and sit around."
Q: "Oh, you were out front?"
A: "Yeah."
Q: "Hanging out."

A: "Uh-huh."

Q: "OK."

A: "And so, they wanted to go to club New Attitude but I ain't know the way."

Q: "Wanted to go where?"

A: "Club New Attitude in Orlando."

Q: "Club what?"

A: "New Attitude."

Q: "New Attitude?"

A: "New Attitude."

Q: "New Attitude, OK."

A: "And they ain't know the way so they asked me to drive over there for them. When I got over there and got to the club, they had done told me what they did."

Q: "What'd they tell you?" the agent asked, letting pass the inconsistent remark about whether it was his companions or him who "ain't know the way" to the club.

A: "They told me they had went down to Winn-Dixie and stole a car and shot the lady and her two children. But rather than me leaving then, because I ain't had no way home, I just stayed to the club with them and I drove back home."

Q: "You drove that car .....?"

A: "Yeah."

Henyard said the trio arrived back in Eustis around 4:30 or 5 a.m.

Q: "OK. Who are these two friends?"

A: "Do I have to say their names?"

Q: "Yes."

A: "Y'all got a tape there?"

The agents, who were certainly paying attention now, realized at this point that Henyard had at least some culpability in the crime, not to mention real knowledge.

Q: "They told you it was a stolen car. You drove the stolen car back. They didn't tell you (inaudible). You're in a police station. We're guided by certain rules, OK."

The agents then read him his rights, telling him that he could remain silent and could have an attorney. They also wanted him to acknowledge, 'I understand and know what I am doing. No promises by us or threats by us have been made to me and no pressure or coercion of any kind has been used against me.' "Now, do you understand what all that means?"

Henyard said he did, waived his rights and kept talking.

Q: "Here's what I think, Ric, Richard. Is it Richard—Richard or Ricky?"

A: "Richard."

Q: "Richard. You knew your fingerprints were on that car and it would be—you know, we were going to find the car, and that, you know—and we—by, you know, fingerprints we're going to come up with you. And guess what, we came up with you, which you'll be arrested for. We got those prints before you came in here, OK? So...."

Q: FBI AGENT: "Who did what?"

Q: SECOND FBI AGENT: "Who did what? It's time now just to tell us what happened, Ric."

A: "I just told you what happened, man."

Q: FBI AGENT: "I'm telling you, we're giving you the opportunity now to tell us what happened. If you don't want to take the opportunity, then you don't want to take the opportunity. You know, I can't—we can't beat it out of you or anything like that, OK? So, we're asking, you know, just to stand up and admit what you did and we'll go from there, OK?"

Q: SECOND FBI AGENT: "Here's the thing. We're going to go— that car's going to be processed, OK?"

A: "Right."

Q: "When I say processed, I mean—do you know what processing a car means, fingerprinting it and they're going to be taking fibers and all kind of stuff out of that car, OK? And then that's going to be later compared to—by our lab or the Florida Department of Law Enforcement Lab for prints, fibers, whatever, you know, is found at the crime scene or whatever persons were in there.

"Now, you—you were in the car by your own admission, OK? Your prints are on that car, as you said, and that's why you came here concerned.

"Also, Emanuel and Alfonso (sic) were in the car, OK? Suppose we go in there and we don't find one of the other prints in that car? Where does that leave you?"

It seemed an opportune time for the agents to begin applying some pressure.

Q: "And, you know, it's—I can't make you any absolute promises whatsoever. This is strictly your conscience. You know what happened. I think there's more to this than what you're telling us and you're looking at a way to exonerate yourself. It's (inaudible)."

A: "Let me ask y'all a question, right?"

Q: "Go ahead."

A: "Y'all do all y'all witnesses like this? I come here to talk to y'all, tell y'all what I know, but y'all still acting like I'm the one that going to get locked up."

Q: "Well, I told you, other information since you walked in here, there's other information coming to us, OK, contrary to what're you're selling—what you're saying, OK?"

The agent, in fact, had said nothing about what kind of information they had been getting.

He continued: "You know, I don't—we don't have a crystal ball here. I mean, we have to—I'm going to have to ask you these questions, OK? And we have information that you're further involved in this than what you're telling us, and we're giving you the opportunity to tell us that.

"Now, if you want to ride it out, then ride it out, OK? But there's tons of evidence going to be coming from that car, and there's going to be tons of evidence that is going to come from her and those kids' bodies, OK? And there's going to be tons of evidence coming from that lady, OK? There's DNA. I don't know if you've ever heard of that, but semen, there's all kinds of evidence; sweat, hair, clothing, fibers, all sorts of things that's going to tell the story, a scientific story, that's going to lead to certain people (inaudible).

"Now, we're giving you the opportunity to tell us now."

A: "Uh-huh. And I suppose if I don't tell you, y'all lock me up, right?"

FBI AGENT: "What?"

FBI AGENT: "No, we're not going to lock you up. I mean, I can't say—you know."

FBI AGENT: "Right this minute, no."

FBI AGENT: "No."

Of course, the agents could have had him arrested on some kind of a charge, including a stolen property charge. But they were telling the truth when they said they weren't going to lock him up right then. They were interested in bigger charges, the biggest, if possible.

A: "No, I'm just saying, I won't be able to go home, right? Will I?"

Q: "Like I said, the evidence will tell us."

The subtle message, of course, was, no, you're not going home, so you might as well tell us what happened. Then maybe (although, not really) you can go home.

The agent, still playing up the strength of possible physical evidence, said, "That woman was raped, OK? A rapist leaves his mark, personal mark that can be identified to a person, OK?

"If you raped her, your mark is there, OK? And I don't care what you say, whether you did or didn't do anything, it's going to be there. If you didn't do it, you haven't got a thing in the world to worry about at all. Nothing. Nothing to worry about. If you didn't do anything other than what you've told us, you have nothing to worry about. But if you did and you're feeling—you're going to feel better for one thing, if you tell us, OK, the rest of the story. We just feel like you've got a lot more than what you're telling us. Do you?"

A: "No, I don't."

Henyard was then asked if he had been drinking. Henyard replied, "We had a few Eight Ball and I was drinking beer."

It's not clear from the taped interview what he meant by "Eight Ball" because the agents did not ask, but it can refer to one-eighth of an ounce, or 3.5 grams of cocaine, which is enough to overdose most people (thegooddrugsguide/sittemap.com). He was probably, however, referring to a Sloe Gin drink by the same name. He went on to say the group was not drinking after 1 a.m., nor had he had anything to drink at the club. Then, the agent asked: "No crack or anything?"

"Huh-uh," he answered.

Later, he would claim to have been drinking and smoking marijuana.

The FBI agent reminded Henyard that he had told him that his friends had picked him up to go to the club around 1 a.m.

"Well, where were you at 10:00 though? The question was, where were you at 10:00?"

A: "At 10 o'clock, I was with Emanuel up at his momma house."

Q: "And he was there?"

A: "Uh-huh."

Q: "Was Alfonso there, too?"

A: "Uh-huh."

Henyard said he was there for about 30 minutes, then went back to the Manors apartment complex, where he said he was later picked up for the ride to the club.

He said Smalls did not go with him to the Manors.

Again, the two agents lapsed into a kind of Abbott and Costello "who's on first" routine, apparently in an effort to try and trip up Henyard.

FBI AGENT: "How long did you stay there, back there at Emanuel's?"

A: "How long did I stay to Emanuel's? About 30 minutes."

FBI AGENT: "Then where?"

A: "The Manors."

FBI AGENT: "No. After you left Alfonso's house, you went back—you said you went back to Lemanuel's, right?"

SECOND FBI AGENT: "No, (inaudible) stayed there together, I thought."

FBI AGENT: "Yeah, but we was still at Emanuel's dad's house."

In fact, Henyard had not said anything about Alfonza's house at this point.

He gave the agents a list of the names of people he said were hanging out at the Manors that night, names that Hart recognized.

"OK. So I can go talk to them and they can tell me what time you got there?" Hart said.

A: "Uh-huh."

Henyard then apparently began to realize that things were not working out as smoothly as he thought they would.

He asked them to take him to his "auntie's" house and said, "Something told me not to come down here."

Q: "No, no, no, believe me."

A: "Y'all doing the same thing."

Q: "No, no, no. Look, who told you not to come down here? Who did?"

A: "I told myself not to come."

Q: "No, no. You're doing the right thing."

A: "How I'm doing the right thing?"

Q: "You are. You are. You are. I'm telling you, if you didn't—Look, we—how would you—Would you have rather the investigation go on? We'd wound up at your place."

A: "Yeah, y'all would have came and got me."

Q: "You know that, and then it would have been a hell of a lot worse."

It was an interesting ploy, a measure to keep Henyard talking. The agent certainly didn't tell him how it could have been any worse.

Henyard replied: "No. Now I'm sitting down here answering all these questions when I could be home."

The agent said it could have been "heavier" if he had not come in, and that agents would have obtained a warrant for his arrest.

"This is in your favor walking in here," the agent said.

Henyard replied: "And the way y'all talking, y'all trying to say I had something to do with it. If I had something to do with it, I'd a came straight out and told you."

The agents, realizing that they were going around in circles, switched gears, asking if he had graduated from high school (no), or if he was working.

"I applied for a job over there to that little fruit thing down the street there, that fruit company. I don't know their name."

The agent asked who drove the car away after he was dropped off by the middle school. He asked this without Henyard telling him that he had been dropped off by the school. He was not dropped off by the school, of course, the car had been found parked near the school.

"I ain't see the car leave."

Then, the agent asked where he parked the car.

Then, Henyard changed the time from 4:30 to 5 a.m., to "about 3:30, 4 a.m."

He said Emanuel was sitting with him in the front seat. Asked what they were wearing, he said Yon was wearing a jeans suit and Smalls was wearing blue pants and a blue and white shirt.

Asked if they had changed clothes during the night, he said no.

He also said there was no other car used by the group that night.

As for the gun, he said Emanuel, without saying why, opened the glove box on the way back home.

"I leaned back, seen the gun, kept driving."

He said the others did not try to intimidate him with the handgun.

"Why do you think they told you?" the agent asked.

"If I'd a did something like that, I'd a told my friends, too."

He said he would have asked them for advice on what to do next.

When the agent asked if they asked for advice, he replied: "They ain't asked me nothing."

Agents then asked him if he had ever seen Dorothy before. The implied question was, did you see her last night?

"Yeah, I seen her a lot. She was a church lady."

Asked what he meant by "church lady," he replied: "Like a preacher lady, you know, like she on Sunday school, teaching Sunday school and stuff like that."

He said he saw her when he would take his 9-year-old nephew to church, and that he had last seen her less than a year ago.

At this point, the tape ends. When the tape player resumes, Henyard asked if his "auntie" was on her way to the station. They told him that she was not at home and that they were going to find her.

Then, there was a shuffling of personnel and tape recorders as the Florida Department of Law Enforcement agents arrived to take over questioning.

Hart remained in the room, somewhat baffled, by the idea of the FBI bailing out of the case.

"I thought, 'You got a guy talking and you stopped him?' I was really floored by that," Hart said. The FBI agents from Ocala decided the local and state authorities should take the case.

The federal agents were replaced by officers with the FDLE and Hart's senior (by four or five months) partner, Scott Barker.

Robert A. O'Connor, a former Seminole County Sheriff's deputy and a special agent with FDLE for three years, had been doing some yard work at home that morning when he got the call to go to Eustis and work on an "abduction and multiple shooting."

He walked in just as FBI agents were walking out.

The FBI told Henyard that because there were overlapping jurisdictions, they were turning the case over to state and local authorities. Murder takes precedence over federal carjacking, the agent said.

"What's you saying, y'all fixing to go, but now I got to stay in here and answer questions with him," Henyard said.

"Yeah. Well, you know, this is—I know this is taking a lot of time out of your day, but you got a—you know, two children are dead, OK? And they didn't hurt anybody, you know? And this is kind of an important thing, and so I mean—I think (inaudible) you know, continue to cooperate," the agent replied.

The agents then repeated their routine about the recent great advances in physical evidence and that if he was innocent, the evidence would clear him, and that it would have been worse if he had to be picked up for questioning "in the middle of the night."

O'Connor asked the FBI agents if they were going to be around for awhile.

"We're not going anywhere," one of the federal agents replied.

"We're not going to bail out," the other said.

But of course, they did leave as quickly as they could.

"I'm convinced that this [jurisdictional decision] was their way to get out of an interview on Super Bowl Sunday," O'Connor said.

Henyard began asking and asking frequently how long he would have to stay for questioning.

"Well," O'Connor said, "we want to get a few things straight and we're going to find out where the truth is coming from, OK? And to be very honest with you, you're going to have to stick around until we determine who—who is telling the truth and, you know, what the truth is, OK? We're not going to hold you here if we don't have to, all right? I'll be very honest with you, but we've got three, you know—two people dead and one seriously hurt and we need—we need to get to the bottom of it, OK? I'm sure you'd understand if you were—if you were the relative of one of those people who was murdered, all right? Let's treat this as—as if it's the serious situation that it is."

Soon, it would be like a three-ring circus for the suspects, and the questioning, which would start at 1 p.m., would last almost four hours.

Smalls and Henyard were in different interview rooms, separated by two empty rooms down a narrow hallway.

Robinson and Aurigemma stood in the middle of the maze, directing traffic, swapping information and updating the investigators on what the teens were saying.

"We knew Smalls was scared brainless," Robinson said.

The technique of roving investigators confused the two.

"They never knew when it was going to switch," Robinson said. The typical response was, "Who are you?"

"Smalls was our pet," Robinson said.

Before the FDLE and Eustis detectives began their questioning, Henyard had at least pretended that he was calm.

"I can tell you something. I ain't going to say that I don't care them two children got killed, but I ain't did it, so why worry about it? I ain't got nothing to worry about," he told the FBI agents.

O'Connor began by asking Henyard how old he was, how far he had gone in school and if he understood "what we're talking about today?" He then read Henyard his rights again.

Henyard said he wanted to start from the beginning, and said he had been with Yon and Smalls starting at 2 or 3 p.m., Saturday at Smalls' house.

He now said they all went to Yon's father's house at about 8 p.m. and stayed there until 10 p.m. "...then I left and went to the Manors."

No longer was his story that he had stayed at Yon's for only about 30 minutes.

He repeated his story of going to the Manors apartment complex around 10 p.m. and again listed his alibi witnesses.

"We stayed up there for awhile 'till about 1 o'clock. That's when Emanuel came by."

They pulled up in a blue Chrysler, he said, wanting to go to the New Attitude Club in Orlando. He said he drove.

"He was telling a good story," O'Connor said of Henyard. "I didn't say anything to dispute it. I was thinking he probably had more involvement. I was watching his body language. He was nervous as a cat."

Q: "What time did you get to the club?"
A: "About 1:50, a quarter to 2."
Q: "OK."
A: "So we got to the club. When we got in the parking lot, they were talking, right? One of them saying, you know, he say they were scared. So I asked what they did."
Q: "Who said he was scared?"
A: "Emanuel."
Q: "Yeah."
A: "He said he was scared. I asked him what he did. He say he stole a car."
Q: "Uh-huh."
A: "He said, 'We shot the people that had the car.' Only I didn't leave because that was my only ride."
Q: "Emanuel is saying this?"
A: "Uh-huh."
Q: "Who did he say actually shot the people?"
A: "Junior shot the two little kids, I know that."
Q: "Junior? Is that Alfonso? Did Emanuel say that or did Alfonso say that?"
A: "Alfonso said that."

Barker then asked: "Alfonso said he shot the two kids?"

A: "The two kids. And Emanuel shot the woman."

Q: "Did they say how it went down?"

A: "They just told me they were waiting outside the Winn-Dixie."

He then went on to describe in detail parking the car when they came back to Eustis from the club, using landmarks and other descriptions.

He said when he awoke that morning his sister told him about police in the neighborhood.

"I asked her what happened. She said some lady got shot last night. She said she ain't know who it is, but the police was there to see the body."

He said he didn't talk to his sister about the crime, but when his saw Linda Miller later, he said he told her, "I was driving and stuff, my auntie said, 'the best thing for you to do is to go down there and talk to them because they gonna get your fingerprints'. I said 'OK.'"

There was more questioning, and again Henyard said he knew "the lady" from church but was not familiar with the car. The detectives then wanted to know how Smalls and Yon supposedly told him about the crime.

"So, they went to, you know, talking up under their breath for awhile. Then they say—Emmanuel say, 'Well, we did something else, too.' I say, 'What's y'all done did? He said they shot the two kids. Eman—Well, Emanuel didn't say it but Junior said he shot the two kids."

There was another round of confusing questions, either because the detectives were trying to get up to speed, because they were from two different law enforcement agencies, or because they were trying to trip up Henyard. Henyard, of course, was trying to keep his story straight, the trap that every liar falls into.

"Ain't nobody said nothing about shooting the lady," an anxious Henyard blurted out.

He said Smalls and Yon did not tell him where the shootings took place or why they shot the children.

Q: "Did they say why they shot the lady?"
A: "I ain't said nothing about shooting the lady."
Q: "You told me before that Alfonso—that Alfonso said he shot the lady."
A: "I say Alfonso shot the two kids."
Q: "OK. And ….."
A: "I said that …."

BARKER: "He said Emanuel shot the lady."
O'CONNOR: "You said—OK, Emanuel. I'm sorry. Emanuel shot the lady. So, did Emanuel tell you he shot the lady or not?"

A: "No. Well, most likely—Well, one of the two did. And when I told you I'd asked, Alfonso told me he shot the lady—the two children, I said, 'Most likely Emanuel shot the lady.'"
Q: "So nobody ever told you actually that—who shot the lady, right?"
A: "Huh-huh."

He then switched the time line again, saying they stayed at the club until 3 a.m. and got home between 4 and 5 a.m.

The detectives asked about the gun, and he said he thought it was a .38-caliber snub nose (the barrel is too long and it is a .22). He said he didn't know who owned the gun.

Q: "Did he say that was the gun that was used to shoot the people, or what? I mean, you know ….."
A: "No."
Q: "So y'all are just—just driving down [U.S.] 441 and he opens up the box and…."

A: "And…."
Q: "…. shows you the box, the gun."
A: "I don't think we was on 441. We came through Apopka."
Q: "Yeah. He just opens it up and shows it to you?"
A: "Uh-huh."
Q: "No reason at all?"
A: "No reason at all."

He continued on with his story about coming back into Eustis and parking the car.

Q: "What did you do with the keys?"
A: "One of them got it, I think."
Q: "Huh?"
A: "One of them got it, I reckon."
Q: "What did you do with them? I mean, you were driving."
A: "I left them in the ignition."

The investigators asked if he had seen Yon or Smalls that morning and he said he had seen Smalls but didn't talk to him because he was in his aunt's car.

Barker asked him what clothing he had been wearing.

A: "I got them on now. White shorts."
Q: "What kind of shirt?"
A: "T-shirt."
Q: "T-shirt and white shorts?"

Hart asked: "No jacket?"
A: "No."

The detectives then began chipping away at his alibi witnesses and his time line. He said some of the young men hanging out in front of the apartment complex left at various times to go to a club in nearby Leesburg.

The investigators again asked him if he was wearing a jacket the night before, which should have triggered an alarm in Henyard's mind. Then again, he might have been deluding himself that the officers were believing his story, despite the obvious big holes in the yarn.

O'Connor asked: "Did they tell you what else happened during this thing when they stole the car and shot people?"

A: "Huh-uh."

Q: "They didn't tell you anything?"

A: "Never told me."

Q: "Were you curious? Did you—What did you think about it when they told you?"

A: "I ain't think about nothing right then. I wanted to come home."

O'Connor's patience was beginning to wear thin.

Q: "Were you with those guys last night when they stole the car?"

A: "No, I wasn't."

Q: "Were you with them when they shot those people?"

A: "No, I wasn't."

Q: "Are you prepared to swear to that in court?"

A: "Yes, I will."

Q: "And swear to the fact that they told you what you said they told you?"

A: "Yes, I will."

Q: "Prepared to go into court and swear up in front of everybody that that's what happened?"

A: "Yes, I will."

Q: "About shooting those people?"

A: "Yes, I will."

Q: "That's what they told you?"

A: "If I have to."

Q: "Did you shoot anybody last night?"

A: "No, I didn't."

Investigators asked him again, and again he denied shooting anyone.

The detectives then asked if he would be willing to give a blood sample for "investigative purposes."

"I'll do it. I got to be in the presence of my auntie."

"That's fine," one of the investigators replied.

"Let me talk to her," Henyard said.

"Sure," the detective replied.

Barker, thinking about gunshot residue, blood and other possible evidence, asked him if he had taken a bath or washed his hands or used the bathroom that day.

A: "Uh-huh."

Q: "Which one of the three?"

A: "All three."

Q: "You took a bath?"

A: "Uh-huh."

Q: "You got up and took a shower this morning and put on the same clothes?"

A: "It's chilly outside these shorts big. If I take off these shorts, these shorts here fall off."

He said he was also wearing the same shoes.

Henyard then answered several questions about the trip to Orlando. Asked if he saw anyone there he knew, he said no.

The detectives stopped the questioning long enough to change the tape.

Because he was a new detective on a small force that required investigators to routinely do things that crime scene investigators do in bigger departments, like dusting for fingerprints, Hart was thinking about the possibilities of collecting physical evidence. He wondered specifically about the possibility of shoe prints being left at the crime scene.

Later, as Henyard was talking, spinning new tales, O'Connor said, "… he put his shoes up on the desk like he's at home."

Hart looked at Henyard's white socks.

"That looks like high-speed blood spatter," he thought.

O'Connor asked Hart if he had any questions.

Hart, who has the personality of the "Energizer Bunny," O'Connor said, literally jumped when he spotted the blood.

"Could I look at your shoes a minute?" Hart asked Henyard.

"Take them off?"

"Yeah."

"They funky."

"They're funky. That's OK. I've been hit with tear gas a hundred times."

"Both of them?"

"Yeah. Let's see your socks, too. I don't mind looking at your socks. Yeah. Let me see them?"

"There's some [expletive] blood on your socks," Hart exclaimed.

"Why you cussing me out, man?"

"Huh? Because you're jacking us around. You're lying. There's blood all over your shoes. There's blood all over your socks," Hart said.

"Where you see blood on my shoes at?"

Henyard then uttered one of the most outrageous statements in the long, shameful history of murder in Florida.

"How you know that ain't no ketchup stain?"

"We'll find out," said O'Connor.

"Well, find out," Henyard said.

"Two dead babies," Hart said.

"Ya'll going to just make me tell the truth, right?"

"That's what we're here for," O'Connor said.

"Start a tape over. I'm being straight up this time."

After looking at the first shoe, Hart realized it had been saturated in blood.

"My stomach fell to the floor," he said.

The blood on the socks was not high-speed spatter, but had caught some of the outpouring of blood when he picked up one of the children.

Hart immediately felt a surge of anger well up against Henyard and had one immediate thought: "You are a dirtbag."

Then, his professional pride and training kicked in.

"I was beyond surprised. It was like walking down the street and finding the winning lottery ticket. How do you get blood on your socks unless you're there? I wasn't worried about a confession at this point."

Henyard began telling a more truthful version but it was still a twisted, self-serving version.

"This is what happened. Me, Emanuel and Junior, all us was talking yesterday, they wanted to get a car. Like I say, I don't know who gun it was."

He told the truth when he said Yon left the store before the car-jacking occurred. And he told the truth when he said it was Smalls who approached Dorothy in the parking lot after she put her children in the car. He also said they took Dorothy and the children to the isolated dirt road. Defendants do tell a story that is partially true, either because they don't want to have to make up every detail, or because they think having an element of the truth in their story will make it more believable.

"But let me tell you straight up," Henyard said, "I did not kill them children. The person who killed them children is Alfonso."

Henyard said Smalls made him pull over and stop the car.

"He told the lady to get out. She got out. He told me to stay in there with the kids for awhile so—and they was sitting on the back of the hood, the trunk, the back. They were sitting up there and I was just sitting in the car listening to music.

"So he came and knocked on the window. Gave me some shoes."

O'Connor asked, "Who gave them?"

"Alfonso," Henyard said. "He gave me some shoes, some stocking things and some panties. So I just put them up underneath the seat of the car, which they still are at. Y'all got the car, I know y'all do."

He said about 15 or 20 minutes later, he returned with Dorothy, put her in the backseat, and got into the car.

He said he and Smalls smoked three joints of marijuana.

"So I smoked three reefer. I was feeling good," he said.

He then went on to tell another set of scurrilous lies.

"So he told me he had, you know—I ain't going to say raped the lady. Y'all going to say it's rape but I ain't going to say it's rape because I heard them talking.

"So I got up, I took her out the door, told her I wanted to talk. I'm paranoid, I'm high and I'm drunk.

"So at the time when I was talking to her, he [Smalls] laid the gun on the back end of the car.

"So she reached for the gun, right, but I grabbed it, and I grabbed it by the handle. And she had it like that there by the barrel part. When she tried to pull the gun—I ain't gonna lie—I pulled the trigger. I think I shot her in the leg. So I laid her on the side of the road. I got scared and I left. We drove farther down the road. Alfonzo...."

Barker stopped Henyard at that point, and said that she was shot three times.

"I only shot her once."

"Did Alfonso shoot her?" Barker asked.

"I don't think so."

"You were there."

"He didn't shoot her. I only shot her one time in the leg. Matter of fact, I could tell you exactly what leg, the left leg. Am I right?"

After leaving Dorothy wounded and lying in a ditch, Henyard said Smalls was "talking crazy" about the children. Henyard claimed he wanted to drop them off someplace and keep going.

"... he went to acting all macho, you know, telling me if I didn't stop the car, he gonna shoot me."

He said he pulled over and stopped, Smalls got out and he called for the children to get out of the car, "and they went to crying. So when the children got out there, he put them in like a little hump in some grass, and he told them to stand right there. And he came back over to where I was and I asked him what he fixing to do. He said, 'I ain't fixing to do nothing, I ain't fixing to do nothing.' He said, 'Keep the car running,' like that."

He said he got back in the car and was listening to music on the radio when he heard two shots.

"I looked back, he was toting one body across the road—not across the road—like a little barbed wire fence thing, threw it over there. Then he came back and got the other one and threw it over there. I asked him where he shot them at but he ain't tell me."

He said they left, went and picked up Yon, went to the club, then went back to Eustis.

"Y'all satisfied now?"

"It's starting to get that way," O'Connor said, knowing that investigators would make Henyard go over the details again and again while they harvested a crop of transparent inconsistencies and lies.

Henyard, for example, said he walked to Winn-Dixie. "I ain't know they had the gun, I ain't going to lie to you, I had a knife."

Henyard also said Yon was carrying the pistol to the store and that it was Yon and Smalls who were talking about getting a car. After about 30 minutes or so, Yon disappeared around the corner of the building and did not return, he said.

"The lady got out of the car, a blue Chrysler, with her two children, walked in the store. He said, 'That's the car we're going to get.' I said, 'OK.'"

He described the bench where they were sitting and where she parked the car.

"So as she came out the door, he was already standing by the car. He was leaning against the pole. And as she came out the door, he went to walking like he fixing to walk off. So she went on the passenger's side, opened up the door, put her children in, closed the door. Opened up the back door, put the groceries back there. And as she was coming around to the driver's side, Alfonso pulled out the gun and told her, 'Don't scream, get in the backseat.' She got in the backseat. Then we went down a little dirt road."

That part of Henyard's story was essentially correct, but then, for some reason, possibly because he thought it would make him seem less culpable, he said Smalls was in the driver's seat and he climbed into the backseat with Dorothy and the children.

He repeated the tale of making Dorothy get out of the car, but added more time to the story. But when he got to the part of the story about how the gun was placed on the trunk and Dorothy tried to grab it, Henyard slipped up.

"So I laid—Alfonso laid the gun on the back end of the trunk."

The detectives, if they noticed Henyard's gaffe, let it pass. They gave Henyard a piece of paper and a pen so he could sketch a diagram of where everyone was supposedly standing during this part of the story.

He repeated his story about how Dorothy grabbed the gun barrel and how he shot her in the leg.

"So I got scared. I said, 'Man, let's go.' I said, 'Come on.' Alfonso said, 'Come on.' So I put the lady over the side of the road, went down the road a little farther.

"And he was talking about something, 'Pull over, man, pull over, man.' And I ... myself, I was wondering what he was gonna do with the kids."

The detectives had him recreate the scene with the gun on the trunk, demonstrating with his hands how the gun was pointed and how, in Henyard's words, "She ain't pull it straight up. She slid it sideways."

He repeated his story about how he was telling Smalls that they should flee after the shot was fired into Dorothy's leg.

Q: "All right. Stop right there. The lady's been shot one time."
A: "That's all I did, shot her one time."

Q: "How did she get shot the other times?"

A: "I don't know. I'm sitting here...."

Q: "I've got to know. She's alive, man."

A: "OK."

Q: "She's alive. Tell me. I need to know."

A: "I'm sitting here tell you all the truth and now y'all still saying I'm lying. I shot the lady one time in the leg. That was it."

Q: "Could it have gone off and hit her in the head? Tell me how she got that?"

A: "It probably did."

Barker continued his probe, dangling investigators' tried and true bait that some detectives call "the out." It usually goes something like this: "I know you didn't mean to kill her....."

Defendants, eager to climb out of the hole they continue to dig for themselves, usually snatch it like the lifeline that it is not.

Q: "All right. When you shoot—when you shot her, I'm sure you were scared then."

A: "I was scared, yeah. I was scared, period, for me grabbing the gun...."

Q: "Right."

A: "...when she grabbed it."

Q: "After that, could you have shot her any other time, not realizing what was happening? I mean, all this is happening quick. Did you shoot her another time?"

A: "Well, the way I was feeling, most likely I did."

Q: "Well, did you or didn't you?"

A: "I'm going to say yeah. Yeah, I did. I shot her two more times."

Q: "Where?"

A: "In the leg, I reckon. She was on the ground. Like I told you, when I shot the first time, the lady fell."

Q: "Uh-huh."

A: "And that just really scared me, right?"
Q: "Right."

At this point, he said he told Smalls that they had to leave and he gave the gun to Smalls.

He said he left Dorothy lying on the ground and they drove off. She wasn't screaming, he said. "The only thing—I heard her say once, she was just saying, 'Oh, Lord, oh, Lord.' That's all I heard."

The detective returned to the topic of shooting Dorothy.

Q: "She was laying on the ground?"
A: "She was laying on the ground."
Q: "Did you put the gun down to her?"
A: "Uh-huh."
Q: "How many times?"
A: "Two."
Q: "Two times?"
A: "Uh-huh."
Q: "You didn't shoot maybe a fourth time?"
A: "No."

He repeated his claim that he did not know where she was shot.

He also repeated his account of how Smalls made him pull over to the side of the road, getting the children out of the car and shooting them.

"And back then, I had a feeling I know what he going to do. So I tried to turn up the radio so I couldn't hear it."

He also repeated his claim that Smalls threw the girls' bodies over the fence, they got in the car, picked up Yon and went to Orlando.

"Now I feel much better," he said, as if telling the partial truth was the same thing as being set free.

The detectives then began asking about the sexual assault.

"I ain't did it. I started to but at the time I started to, that's when she grabbed the gun."

As a way of explaining his state of mind, first he claimed he was drunk, then he said he was not drunk but high.

The investigators kept hammering away at him, getting him to admit his involvement more and more.

Q: "So you admit to shooting her?"

A: "Uh-huh."

Q: "Three times."

A: "Yes."

Q: "You admit to taking the car with them, right?"

A: "I ain't going to say I took it, but I was there when he took it."

Q: "All right. You were with him…"

A: "I just got in the car."

He again repeated the story about Smalls driving the car out of the parking lot.

The officers tried to get him to stop trying to weasel out of taking responsibility for trying to kill Dorothy.

"Tell me the truth. I mean, did you mean to kill her?" a detective asked.

"No, I did not," he said.

The two also argued about how many times he shot her and whether the detective first said she had been shot more than once or whether Henyard had said it.

"When we get finished talking, I want you to rewind that tape," Henyard said.

Eventually, Henyard admitted helping get the girls out of the car, but he denied moving their bodies. And he claimed that he knew Dorothy was alive when they left.

The detectives then had him go over the crime scene with a hand-drawn map.

After Smalls dumped the bodies, he simply said, "Let's go get Emanuel," Henyard said.

"What did you say?" a detective asked.

"Man, I was too scared to say nothing to that man. After I done seen him shoot them kids, he probably would have shot me, too. He said, 'Let's go pick up Emanuel.' I said, 'OK.'"

He said Smalls told him to get Yon and a change of clothing, because his clothes were covered in blood.

Henyard then launched what he thought was a plausible story about the blood.

"And then the lady's stuff was up under the seat. Something else had blood on it. That's how I got the blood on my socks and shoes."

After a time, there was about a 10-minute break in the questioning, and the detectives started a new tape.

They began asking questions about clothing.

Hart said, "You were wearing the blue—the blue jacket with the gray hood."

"White T-shirt," Henyard replied.

Q: "All right. Now, we're going to interrupt you right here and show you some clothing and see if you recognize it, OK? This is a detective from the Eustis Police Department.

"Do you recognize that?"

A: "My coat."

Q: "That's your coat?"

A: "Yeah."

Q: "OK. That's yours. And what is your name?"

A: "Richard Henyard."

Q: "OK. You were wearing that last night?"

A: "Uh-huh."

For the record, the investigator noted on tape, Henyard had identified a denim jacket with a gray sweatshirt hood.

He went on to identify other articles of clothing.

What he must have known at this time, was that the "auntie" that he had been asking for, Linda Miller, had turned the clothing over to police. The stolen car keys were in the pocket, and so was a holster and unspent .22-caliber bullets.

Henyard identified the clothing that Smalls had been wearing, a lightweight "silky" material that he identified as being "light brown," but others said was green.

O'Connor, pressing hard now, told Henyard that crime scene technicians could get fingerprints off bodies.

"I'm going to find your fingerprints because you helped to throw them over—over the fence, didn't you?"

"No, I did not," he said.

Henyard then identified more clothing worn by Smalls.

Q: "You know, at this point in time, it's bad enough that you're—that you're here, OK. And I appreciate the fact you coming clean with what you've come clean with, all right?"

A: "Uh-huh."

Q: "But—but if it's there, let's do it all, OK? He's trying to put the hat on you, OK? Now we're talking—now we're talking—we're talking you killing the two kids. Now we're talking you helped him toss them over the fence. Now we're talking you raping that lady, too."

It was the first reference to detectives also talking with Smalls. It's another classic squeeze play. In the true-crime movie classic "In Cold Blood," for example, the two suspects pass each other in the hallway of a police station, each trying to read the eyes of the other and wondering, "What did you tell them?"

"There ain't nothing to talk," Henyard said, "but I did help him get the bodies over the fence, but I did not kill them kids."

"Talk is going to put you in the electric chair, my friend, that's what it is going to do. That's what it is going to do, it's gonna put you on death row. Now you better start telling me what happened," a detective replied.

Henyard insisted he had been telling the truth, but the detective pointed out that he had "conveniently" left out the part about him helping toss the girls' bodies over the fence.

"I ain't getting no murder charge, man," Henyard said.

"Oh, yeah? Well, that's....."

"I did not kill...."

"Well, that's what you're looking at right now, sport. Believe it. Get it right."

He then admitted to carrying Jasmine's body.

Following a pattern now, investigators kept repeating their questions until bits and pieces of the story emerged.

Q: "You didn't do anything to stop him."

A: "What I supposed to do? Run up on the man with a gun?"

Q: "You gonna let two little girls be killed?"

A: "I'm not fixing to run up on no man with no gun. The man was already acting stupid. But like I told you, when he told me to pull over, this is his exact word, 'Pull over or I will shoot you.' What am I supposed to do, keep going?"

He admitted to helping get the girls out of the backseat in what must have been the heart-breaking truth, as far as it went.

"Were they scared?"

"Yeah, they was scared. They was crying. All the time they was in that backseat, they were saying, 'I want my mommy.'"

Asked what he told Yon, he replied: "We told him that we shot— I shot the lady, but we didn't say nothing about the baby. I did not tell him babies was involved. Well, he should know because we told him three people was shot. I ain't tell him children was involved."

He said the trio stopped off in Plymouth on the way to Orlando. Yon wanted to see a "homeboy," Henyard said, and Yon told him about the crime.

Henyard talked about going to Smalls' house and picking up Yon and asking for a change of clothes.

The discussion returned to Smalls' assault on Dorothy, which Henyard did not classify as rape, although the detective pointed out, "But he had a gun."

The detectives began bearing down, asking details about how Henyard had also assaulted her, despite his denials.

"The only thing I did was kiss her," he said, when she was saying 'Oh, God, oh, God, please help me,' and while the children were crying.

"Y'all ain't gonna hurt me?" he said, quoting Dorothy.

"I said, 'no.'"

"She say, 'Y'all, please,' she said. 'Y'all please let me go and my children. Y'all can keep the car. I cannot identify y'all.'"

He noted that she was calling on God for help.

"I just kept telling her, 'We ain't gonna hurt you.'"

He claimed he had not originally intended to commit the crime of rape, but "after I got finished smoking that reefer, that's what I wanted to do."

He also tried to deflect the accusation that after he shot Dorothy, he either thought she was dead or was leaving her to die.

"Well, I knew she wasn't dead. When I came back by, she wasn't there."

O'Connor then pushed Henyard on the decision to eliminate the other two witnesses in the crime.

Agent O'Connor, convinced that Henyard shot the girls, was using every interview technique he could think of to get him to confess.

O'Connor had been carrying a photo of Dorothy and the two girls in his shirt pocket.

"I took out the pictures, and I grabbed him. He stunk, he was really nasty," O'Connor said.

"Look at these two little babies," O'Connor said. "He starts crying. 'They're dead, gone,' I said."

At one point, O'Connor said he was crying himself.

"I did everything I could to pull it out of him," O'Connor said.

He said he told him to "get it off your chest," and every other "cliché" he could think of.

"Why did you shoot them?" O'Connor asked. "I want to know, Richard. Do it for their family, if nothing else, do it, do it—don't do it for me …."

He also urged Henyard to confess for his own sake, and said he couldn't make any promises but it might go easier for him in the justice system if he confessed.

"I knew that if he was ever going to tell me about it, it would be at that point."

At one point, the special agent indirectly challenged Henyard's "manhood" as he put it, suggesting that there was no way that Henyard, who he referred to as "a man," would allow "a boy" to run the show.

For example, O'Connor said: "I don't think a 15-year-old kid is a grown man enough to shoot two kids."

"That's what you think, man," Henyard replied. "But I'm gonna tell you something. When you're black and you got a gun in your hand, you think you're the world. I should know, I been there."

It was risky, he acknowledges now, because interrogators spend so much intensity and time building a rapport with a suspect they don't want to lose it.

There was a reason for taking the risk, however. During the interview Henyard admitted that he knew who Dorothy was.

O'Connor realized that Henyard may have shot Dorothy because he was afraid she could identify him. And if he could fall into O'Connor's ego trap and admit that he had the gun and not the younger Smalls, then it would be a damning admission.

O'Connor hammered at Henyard with the questions again and again, but Henyard would not budge on the murder of Jasmine and Jamilya.

Henyard finally did admit to the rape, however. He had initially denied it during a voice stress analysis pretest.

Voice stress analysis, like a polygraph examination, is not admissible in court but can sometimes be useful in putting psychological strain on a suspect to tell the truth.

The equipment uses radio waves to chart responses to questions.

"When a person ... has psychological stress or is showing deception in his response ... the FM frequency in the voice wavelength dissipates out of the voice pattern picture," said FDLE Agent Robert Tippett in a deposition.

During the actual analysis, Henyard showed a "non-deceptive response," he said.

"... I had sex with the lady," Henyard admitted. "And as I was leaving, that's when she grabbed the gun.

"... she was trying to snatch the handle out of my hand, that's when the trigger got pulled. And like I said, I freaked out and I shot two more times."

Asked if he shot her in the head, he replied, "I don't know where I shot her...."

He later blamed the frenzied shooting spree on being high, and then said, "I just, I lost my mind, man. It just left me."

He said, "I caught myself on the third time. The fourth, I was gonna pull the trigger one more time but I just caught myself, jumped in the car and left."

But he steadfastly refused to admit that he later shot the girls.

He admitted that he picked up Jasmine and moved her out of the car.

"I got out the car. When I picked her up, she just grabbed me, just went to crying, 'I want my mommy, I want my mommy.'

"I wanted to do something but I couldn't. That man had that gun, OK? If he hadn't had no gun, if he had anything else besides a gun, I would have did something, but I ain't fixing to run up on no gun, OK?"

"You may as well have killed them," O'Connor observed.

"How you figure that? I ain't pulled the trigger. I ain't point the gun at them."

"You may as well have killed them," O'Connor repeated. "Let's get out of here," he said to his fellow law enforcement officers.

"That'll end this tape," Barker said.

But it wouldn't end Henyard's culpability. And it would be science, not some fairy tale, that would send Henyard down an evidence path of no return.

Broken Lives

The search for the gun would eventually prove fruitful, and it would shed light on the suspects' repugnant, dysfunctional lives, a sharp contrast to the one led by Dorothy and her family.

Longtime prosecutor Gross is a 5-foot-7, energetic, engaging, sometimes sarcastic man (he loves "The Simpsons"), and he uses humor to cope with the horrors. He is a middle-aged workaholic who specializes in convicting people of murder, and he does it very well. So, it was no surprise to investigators when he not only showed up at the crime scene, but joined in the third and final interview of Henyard, and ended up later helping search for the murder weapon.

Investigators learned that the missing gun had been stolen by Henyard from a man he called his "grandfather." Luther Reed, in fact, was a friend of Henyard's mother, and had bailed her out of jams in the past.

Reed was forthcoming. Two days before the shooting, Henyard had come by for a visit, and when he was fixing Henyard a bowl of soup, the young man had stolen the gun from beneath his pillow, Reed said.

Gross, who was given permission to search the apartment, was stunned to find in the filthy apartment a large splotch of dried blood on the floor upstairs. He was skeptical when the old man told him it was from a raccoon he had shot and butchered. He used the pistol, a nine-shot J.C. Higgins Model 88 revolver, for hunting, Reed claimed. Indignant at the questioning, he led Gross to his kitchen and to the refrigerator, which was padlocked, despite the fact that he was living alone.

"There's the meat," he said, pointing to a package inside the refrigerator.

Disappointed but not ready to give up, Gross noticed a large trash bin within eyesight of the apartment window. Thinking that Henyard could have tossed the gun into the bin from the window, Gross decided to go "Dumpster diving."

What he found was a bit of a shock.

"There, smiling up at me, was the rest of the raccoon," he said.

Dave West, who was the lead agent in the case for the FDLE, would not have been amused by the raccoon story, if he knew about it. He had been pushing Gross to get a search warrant for Smalls' home.

Gross balked, not because he didn't want to search the house, but because he was afraid there was not enough legal grounds to get a judge to sign a warrant.

Finally, by Thursday, Gross tried and succeeded in getting a judge to sign a search warrant.

Later, during a deposition, Smalls' lawyer, Jeff Pfister, questioned State Attorney Investigator Pat Kicklighter about the warrant.

"Why did you think the gun was at Smalls' house?"

"By the location of where the car was found, where Smalls' house is, you're just a few doors down from there. We just had good reason to believe there's a possibility that they would not throw the gun away," he said, though he did not elaborate on why he thought they would not ditch the gun.

The house was a small, narrow, "shotgun" type of house (if you fired a shotgun, the pellets would hit every inch of the interior). When Gross arrived at the home, he got permission to search after suggesting to Annette Smalls that it would be safer for the children if she got the kids out of the house. He then pulled the search warrant out of his back pocket and said, "And by the way, we have a search warrant."

It wasn't unusual to find her at home. She didn't work, she would say in a sworn statement. A widow, she was drawing Social Security survivor benefits.

"He got shot somewhere in North Carolina," she said of her late husband.

"I just remember it was so revolting," Gross said of the living conditions. Clothes were piled up everywhere, Kicklighter pulled out a dirty diaper from beneath the couch and Gross almost sat on a newborn infant nestled in the couch cushions in the darkened room. At least two of the young girls in the tiny house had babies.

One striking feature of the house was a broken bathtub faucet that allowed water to pour out continuously at a high rate, Gross said.

Searchers found a crack cocaine pipe and other paraphernalia, but their focus was on trying to find the murder weapon.

The search finally led to a back bedroom that Yon had been sharing with Tamara.

There, under a chair piled high with clothing, was the gun lying on the floor.

Jeff Pfister, the defense attorney who would defend Smalls at his trial, was struck even years later by the picture of the broken faucet gushing water down the drain.

"I have to fix the faucet at my house when it's broken. I just thought, 'what a waste,' and how symbolic it was of what their lives were."

CHAPTER 5

Poor But Rich in Love

Dysfunction junction, crazy, waste, tragic and poor are all are terms that can be used to describe Henyard's and Smalls' lives.

Godly, focused, family-oriented, hardworking and loving are terms that could be used to describe Dorothy and her family. And so are two of the words used to describe the killers: tragic and poor.

Dorothy's family is so different it almost defies imagination. Why? One key reason is Dorothy's mother, Elsie, a soft-spoken, tender-hearted woman who dearly loves her children and grand-children. When the children were growing up, she worked hard cleaning and doing other jobs for a mobile home manufacturer. She dished out what food she could scrape together, and even more important, lessons from the Bible that was propped up on the kitchen table.

Before school, after school, and every time she could get the family to church, she made sure Dorothy and her five siblings were bathed in prayer and scriptures.

She especially focused on one theme: "Be kind to one another." She cited Ephesians 4:32, which reads: "Be kind and compassionate to one another, forgiving each other, just as in Christ God forgave you" (NIV).

Self-esteem was important, too.

"They were poor but didn't know it," she said.

"I kept them clean and in school looking nice," she said.

"I always bought bread, butter, milk and potatoes," she said, making sure the family at least had that much. "It may not have always been what they wanted to eat, but we ate."

The family had been brought to the brink in 1972.

"It was very tough," Elsie said. "My husband left me with six children in school."

She gathered the children and told them: "We're going to have to do without a lot of things but I'm not going to lose the house."

"There were times when we asked for stuff," Margaret said. "Afterward, we knew not to ask."

Elsie lived up to her promise about not losing the house, but did lose some things, including the family car.

Some of the children said they wanted to quit school to help support the family.

"No, you stay in school," she told them. "Be something," she told them.

Today, sister Ozietta is a supervisor in the Marion County Clerk of Court's Office, brother James works for the city of Wildwood, Denese is in home health care, Gene is in construction, Margaret is a registered nurse at one of the finest hospitals in the country, and Dorothy is a teacher and a pastor.

Each had their own reaction to the marital crisis. Margaret became fiercely independent and urged her siblings to do the same.

"He doesn't love us. We need to go on," she would tell her brothers and sisters.

"I wasn't going to let that stop me from taking care of the family. I never wanted to be dependent upon some man," said Margaret, who was always trying to come up with lucrative business ideas and later became a happily married woman, mother and registered nurse.

She said her brothers longed for their father's approval and companionship.

Margaret, who is only a year older than Dorothy, was protective, not only of Dorothy but her other sisters, as well.

To one of her future brothers-in-law, she said: "If you're not going to treat her right, leave her alone."

Ozietta, who was in the third grade when her father left the family, said she remembers her mother working hard to support the family.

"She worked all the time, scrubbing floors for others, picking oranges, whatever it took," Ozietta said. "She made sure we had some food to eat and no holes in our shoes."

Margaret, the oldest girl, found herself as a kind of surrogate mom and disciplinarian as she stepped in to help raise the family.

"Mama was always so easy going. She would say, 'Arthur Gene, I wish you would take your feet off the furniture,'" she said, imitating her mother's soft-spoken, sweet-natured voice.

"Get your feet off the sofa!" Margaret would say.

"Margaret, don't yell at the child like that," Margaret recalls, chuckling, and again imitating her mother's soft voice.

Each child contributed to the family as best they could. The girls cleaned houses, for example, and the boys harvested watermelons or helped operate crop irrigation systems. Sometimes after school, everyone picked oranges. During the Christmas holidays, jobs were available at a citrus packinghouse. Money was placed on the kitchen table or clothing or other items were purchased for their mother, since she didn't like to spend any money on herself.

The split had been brewing for some time.

"He had been raised in the church but quit going," Elsie said.

And he went from being a hardworking farm irrigation worker to running in a fast crowd.

"It was the women," she said.

"I told him, 'When your money's gone your friends will be gone. If the children will, they're the only ones who will take care of you. The Bible doesn't lie, you'll reap what you sow.'"

It was painful for the children. One of the girls came home one day crying and asked: "When will daddy start reaping what he sows?"

Denese, who was the youngest and only 7 at the time, was not as hard hit as the others by the loss. Her strongest memory of that time was her father packing an old leather suitcase.

"It was strange. It was hard. But he was not part of our life anymore. He was just somebody that had kids. It was hard on mama."

They would be confronted by other children with tales of what their father was doing, or told that he had given them money when he had only given their mother $20 to take care of all the children's needs for the week.

Ozietta remembers being teased unmercifully by other girls about her father's alleged sexual exploits.

"I was in classes with girls whose mothers slept with my father," she said.

Because Margaret was about six years older than Ozietta was, she was too far removed to come to her rescue.

"I had to rely on God a lot," Ozietta said.

"You can't believe everything people say," Elsie would tell the children.

"I never talked their daddy down to them," she said.

"When they found out what kind of daddy he was, they were adults," she said. One of those times for Dorothy came when she visited her father in prison, where he was serving time on a drug charge.

"I cried more for my children than for what he was doing to me," Elsie said.

"I was so glad when the kids were grown and they didn't need him."

She was right about reaping and sowing—and forgiveness.

When he became ill and his kidneys shut down, Margaret took him to the hospital in Orlando in her car.

"If not for Mama, you wouldn't be in my front seat right now," she told her father.

"You don't have to wonder what Margaret's thinking. She'll tell you," laughs Elsie, who became Elsie Thomas when she remarried in 1978.

Dorothy's father would end up getting a kidney transplant. And he would undergo a different kind of transformation, too.

"He's turned back to the Lord now," Elsie said, and is faithful in his church attendance.

"To me, that's great."

Arthur Gene Reid, the fourth born child in the family, is 50 now, a proud father of five and a grandfather.

He acknowledges his mother was the spiritual leader of the household.

"She was very, very strong," he said. "Still is."

"All day Sunday was church day," he said. "Whatever was going on during the week, we were there. Sometimes, we traveled to other churches."

There would only be 50 to 60 people in attendance at the rural church on Sunday mornings, but church was the center of their social lives.

"We were outcasts," Ozietta said. "We were from Tennessee. Mama didn't have any family here. We could either go to church or Mama could do what other women in the neighborhood were doing.

"We were in church all the time, Wednesday and Friday night, Sunday, Sunday night. Sunday, we were in church all day."

It wasn't just an opportunity to hang out with like-minded people, however. Spiritual seeds were planted, seeds that would change Gene's life and others, often in miraculous ways.

When he decided to act as Dorothy's personal bodyguard after she was shot, he went with her everywhere she went. Because

Dorothy went to church every chance she got and spent the rest of her time around other Christians, it began to rub off on him.

"When something happens, it's time to look over your life," he said.

He also said, "Being around a lot of positive-thinking people and people trying to live according to the Bible makes you think about how you have been living your life.

"What benefit am I getting from friends who just accumulate things?" he remembers asking himself.

"It did have a big effect on my lifestyle," Arthur Gene said. "I changed my lifestyle. I did accumulate a few things: a wife, children, a home.

"We're just blessed," he said.

The tragedy was a life-changing event for Ozietta, too.

"I wasn't saved, was not in a church. I was just doing my own thing. I thought, 'Here's a woman who was doing nothing but living right. If God allowed this to happen to her....'"

"This was my wake-up call. [I thought] I'd better get it together. I'd rather be living my life for Him," she said.

Denese relied on those lessons from her childhood about the power of prayer. "It instilled the idea of staying strong in spite of everything," she said.

Already a believer, she said the tragedy brought her into a closer walk with God.

The tragedy also brought the family closer together, Ozietta said.

"Elsie taught her children to love each other," Emma said.

"Kids are ignored today. Parents don't have a relationship with their children. They don't spend enough time with them.

"You need family and church and family and church," she said.

Rosalyn Lewis agrees that parents need to stay close to their children.

"I would ask parents to take better checks on their teens," she said. "Even preteens and their peers," she said.

There is more opportunity to get into trouble now than ever before. They may be doing things you wouldn't dream of, she says.

"Kids are raising themselves," she said.

"Don't let them run the streets. Always know who they're with and listen to the children. Talk with them."

Of her two sons and her daughter, she admits that when they were growing up, "I would spy on them. I would want to know what's behind the door, what's in their sock drawer, what's under their mattress. I would say, this is my house, you're living under my rules."

She also keeps tabs on her grand and great-grandchildren. "They're good children, but they're growing too fast," she said, referring to the society that we live in.

Dorothy's family was fortunate because even though she was raising a family without a husband, Elsie made sure the children were well grounded.

"Mama is still the glue, still the centerpiece," said James Reid, 55, the oldest of the family.

"All she wanted us to do was behave. Don't lie or steal. That was her pet peeve. If we were wrong, we were wrong, but she never shunned her love for us. She was there for us, but not to uphold what we had done.

"We didn't have nothing much coming up. She just wanted us to be happy."

Part of that happiness, Reid said, was instilled in them so well, it still holds up to this day.

"We fussed, the ordinary things, we all had our own personalities," he said, "but we're a family and we try to look out for each other.

"We came out fairly well. My hat's off to Mama," Reid said.

Childhood Illnesses

Dorothy seemed to be blessed from the time she was an infant.

Born in the little town of Medon, Tennessee, Dorothy would grow up to have her mother tell her that she was a joy to her family. She did, however, provide some anxious moments.

"My mom said when I was an infant I would smile all the time. One day I stopped smiling and didn't smile for about a month. My family thought I was going to die. After much prayer, my smile returned and my mom knew that life was being restored to me.

"It seemed as though something was always happening to me," she said.

Elsie says that when Dorothy was 3, a 7-year-old cousin accidentally dislocated her leg while he was sweeping the floor. But when everyone was praying for her, Elsie said they could hear the sound of the leg popping back into place, and she was fine.

The family moved to Florida when she was 2.

Once she started attending school, she was frequently sick. When she was 10, she had to be hospitalized for a few days with a strain of intestinal bacteria, and when she was a teen, she complained of weakness in her legs to the point where she had to use crutches.

Doctors were unable to find the cause of the weakness, but after about age 16, she became a healthy teenager.

Character Building

Dorothy was teased by her siblings as a "goody two-shoes," Elsie said.

Margaret concurs.

"Dorothy was always so good, so kind," she said. Maybe even a little too good. "Dad would tell her, 'You tell me if they cut up'."

Dorothy's handwriting bears an uncanny resemblance to her mother's, a fact that was not lost on Margaret, who once asked her teen sister to forge a note so she could skip a class.

"She wouldn't do it," Margaret said. "She cried because I was mad at her," she added.

"She couldn't stand for anyone to be mad at her," said Ozietta, who admits that if she wanted to borrow her car all she had to do was to act as if she was angry with her.

"Margaret used to tell her, 'Let them be mad at you. That way you don't have to worry about them doing the wrong thing,'" Ozietta said, laughing.

"She was always a proper person. She always tried to keep the peace," Elsie said.

As a teen, Dorothy got a job as a receptionist at the mobile home plant where her mother worked.

"In 1978, I began to walk a closer walk with the Lord," Dorothy said. Elsie was the acknowledged family spiritual leader, but like most teens, Dorothy said she sometimes thought, "Whatever."

"I wanted to do what my friends were doing," she said.

Once, when she was about 17 or 18, Dorothy decided she wasn't going to go back to church, Ozietta said.

"We call it backsliding," she said.

One night, Dorothy went to a party and was seen standing near a group of people and holding a cigarette. A young man walked up and said, "Dot Reid? What are you doing out here?"

"I'm going to a party, what are you doing out here?"

"You don't even look right being out here. You need to go home!" said Ozietta. .

It wasn't long after that that Dorothy went back to church.

"I just wanted to do the right thing," Dorothy said.

Dorothy said it wasn't too long after that she reached a real watershed moment of faith in her life, when she turned 21.

Dorothy's family notes that she has always had a tendency to think of others first, which is another sign of spiritual maturity. Matthew 22:39, for example, commands Christians "to love your neighbor as yourself."

"She was always the sweetest, hardest working person. At birthdays or Christmas she always gave the nicest gifts," Elsie said.

"Dorothy, that's a little too expensive," her mother would say.

She could not be talked out of spending her hard-earned money on others, however.

"She was a good girl. She did whatever she could for people," Ozietta said.

"I used to be jealous of her. I thought everything came easy to her. That was not the case. That was just in my mind," Ozietta said. "She was the favorite among the siblings."

"Everybody loves Dorothy," Denese said. "If you don't love Dorothy there's something wrong with you."

Dorothy's concern for others was evident even in her darkest crisis.

"As soon as I walked into Dorothy's hospital room, she said, 'Hi Mom.' She was always worried about how I was doing," Elsie said.

Yet, the family was worried about her. "We didn't know what was going to happen when she came home," Elsie said.

The day she finally returned to her own house, a 6-year-old girl came over from across the street, looked up at Dorothy and said of her older sibling: "My brother killed himself last night," Elsie said.

"Dorothy went right over there to console her," she added.

Lewis

It was in the early '70s that Dorothy met the man who would later become her husband.

His name was James Arthur Lewis, Jr., but she called him Lewis when they became reacquainted in 1982. They dated two years before getting married.

"While dating and in the beginning of our marriage, Lewis used to make me laugh and he appeared to be very caring," she said. "I found out the hard way that people do change after they get married.

"In about two months into our marriage, Lewis changed. It seemed as though I wasn't good enough for him, and no matter what I did he had something negative to say."

Over time, she said, he went from being "self-assured" to "arrogant."

"The first year of our marriage, I suffered from mental abuse. It wasn't until I became a mother that I didn't allow his words to hurt me so badly. I didn't let the negative things he said about me being a wife come between me being the best mother that I could be.

"This type of mental abuse went on for the first three years of our marriage, and in 1987 Lewis became very ill." Lewis, who had been diagnosed with lupus before he married Dorothy, harbored a fear that he would die by age 30.

The chronic inflammatory disease, in which the immune system attacks tissues or organs, can have multiple symptoms, including anxiety.

"He said he didn't feel like himself, like he was going 'schizo.' Of course, that's not what it was," Dorothy said.

"After recovering from that bout of illness, Lewis had a different attitude. He was the man that I fell in love with. He was a good husband and a good father to Jamilya, who was born on November 1, 1985.

"The year 1989 was filled with joy and sadness. We became parents of our second child in February, and in September, we moved from Wildwood to Eustis, where we bought our home. We were so happy.

"On December 23, Lewis came home from work with flu-like symptoms. Jokingly, he accused the girls and me of giving him our colds. The next night, at about 8 p.m., I was preparing to take Lewis to the emergency room to get an antibiotic or some kind of treatment for what I thought was the flu. Just as we were leaving the house, he began to slur his speech."

His condition worsened when he reached the hospital.

"A nurse told him to lie down on the bed, and he said, 'OK.'"

It would be the last word he would ever speak.

The hospital staff ran several tests on Lewis. One of the things they discovered was that his heart was enlarged, leading one doctor to speculate that he had had a stroke.

The real terror would come at 4:30 a.m. on Monday, Christmas Day.

"He was in one of the ER beds. I was standing next to his bed watching him when I noticed his breathing," Dorothy said. "He inhaled, but I didn't see an exhale. I started screaming for the doctors to get in the room to see about him.

"I was removed from the room, and Lewis was hooked up to a breathing machine. I was told that he didn't have any brain activities. It was then that my husband died, but I was in denial."

She had him flown to a hospital in Gainesville where other tests could be administered.

The physicians, who eventually diagnosed the illness as pneumococcal meningitis, were blunt.

"Doctors came in the room. A doctor said, 'Your husband is gone. There's no life in him. We're going to have to take him off the breathing machine. That's just a shell right there.'"

It angered Margaret.

"You can't pressure her to take him off life support," the protective sister said, but the doctor in charge of his care persisted.

"You're going to have to make a decision," he said.

Dorothy agonized over the dilemma, even when the doctor told her that no other hospital or nursing home would accept him as a patient.

"I couldn't do it," she said.

She went to a church service. It was Friday night.

"I told them I needed a miracle to happen. I wanted a prayer line, where we would join hands. I wanted Lewis raised and returned whole. I said, 'If there are any doubters, I don't want you in the circle.' I was going by what Jesus did when he told unbelievers to get out of the house when he was curing a little girl" (Mark 5:35-43).

"As we were praying, a still voice, a quiet voice said, 'No.' I fell to my knees and said, 'Please don't tell me that.' And I heard 'No,' again.

"That's when I accepted that he was gone."

She went to the hospital the next morning and told the hospital not to do anything until his family could come down from New Jersey to say their goodbyes.

The next day, on December 30, he was dead. He was 31.

"So, there I was, a single parent with two children; Jamilya, 4, and Jasmine, 10 months."

There was more bad news. Margaret had been urging Lewis to buy a life insurance policy for his young family, but when she went back to the couple's home, she could see the policy spread out on a table for his inspection—without his signature.

Times were tough, and not just financially. Dorothy said she went from asking "how could this happen?" to periods in which she just wept for hours.

"I cried because Lewis was gone and because God was making ways for us," she said.

Shortly after they got married, Lewis had bought a small pickup truck.

"I would never drive it. It was his and I had my own car," she said. But when her car broke down she would drive the truck.

"I would be crying and saying to God, 'but you're still making a way for us.' One car is down but Lewis left us with this truck. There were so many mixed emotions," she said.

"For about a year after he died I would go out to his grave almost every day on my lunch break and just talk. It was like I was kind of angry with Lewis because it seemed he didn't put up much of a fight. I would say, 'You didn't even try to fight this.' If he got a little scratch on his finger he would say, 'Dorothy I got a scratch on my finger.' He was that kind of guy. He couldn't stand pain. And then for this to happen, he didn't complain. I couldn't figure it out."

No one in the family expected Lewis to die, said Ozietta, who was at home on leave from the Army at that time.

"We thought he just had a cold," Ozietta said.

"We couldn't imagine that anything was seriously wrong. We're like Margaret, we can't stand wimpy men. We thought he had a cold and was acting like a baby."

"Dorothy really beat herself up over making remarks like that, but we didn't know," Ozietta said.

There were more worries.

"About six months after Lewis died, one night Jamilya came down with a temperature of 105 degrees," Dorothy said.

"I wanted to take her to the ER, but she refused to go. She was crying and said: 'I don't want to go there because daddy went there and never came back home again.'

"I lost it. All three of us were crying.

"So I called Lewis's aunt, who was my pastor at the time. She came over to help me pray and take care of Jamilya through the night. I began to pray, and I gave Jamilya sponge baths along with medicine to break the fever.

"When the morning came, Jamilya's fever had broken and never returned," she said.

It wasn't the first time Jamilya had worried her mother. At the age of 2, Jamilya was hospitalized because she was diagnosed with pneumococcal bacteria.

In 1990, during a regular visit to Jamilya's doctor, Dorothy mentioned that Lewis had died of meningitis. The doctor, worried about the ability of the children's immune system to fight off meningitis, ordered tests. Jasmine's test results were good, but Jamilya's immune system resistance was very low.

The doctor prescribed amoxicillin and recommended that she take it for the rest of her life.

"About two years after Lewis' death, I saw that I was able to maintain our home, so I quit a job of 15 years to go to college full-time in hopes of making a better living for my girls and me. During this time, I had to be on a strict budget because the only income I had was from Lewis' Social Security," she said.

"Being a single parent raising two daughters had its good and bad days, but the good days outweighed the bad. I never regretted being a mother to my girls; I loved them so much and they gave me joy. After the passing of their father, I had to be strong for Jamilya and Jasmine. It was because of them that I had the courage to go on."

That courage would soon be tested beyond human limitations, however. Fortunately, for Dorothy, she would not be relying on her own capabilities.

"God is my strength, my everything," she said.

CHAPTER 6

"Spiritual Surgery"

Shock, fear, living nightmare, self-recrimination, depression, search for meaning. They are all descriptive words, yet they still fall short of describing what Dorothy was going through in the dark days after the bright lights of Jasmine and Jamilya were snuffed out by their ruthless killers.

Despite the best, loving efforts of her friends and family, Dorothy—like every crime victim—would ultimately have to figure it out for herself. This journey, which no one would ever voluntarily take, would ultimately prove to be inspiring to others.

It wouldn't be easy. First, there was what she called a feeling of "blah" in the days immediately following the crimes. She was just going through the motions and she wasn't her normal, easy-going, sweet-natured self.

"Ornery" is the word that her family used when she balked at wearing the dress that had been picked out for her for the funeral. And it is the word they used when she became uncharacteristically angry when there was a mix-up with the arrival of the funeral home limousine and she said she wasn't going to go the funeral.

It is clear she was in shock and was depressed.

"It would have been abnormal if she hadn't been depressed," Snitkin said, though she said she would not have described Dorothy as clinically depressed.

It wasn't just the psychological trauma of losing her children that Dorothy had to deal with. She had sustained gunshot wounds, mostly head wounds, that surprisingly did not kill her. She was left, however, with what she thought would be severe, permanent injuries, including the loss of smell and taste. She was also disfigured by the point-blank wounds. Her teeth had been shot out, leaving the already reserved young woman feeling vulnerable to the point that she constantly put her hand over her mouth. And for a time, she had a visible wound on her forehead.

Left largely unspoken by some of her friends and family, but just as traumatic, was the fact that she had been brutalized by two young males in the most impersonal, demeaning way possible, and probably within view of her terrorized, young children. Dorothy herself wrote about it, in a required victim statement to the State Attorney's Office seven months after the crime. She wrote, "Even during the actual rape itself, my primary concern was for my children. Although I did everything I could to protect them, even seven months after this all occurred, I feel awful at the thought of how frightened my two little girls were during the abduction, during the rape and later when they were taken without me."

Dorothy would need a series of surgeries for her gunshot wounds. Once she was discharged from the hospital after her initial stay, it was agreed that she should stay with her godmother, Emma, in nearby Ocala.

Even the simple things were hard, Emma noted.

"She couldn't eat anything but soft food because her teeth were shot out." Emma recalls that she fixed mashed potatoes, mashed peas, and whatever else she could think of for Dorothy, whose appetite was so diminished she had to be coaxed to eat.

Tyranny of Fear

Dorothy was also uncharacteristically afraid.

"It is almost impossible for anyone who did not experience what my children and I experienced to understand fully how this event affected my family and me."

She wrote, "This event has robbed me of my life, my children and my physical emotional well being. It ... left me in a constant state of fear."

"She was scared of the dark," Emma said. "She had to have lights on all the time."

And she slept fitfully and only then in brief time spans.

"That was a very bad time, a very bad time," Emma said. "She wouldn't let my husband go out at night."

Dorothy also wrote in her statement: "My daily life has totally changed because now I live my life in constant fear. I do not go anywhere alone unless it is absolutely necessary. I am constantly looking over my shoulder to make sure no one is following me. I try to avoid being alone, even at home. When I am at home, I keep the curtains closed to avoid anyone knowing that I am home by myself, for fear that a bad event can occur again."

Though a home health nurse would make visits, one night Emma had to take her to the hospital because the nurse was unable to get an intravenous line started in her arm.

"There were some boys there and one of them had a hood on his jacket. That did it," Emma said.

"I was standing at the receptionist desk in the ER waiting to see a nurse," Dorothy recalls.

"I saw a guy with a red hooded jacket on coming toward me, and I automatically thought about my attacker because he wore a hooded jacket the night of my tragedy. I wanted to scream, but I didn't want to make a fool of myself. I must have looked terrified, because the receptionist said, 'Are you alright?' But I couldn't speak. Then she took me out of the waiting room into a private room to wait for the nurse. I was shaking all over, and overwhelmed with fear."

Ozietta remembers visiting with Dorothy after the frightening flashback.

When frightened, Dorothy would whisper, Ozietta said. "She said, 'Ozietta, I almost lost it…. Everything just came flooding back. I wanted to run but I couldn't.'"

Ozietta told her, "It's OK to feel what you're feeling. I can't imagine going through what you've been through. Don't beat yourself up."

Elsie stayed with Dorothy during the day while Emma worked, so Dorothy would never have to be alone. Ozietta, who visited Dorothy every day on her lunch breaks or after work, would take her sister's emotional temperature and react accordingly.

"Sometimes, if Dorothy didn't want to talk, I would just hold her hand. Sometimes I would sing. She always loved to sing."

"Brick Wall"

Emma wasn't the only one being supportive.

Arthur Gene, his protective brotherly instincts riled up and his street-smart antennae raised, became her bodyguard. When she eventually returned to her house, he slept on the floor outside her room each night and accompanied her everywhere as a formidable-looking shadow.

"That was my purpose, to be wherever she was," he said.

Was there a credible threat to her at that point? Perhaps not, he reasons in retrospect.

"It's just that she didn't want for nothing," he said, and "if anything did come up, they would have to come through a brick wall [to get to her]."

Gene, who wore a "do-rag" scarf on his head like the ones bikers wear, was only too happy to give off scary vibes.

"I'm not the type of person who smiles all the time. I gave the impression, 'This is not somebody you want to play with.'"

He got the message across—almost too well—his mother said. "He scared some people."

But it was a comfort for Dorothy; tucked in between the fierce, protective attitudes of her family and others, she felt safe enough to begin recovering.

"In the first six months Dorothy was not left alone for 10 minutes," Snitkin said.

"If she went to the doctor, you had to go with her. You couldn't leave her side," Denese said. Things eventually got better.

"I watched her grow," Denese said. Eventually Dorothy would start saying, "It's OK, I can do that by myself," including going into stores.

Family Trauma

Typically, Dorothy was thinking of others, and was concerned about how the trauma had affected her family.

"For their part, members of my family have tremendous emotional pain," she wrote in her statement for prosecutors. "For example, one of my sisters cannot even talk about this event. I have another sister, Margaret, who has been a tremendous help to me, both emotionally and physically. Margaret is filled with anger about this event. Even in the early stages of this whole event, the fear was immediate. Margaret said that for the first three hours I was in the hospital no one in the family knew where my two children were and what had happened to them."

One of the ones who was shocked and upset was James Reid.

"I was in the Marion County jail when it happened," he said. "There was a news flash that interrupted a ball game. I looked up and saw my mama's face and my mama's car. I just said, 'That's my mama.'

"They showed pictures of my nieces. I got hold to the guard. There were some guys who wanted to turn the channel on the TV, but there was a bunch of good guys standing behind me."

It would take awhile, and after some frantic worry, he was eventually able to make a call and find out that it was Dorothy, not Elsie, who had been brutally attacked, and that the girls had been murdered.

Reid, who was in jail on a domestic violence charge, was allowed to attend the funeral, and it was a short time after that that he was released from jail, stunned and furious at what had happened to his family.

"It hit me like a rock," he said. For one thing, there was only a three-month difference in the age of his youngest daughter and Jamilya, something that still upsets him.

Dorothy, in her victim impact statement, repeated the fact that Margaret was angry, adding: "Although nothing physical was taken from her, she suffers from an enormous sense of loss because the killing of my children was so needless and so senseless."

Dorothy said her traumatic experience made an impact on her sister.

"It has also affected the way Margaret looks at young boys and men, being very cautious of anyone who is around her," she wrote.

"God Didn't Do This"

Not surprisingly, one of the first steps in Dorothy's recovery was to fall back on her faith.

First, she had to get past those who didn't have the same kind of experience and understanding of God that she had.

Some, for example, would ask: "How can you trust God after what He did?"

"God didn't do this," she would reply.

"So many victims are so mad at God for letting these things happen," Snitkin said. "Dorothy never said that to me."

Elsie has said the same thing, and quotes Dorothy as saying: "Why get angry with God? I can't beat Him."

Instead, Dorothy favored her mother's attitude.

"He's been good throughout the whole thing," Elsie says. "If we can't get over it, we'll just get through it. We're always going through things. He doesn't leave us hanging, there's always a way of escape."

Dorothy had a unique perspective on the death of the girls.

"I didn't question God on this one. Now, I did question God about Lewis as to why didn't Lewis fight. My thing was, He could have saved them it if He wanted to. So, my thing was just accepting it. Help me to accept it and go on."

She did her best to think of things in a positive vein. Perhaps God needed or wanted the girls more than she did, she thought.

Maybe He was protecting them from some future horror by taking them now.

They may have grown up only to have been permanently scarred by the crime they witnessed against her, she noted.

Denese has tried to analyze the "why" question, and agrees that the girls may have been irreparably harmed by the trauma, had they lived.

"They were such little angels. They never knew anything about tragedy or anger," she said.

Dorothy was allowed to survive so she could tell her story, Denese said.

Still, Denese admits that initially, "It was hard not to be angry with God. He could have stopped it," she reasoned.

Some people offered their own views on why the girls were not spared.

"God loves rosebuds, too," a friend wrote to Dorothy.

Rosalyn Lewis, who prayed for Dorothy and asked others to do the same, also prayed for herself, including when she attended the trials.

"God, give me the strength to get over it," she prayed. "And I have," Lewis said.

Lewis said she didn't try to make sense of the tragedy.

"I have faith enough to believe that everything happens for a reason. I don't go around doubting God. I was just happy to know that the ones who were responsible were caught," she said.

Power of Prayer

But how did Dorothy stay positive? How did she stay sane?

"I believe it was because of the strength that others were praying for me," Dorothy said.

"I don't doubt that at all," Snitkin said.

Dorothy's mother was certainly asking God for mercy.

"Lord, she's hurt enough. Don't let her hurt anymore," Elsie prayed.

Dorothy prayed for herself too, asking for strength, "to get through this and not feel sorry for myself."

Were her prayers answered?

Not only did she get through it physically, "but that's why I have a sound mind," she said.

"People would say to me, 'You're such an amazing woman.' And I would say, 'To God be the glory,' because there was no way on earth for me to do it on my own," she said.

Dorothy, who likes to talk about how God performed "spiritual surgery" to soothe her soul, says there was no writing-in-the-sky moment from God saying everything was going to be OK.

"I was just taking it one day at a time."

But she also had a sense that because God is faithful, He would get her through it.

For one thing, there was what she called "an outpouring of love" from the community. A local Moose Lodge started collecting donations to help her meet her expenses. Her electric and cable bills were paid. A dentist worked on her teeth for free, the nickel-sized powder burn on her forehead eventually disappeared, and she was able to get her sense of smell and taste back.

Why Spared?

She had to face another normal but tough question that some survivors can never come to grips with.

"There seemed to be some reason that I was spared," she said. The question was why?

"I figured that God considered me so that He could be glorified, so that I would be the instrument that He used to let people know that He is God. He is God in that, 'Here's a lady who was shot, raped, thrown in the bushes and left for dead. And I am God, that I can raise this person, allow her to walk and knock on somebody's door and tell them what happened to her, explain to the officers what happened, and spare her life.'

"Who else but God? And when I share this message about what God has brought me from, and how He has shown me with a sound mind and spared me, who else but God?"

She believes there is no way she could have survived or gotten stronger on her own. "No way, no how. To God be the glory," Dorothy said.

Margaret had a hard time coming to grips with the tragedy.

"It just seemed so surreal," she said.

"How could God allow this to happen? He could have stopped the enemy."

Meanwhile, Dorothy was telling everyone she didn't want to hear about Job, and neither did Margaret.

"God didn't have to allow this to get glory," she reasoned. "Don't talk to me about this," Margaret told a fellow church member.

When a church leader cautioned her not to be angry with God, Margaret corrected him.

"I didn't say I was angry at God."

But she acknowledged that she didn't really understand it.

"Some things we'll never know," Margaret said.

But it was Dorothy's belief—that God could turn her tragedy into a blessing for others—that would shape her life and the lives of others.

"I had accepted God's calling to teach God's Word before this tragedy," she said.

By about 1991, her pastor had consented to let her deliver the Sunday morning message on the fourth Sunday of the month, which was dedicated to the youth. She would also be asked occasionally to speak at women's day programs.

But two years after the Super Bowl weekend tragedy, there was an even more powerful demonstration of God's power and mercy that she could talk about, she reasoned.

But the first thing that had to happen, she knew, was that she had to overcome the fear that now gripped her so intensely.

Bold Spirit

"God, you spared me for something," she prayed, "and I can't do it if I'm going to be scared."

It wasn't just the trauma of the crime that worried her. By nature she was introverted. It was then that she discovered a Bible verse that would help her. The verse, 2 Timothy 1:7 reads: "For God did not give us a spirit of timidity, but a spirit of power, of love and of self-discipline" (NIV).

Each time she addressed a group she would talk about God's power and mercy. Soon, other churches began to hear about her incredible story and asked if she would talk to their congregations.

When she appeared, if the crowd did not recognize her name, the introductory remarks would clue them in.

Some would come to hear her speak out of curiosity. It was unnerving but Dorothy would use it to break the ice.

"Alright, just look at me. Here I am, just get the staring out of the way," she said, laughing.

Sometimes she would be asked to speak to drug rehabilitation groups, and always with the same message.

"If you want to be delivered, He will deliver you. Look what He did for me."

"I would talk about when I got shot in the head. When the head goes the body is nothing. So when the enemy [Satan] saw that that didn't kill me, he would figure, 'Surely she will die when she finds out her girls died. I'm going to get her one way or the other.'

"I would tell them how prayers were prayed, that I would not have any more pain. My mom prayed, 'Lord, she's hurt enough, don't let her hurt any more.' My godmom prayed that prayer," she said, adding that church members and others also offered up the same prayer. 'Don't let her hurt anymore.'"

People see her as a "walking miracle," Ozietta said. People who might not be familiar with her story are enthralled with her testimony, she said.

"People are just amazed. She's a ball of fire anyway. She'll say, 'I'm not telling you this to feel sorry for me.'"

Dorothy tells people she is telling her story to show how awesome God is.

"People come away with hope," Ozietta said.

Of course, prayer is a crucial part of her message.

One of Dorothy's favorite scriptures today is the second sentence in James 5:16, which reads: "The effective, fervent prayer of a righteous man avails much" (NKJV).

Were the prayers for physical or mental healing?

"I believe that prayer was mentally. I still have physical pain.... That's why I have a sound mind. And I share with the people that I believe God performed a spiritual surgery on me because He took the hurt away. I can honestly say He did that."

Counseling

There were attempts to line up earthly help, too, with varying levels of success.

The first such effort was through a psychologist recommended by Snitkin.

The first thing he did was to shut his office door for privacy.

"I was very, very nervous. I was being shut up in this room with a man I didn't even know.

"He would ask me questions like, 'Well, how do you feel?' And, 'If you could talk to the girls what would you say to them?'

"He asked me something about God. And I said to him, 'It's a miracle that I'm alive.'

"He was like, 'Well, why would you say that?' I said because it seems like that if anybody should have died that night, it should have been me, based on where I was shot and the number of times I was shot, so yes, it is a miracle that I am alive.'

"This guy, apparently, didn't have any sense of Christianity, or so it seemed, so he wasn't helping me."

Later, she went with him to a grief support group. "Going to these meetings, I found them so depressing."

She was amazed at the people who went to the meetings. In some cases, people had suffered the loss of a child "years and years ago," she said.

"They were crying on each other's shoulders and not even trying to pick themselves up. I'm like, 'This is so depressing.'

"I didn't want to tell Greta. I didn't want to hurt her feelings, so I would continue to go there once a month."

One night, fiery FDLE Agent David West, who would become a friend of Dorothy's, went with her to one of the meetings.

"He was just listening to all the stories of the people being sad, and [after the meeting] he was like, 'Dorothy, these people here are just draining your energy.'

"I love Dave West," she says, laughing.

West, for his part, describes her as a "personal miracle to behold."

She was and still is an inspiration, West said.

"I was a big boy with a badge and a gun and I was trying to be her helper and protection and I came away stronger after being with her."

Dorothy, of course, realized that West was right about the sessions not helping her.

"But then I realized well, maybe I'm helping them. Here, I've just gone through this and God is carrying me through this, so hopefully I was giving them some hope.

"I saw that counselor one other time and he noticed a big difference in me from the first time. I said, 'You know, I'm coming to you this second time to let you know I am doing fine. God is helping me through this and I'm not feeling sorry for myself. And I want to go on and do whatever I need to do and I don't want people to feel pity for me because I don't want to feel pity for myself. Because no one wants to be around a pitying person all the time.'

"And he was like, 'Wow, you really have come a long way.' And I said, 'To God be the glory.'

"So I didn't have to go in his office anymore. He did go ahead and continue the meetings with the other victims. We were all in the room together."

Brock

It was then that a friend told Margaret about a Christian counselor. The friend had already talked to Hugh Frazier Brockington II.

Highly intelligent, the holder of a doctorate degree in Christian counseling, Brock, who was 38 years old at the time, was and still is as energetic as he is smart.

His father, the Rev. Hugh F. Brockington, Sr., Ph.D., of Metropolitan Missionary Baptist Church, was a key civil rights figure in the Cocoa area in the late 1950s and '60s. The former builder and pastor of Mount Olive Missionary Baptist Church in Fort Pierce, Florida, coordinated his political efforts through the Civic League and other organizations to make sure people in the black community knew who to vote for, as Brock put it.

It was a dangerous, turbulent time. Famed civil rights pioneer Harry T. Moore and his wife, who also lived in Brevard County, were killed in 1951 when someone planted dynamite beneath their house, and the Klan was active in the 1960s and making some ugly headlines in nearby St. Augustine and other places in the state.

In the 1960s, Brock's father received calls from President Kennedy, Vice President Hubert Humphrey, President Lyndon Johnson and the Rev. Martin Luther King, Jr. Brock's father sometimes visited with the famed civil rights leader in Atlanta, especially when he had revivals.

Brock traveled with his father late at night to help coordinate efforts for elections. "My father received calls related to city, county, courthouse, state house up to the White House," Brock said.

And if the Rev. Billy Graham was coming to the area, his father received a call, Brock said.

"I remember there was a telephone switchboard on the bookcase in my father's office," Brock said.

Lake County had a hateful legacy in those days. It was so well-known that Brock's adoptive mother, Collis Lee Sutton Brockington, would later beg him not to move there. She died in 2001. Brock's biological mother, Dorothy "Dot" Wilks, is still living.

In 1949, four young black men were arrested and charged with attacking a farmer and raping his wife in Lake County in a notorious, nationally known case, the "Groveland Four."

A posse killed one suspect before he could be arrested, and the National Guard had to be called in to restore order when black communities were attacked by mobs. Thurgood Marshall, who would later become a U.S. Supreme Court justice, was the NAACP defense attorney. Sheriff Willis McCall shot and killed one defendant on the ride from state prison to a retrial, saying he was trying to escape. But the other defendant with him that night survived his wounds and said the shooting was unprovoked.

It took years for the stigma and the fear of Lake County to subside.

Brock remembers his parents carefully taking some roads and not others while visiting relatives.

"I do not remember traveling U.S. 441 until the late 1960s with my parents," he said.

"Today I can honestly say that Lake County does not appear to be the Lake County that I grew up hearing so much about. The citizens of Lake County who are people of color have been so gracious to me and my family and we are so thankful. In every ethnic group we have the good individuals as well as the bad individuals, but the good always outweigh the bad," he said.

Hate was a foreign concept to Brock.

"I grew up in a family that shared love," he said. There was plenty of love to go around. An only child, Brock nonetheless grew up with his "godsister," Lydia Stacey Reynolds. He also describes his father as "a community servant."

It was not unusual to go to church and find that his father had given a homeless person permission to spend the night there.

Something that was unusual, however, was that Brock's father sometimes swapped places on Sunday morning with the Rev. James Sawyer at the First Baptist Church of Cocoa.

"This was unheard of," Brock said. "A black preacher and choir preaching and singing in an all-white church on Sunday morning, and the white preacher and choir in a black church? This was race relations at its greatest," he said.

There were some other breakthroughs before the color barriers finally came down.

"Sheriff Rollin Zimmerman would stop by our home for dinner or to chat at least once a week," Brock said. And Bill Nelson, who is currently the Democratic U.S. senator from Florida, would call his father.

During the '60s several white families worshipped at Rev. Brockington's church. One family, the Jordans, became members and purchased Bibles for every child that attended Sunday school. Mrs. Betty Jordan later became the godmother of Hugh III, Kristopher Keith and Nikia. Kristopher was given the middle name Keith, in memory of her son.

Many other white families supported Brock's father's ministry.

The Rev. Brockington, meanwhile, recruited doctors to serve the black community.

It could be tough growing up, he said, because everyone knew his parents and expected him to live up to their high standards. If he missed the mark he could be spanked by everyone from the principal to his neighbors—before he got home, and was disciplined again.

"They made sure I did what I had to do," he said.

"The word abuse did not exist until integration was created. Prior to integration it was applying the board of education to the seat of understanding, and it got some understanding," Brock said.

"This is why we did not have many blacks in jail during those years. Disrespect and crime was minimal in the black community during those years. Prayer was in the schools and our teachers were seen as role models because they were the ones that educated everyone. Teachers did not fear getting into trouble for spanking a child in the black community because it was a community raising the children. This is not true today," he said.

Brock was among the first black children in the area to desegregate the local public schools.

Brock first stepped up behind a pulpit as an interim pastor in 1986 at The Greater Union Missionary Baptist Church in DeLand. A few months later he accepted the call from Mount Moriah Missionary Baptist Church in Plant City. The building was condemned and gutted with only four walls standing.

Brock, however, said he had a vision that God had given him, and the building was redesigned with the help and blessings of faithful members.

In 1998 Brock wrote and published Brockington's Manual: *What Every Pastor and Layman/Member Should Know About the Local Baptist Church,* and *A Model Church Constitution and By-Laws for the Local Missionary Baptist Church,* which was adopted and used by many churches. In 1994 he would write a book with Dorothy called *Reclamation and Rededication Through Synergistic Unity.* The book was used as a blueprint for addressing needs in Altamonte Springs, and is still in use in Eustis. One of his first counseling assignments was at Lake Correctional Institution, where he worked with the state prisoners who had alcohol and drug abuse problems.

"For all the schooling I had, I got a real education there."

When Dorothy was still in the hospital, a friend had asked Brock to meet with Dorothy so he could counsel her.

But the normally self-confident man's first thought was, "What could I possibly say to her?"

He also thought, "I don't want to push myself on anyone."

After some convincing, however, he agreed to at least offer his services. He went to the hospital to see her but could not get past Margaret.

"No, she doesn't know you so you can't come in," she said.

He was persistent, however.

"He came one other time when Margaret wasn't there and mom let him in the door," Dorothy said.

"She was bandaged up and not comfortable being around any-one," Brock said. "She didn't want to be bothered."

Later, he learned that Dorothy was not being helped by the counselor who had been seeing her.

Brock, who apparently does not have a prejudicial bone in his body, had a theory. He told Margaret: "White counselors don't always know how to deal with black people. Our communication is differ-ent a lot of times."

Margaret heard him out and asked Dorothy if she wanted to meet with him. An agreement was reached for the two to meet at Margaret's home in Orlando.

"I told her I would do it for nothing," he said, referring to coun-seling fees.

When he met with her he was struck by one thing immediately—she was blaming herself. She was blaming herself for putting the girls in the car before she could get to the driver's side door, and blamed herself for the entire incident, it seemed.

Then he asked her: "Well, what could you have done differently?"

The answer was simple—nothing.

Snitkin would later hold a town meeting in Eustis to talk about the crime that had rocked the community.

One man asked the question: "Why didn't she just run when she realized what was happening?"

"Because her babies were in the car," she said.

Why did the man ask the question in the first place?

"Blame the victim," Snitkin said.

"I thought that I could protect them better if I was with them. I thought if I ran away, the girls would get out of the car, and those guys would hurt them. I was told, 'Just do what I tell you to do and no one will get hurt,'" she would say years later, still second-guessing herself somewhat.

And Brock gave her something the other counselor did not: Scriptures that assured her that God had never abandoned her. It was part of what he calls "RAW," therapy, or "Reality Action Word."

It took a little while for Dorothy to let go of the self-blame game. One of the turning points came when he pointed out that she had been willing to give up her own life to save the girls.

"That helped me. My self-esteem was coming up," Dorothy said.

He also asked some questions in an effort to find out where she was in the grieving process and talked about the various stages that the bereaved typically go through. He was impressed that she knew about the various stages.

Asked to rate her healing on a scale of 1 to 10, she said she thought she was an 8.

"I told him that God was really carrying me through this. I could relate to the 'Footprints in the Sand' picture, the popular poem that talks about how Jesus not only does not leave us alone in times of trouble, but carries us during those times."

Brock is familiar with people who go through the decades-long grieving process like the one Dorothy witnessed in the support group. That level of pain causes stress, anxiety and depression, he says. It causes wear and tear on the body and spirit.

"Textbook counselors" as he calls them, tell patients about five stages of grief that they must go through. He disagrees. Not everyone mourns the same way, he says.

"God does not want His people to maintain a life filled with grief but a life filled with love for release and relief.

"Because she has a strong spiritual connection, she made it a lot easier," he said of the healing process.

Besides his formal education, Brock was able to draw on another one of his family's legacies for wisdom about how to handle grief.

Brock had worked for a time for Stone Brothers Funeral Home of Cocoa, owned by Richard and Rudy Stone, and had grown up with the Samuel Gaines family, who operated the funeral business in Fort Pierce, Florida.

"When my father took ill and later passed in 1983, Mr. Rudy saw something in me and treated me as if I was his biological son. One day, while working in the morgue, I told him that I was going to quit school. He hit me in the chest and said, 'Over my dead body!'"

Later, when Stone was on his deathbed, he told Brock that he loved him as a son and told him how proud he was of him.

After Stone's death, Brock set out to return the favor for all his kindness by seeking to become a mentor to Stone's son, Rujay.

"Beautiful Spirit"

In talking with Dorothy that first time, Brock saw no evidence that she was ever mired in the first three steps of the conventionally described stages of mourning: denial, anger and bargaining.

Dorothy has her own explanation, including overcoming the potentially crippling step of depression: "God is still carrying me through this," she says. Brock and Dorothy say her faith carried her through to step five—acceptance.

Brock likes to talk about three steps of healing: "Recognizing God and Jesus as the Healer, ask for help and developing a faith walk."

As he puts it, "She is a living testimony that individuals do not always experience the five stages of grief."

He also showed her a book that he had written the year before, *Introductory Tools and Strategies for Counseling and Motivating Special Populations.*

When the initial session was over, he left.

"Ohhh, I think he likes you," Elsie said.

Dorothy brushed that observation aside very quickly, however. Her head was bandaged and her teeth were not fixed yet. "How can he like me?"

In the second session, she talked about a fear of being out in a crowd, especially with young black men who reminded her of her attackers. To help her overcome that fear, he later invited her to attend a football game in Orlando with another couple.

By the end of the second counseling session, Brock told Margaret that he would have to "back off" as counselor because he "shouldn't be having feelings like that for a patient."

"I saw myself becoming emotionally attached," he said.

Asked what attracted him, he smiles and says, "Just look at her!" Among other things, he was struck by what he described as her "humbleness, spiritual contact with God, non-wavering faith, her compassion, and her inner and outer beauty," as he put it.

"She cared about others even in her situation. She had a beautiful spirit about her," he said.

So, the counseling relationship ended and another kind of bond blossomed. He went from being "Dr. Brockington" to "Brock" or "Precious Heart," or whatever loving name she chose.

Waxing poetic, he says, "To this date she continues to make my heart create its own rhythm with a flutter, my mouth stutter, and resurrect a spring of joy like no other. When I look into her eyes I can see love and hope. She is my Queen and my woman in the Royal Priesthood that God has given unto me."

He offered encouragement and they became friends. He became a regular fixture, including at family gatherings and church events.

He had won over Margaret, which was crucial.

"It seemed to her that he was bringing me some kind of joy," Dorothy said.

It had been three years since Lewis had died.

"What helped her was meeting Brock," said Snitkin, who remembers the day Dorothy told her that Brock had asked her to go to dinner.

"Go to dinner with the man," Snitkin advised.

And when Dorothy told her that he was "so nice," Snitkin gave her some additional advice: "You ought to cultivate this one."

The romantic relationship would take a long time to develop.

"It was a year before I let him kiss me on the lips, a little smack," Dorothy said.

"He was very, very patient."

Brock called it "careful dating."

"In a situation like that if you hold her it is to show her that she is safe, that she could feel safe. It was hard when my emotions would kick in."

Meeting Dorothy, he said, is proof that "God will meet your needs and wants.

"Dorothy made me understand that on the side of every good man is a good woman and not 'behind every man is a good woman,'" he said. More than a partnership, "we are one," he said.

Thrilled that he has found the love of his life, there was a part of his psyche that was bruised from two previous marriages.

"I had to learn that I'm not perfect. I made mistakes."

He is proud of the fact that he is now the father of six, ranging in age from 12 to 38. Two were the children of one of his two ex-wives, but he considered them to be his own and did as much parenting as he could long-distance when they moved to Detroit.

Expanded Family

Hugh III is 25, and has been a model and an actor in Hollywood, California, for five years.

His father and "MaMa Dorothy" as he calls her, "have been very supportive of it," he says.

"If not for them, I wouldn't be here."

He came to know Dorothy when he was in the fourth grade.

Every other weekend, he would alternate between his mother, Janice, in Lake Mary, Florida, and spending time with his dad and Dorothy. Friday nights were spent eating pizza and watching family TV shows.

He credits his mother and father and Dorothy for giving him a peaceful childhood because they never used him as a pawn like some divorced families do with their children. In fact, Dorothy was careful to include Hugh's mother in her family's gatherings, and they were always cordial and willing to come together for special family events, he said.

He laughs and says, "I really feel like I'm turning into my parents. My dad repeats stories; I know I do the same thing."

Even stranger, considering that he is in the heart of Tinsel Town, he finds himself actively studying the Word of God.

"What am I doing going to church and Bible study?" he said. "I'm in Los Angeles. I didn't think this would happen."

He is the lead singer in the Grammy-nominated choir at West Angeles Church of God in Christ.

He remembers when he first met Dorothy and she seemed "a little timid," he said. "She was very nice, very sweet," he said.

Homecoming trips now reveal a much different person, he said.

"When I see her [preach] in church, she's wild, she's on fire for the Lord," he says. "She gets very excited. She goes full out with it and she doesn't care."

Not surprising, the young actor, model and dancer, uses the "full out" dance term to describe his dad, too.

"If he has a vision, he goes for it. If it doesn't work as planned, he is unfazed. He gets up the next day and goes full out again," Hugh said.

"I'm not there yet. I hope to be. Because I think I am getting to be more like him, I think I will be."

He said he and Dorothy always check on him to see if he is staying on task and is busy.

He has been busy. He has done modeling jobs for Target, Apple, Nokia, Keds and Activision, which produces Tony Hawk's skateboarding game. Recently, he had a speaking part on the popular Nickelodeon TV show "Drake & Josh." He's also appeared in Britney Spears' music video "If You Seek Amy" as well as Disney's Ashley Tisdale's "Kiss the Girl."

He has trained with dancer/choreographer Kevin "Tony Czar" Colin.

It is a strange sensation to see yourself on a giant advertising poster, he said. "It doesn't seem real."

He said Dorothy and his father embarrassed him a little when they attended his sister's wedding in Detroit not too long ago when they saw his picture in the Apple Store at the Somerset Mall in Troy and began telling others and taking his photo next to the poster.

One of his big dreams now is to study real estate development at UCLA so he can build parks and environmentally friendly "green" buildings.

He said he wants to do something in life to tie it all together, perhaps using fame to become a philanthropist.

Whatever it is, he wants to go "full out."

His brother, Kristopher Keith Brockington, 23, remembers the first time he met "MaMa Dorothy." He was about 6 and he was taken with her kindness and the way she treated the brothers as if they were her own sons.

When Dorothy and Brock were married "it was all good," Kristopher said, "because we now have an extended family with

Granny (Dorothy's mother). Dad said Granny is just like his mother. She treated us like we are her grandchildren."

Every other weekend he and his brother would both stay with Dorothy and their dad. They did family things and went to church. Dorothy and his dad encouraged the boys to play the drums at church. He grew up as a child with a full set of drums. His mom and dad played the piano and Janice was a lead singer with The Florida Mass Choir. Today if they have a family gathering, moms Janice and Dorothy may sing, with his stepfather, Veit, playing the piano.

He said he was pleasantly surprised to see Dorothy play the drums at church.

He noticed that in the beginning Dorothy was very cautious about going places. After Joshua was born she became more relaxed about going to various places, he said.

"She never disrespected us and treated us equal. She cooked spaghetti because we really liked it and [she] makes some mean Dorothy Burgers. If we wanted something she was always willing to do it for us."

If he needed help with school work she did her best to help him understand it, he said.

Once, after going on a ride at Busch Gardens, Dorothy became ill, but typically, for Dorothy, she encouraged the concerned boys to go ahead and have fun.

Kristopher said that it is "cool" that his family does not get upset with each other and how all four parents come to an agreement on what is best for them.

"If my dad found out that someone was giving me or my brother a problem he dealt with them and that was the end of it. Even today he doesn't play, especially when it comes to Joshua. Dad has always told us we are somebody, we are leaders, we can make things happen.

"Dad taught us to be respectful. Dad identified us as 'YAVIS'— young, attractive, verbal, intelligent and successful."

Kristopher is the father of Kristopher Aerial Brockington, who was 18 months old at the time of this writing. A doting grandparent, Dorothy likes to take her share of time with the other grandparents, and likes to take little Kris with her wherever she goes.

Kristopher looks up to his father.

"He's very good with people." Referring to the group home he operates for troubled children, he says, "He can take the worst kid and have him say 'yes sir' and 'no sir.'"

Despite divorce, his family has gotten larger. "Everybody's gotten closer. That's a blessing," he said.

Kristopher works with his stepfather, Veit Renn, a multi-platinum songwriter and record producer in Orlando.

A business major at the University of Central Florida, Kristopher is a recording engineer at Renn Music Productions. He was taught everything about production—vocal editing, mixing and engineering—from the ground up by his stepfather who accepted him as his son.

The company has worked with such groups as the Back Street Boys, 'N Sync and has produced 20 songs with Jennifer Hudson. The company produces all kinds of music—including pop, rock, gospel, hip-hop, soul and R&B.

Because of his training, he also runs the studio.

Veit, Janice and Renn Music Productions wrote and produced the theme song for New Directions Family Worship Center as a family gift for the church dedication.

Perhaps the greatest contribution that Dorothy ever made as a stepmother came when she counseled Nikia Brockington.

Nikia, 32, who lives in Detroit, came to know Dorothy when she was about 16.

"She always accepted me like I was her natural daughter."

Her father and her mother, Glenda, were divorced when she was very young.

Dorothy, she said, has always inspired her because, "she'll talk you through it," whatever "it" is, even if it means putting aside her own best interests.

Dorothy's love, faith and strength would be put to the test when Nikia was 20 and her boyfriend of two years (they knew each other since grade school) was murdered during a carjacking.

Nikia said that despite the fact that it must have triggered some terrible memories for her, Dorothy and her father would listen to her "cry and cry" on three-way telephone calls.

Dorothy could say that she knew what Nikia was going through, as few people could.

"It can only get better, the pain will subside," Dorothy said.

"She knew exactly how I felt. She lost two children. I lost a boyfriend. I knew if she could make it I could go on."

Nikia said it is hard to put into words how she feels about having Dorothy in her life.

"I have the best of both worlds. I have the best dad and the best moms. I couldn't have it any better."

She believes that it has made her a better person.

"She's done so many motherly things for me," she said of Dorothy. "I'm so grateful."

Nikia's friends who have learned about the tragedy in Dorothy's life have been amazed.

"It was like, 'She's so graceful and so beautiful. She's not bitter. She's not mad at the world.'"

Nikia is even more amazed.

She can be so enthusiastic about preaching. But there's nothing flashy about her, she said.

"She carries herself so well, so Godly, and she's humble at the same time," Nikia said.

"If I can be half the woman she is….," she said.

Nikia, who describes herself as a spiritual person, is the troop leader for the Girl Scouts in her church.

A registered radiologic technologist, she plans to get a degree in allied health science, get married, have a family "and continue to be happy."

They are three ambitious, talented, well-grounded and very impressive young people.

'Future World Leader'

Joshua, the youngest at 12 years of age, may be the most confident, ambitious member of the family.

He may be slightly built, but he is also serious, wise beyond his years and soft-spoken. He is also bold and ready to take on the biggest challenges.

"My parents tell me I can do all things by putting God first," he said in a September 2009 letter to President Barack Obama.

"I am writing you requesting to meet you and your family at your home, which is the White House, if you can find time in your busy schedule next month. I would like to visit our international family man role model in his home, which is my future home."

Like every other person before him seeking a meeting with the chief executive, he pointed out that he was a supporter.

"At my school I campaigned hard for you and you won the Presidency at my school," he said.

Joshua pointed out his many awards, including the President's Education Awards Program, and said the reason he would be in Washington, D.C., would be to attend the People to People Leadership Program World Leadership Forum. U.S. presidents are honorary chairmen of the program.

"My father and mother always tell me I am a leader and not a follower," he said.

He then added: "This is history because you are our 1st [African American] President and I know I can also be President."

He described his parents in the letter, including: "My mother is presently writing a book about her life story about how she overcame her Fear and her Faith in God."

He continued saying, "Someone from 'The Oprah Show' called and spoke with my mother. I hope we will able to go on 'The Oprah Show' with my mother to promote her books, my father's work and I will be discovered as a musician, and a young/talented/intelligent/ educated actor. I will own my own business and take over my father's.

I am also going to be a writer like my father, who has written several books, and my mother."

He also wrote, "Once I introduce myself I am remembered."

He's right about that. In 2005 he won five awards at the International Modeling and Talent Association in Los Angeles. He was told that if he stayed with Hugh III, they would likely be discovered. They ended up signing with The Hines and Hunt Agency in Burbank.

"We were all getting ready to move out to Hollywood when we were called into this ministry here," Brock said.

Included in Joshua's letter to the White House was his account of seeing the president at the convention center in Orlando in May of 2008 and returning the next day to see his plane.

"I know you may not remember this but I was the only boy standing and waving my hands near the road at the entrance before your motorcade went through the gates to your plane."

He then asked if he could have a letter or autographed picture of his family "with your presidential seal?" he asked. "What about Presidential Cuff Links or something for history?"

He signed the letter, "Your Future World Leader Joshua Caleb Brockington."

The White House responded with two notes, one acknowledging his receipt of the presidential award and the other, addressed as "Dear Student" thanking him for his note.

"Each day I am inspired by the encouraging messages of hope and determination I have received from students across the country. America needs young people like you who are studying hard in school, serving your community, and dreaming big dreams. Our country faces great challenges, but we will overcome them if we work together."

Both notes were affixed with the president's signature. He also got a picture of the family's dog, Michelle Obama and the girls. Her signature was affixed to her picture.

Joshua is already showing his versatility. Besides being active in student government, he takes karate lessons, plays basketball and has played the piano for six years and also likes drums. He can read notes but he can also play a song after hearing it one time. He plays the keyboard for the church services every Sunday.

A high achiever since pre-K, he is an honor student and is learning how to be an entrepreneur. At a recent meeting of the National Conference for Preventing Crime in the Black Community, he struck up deals with vendors to sell their products for a percentage or samples of their products. He made over $200 the first time and returned the next year to continue his efforts.

"My father always told me, 'I don't get what I deserve but I get what I negotiate,'" he said in his letter to the president.

He also has a deep appreciation for his family.

"I think that my family is the best family there is," he said, "because everybody in my family cares for you and they will do what they can. If you're hurt, they'll comfort you. If you're happy, they will be there with you," he said, especially his parents and grandmother.

"I think our family is the coolest ever."

Brock and Dorothy's marriage, like all marriages, has had a few bumps in the road, but nothing that communication, compromise and love couldn't solve.

"This happens to everybody," Dorothy said, sounding like the marriage counselor she has become. "You just work through it.

"We have a good marriage," she says.

New Directions

They are a team in every way, including their co-pastor duties.

After they got married in 1994, he found himself moving from a more traditional view of churches to what he viewed as the less inhibited, more charismatic style embraced by Dorothy's Pentecostal or "holiness" style of worship.

By 2001, he had grown tired of the traditional setup, with individual churches bringing in money to an affiliation, only to have it go broke because the organization had spent all the money without saving any for repairs on a building that had been jointly funded.

"I knew there had to be more to it than that."

He told his congregation that after the church had been remodeled God was leading him in a different direction.

So, in May 2005, after serving 10 years as pastors of Stanton First Baptist Church in Weirsdale, he and Dorothy started their own ministry—New Directions Family Worship Center—in a one-car garage.

Through a series of what appears to be God-orchestrated good fortune, with milestone transactions taking place with a handshake instead of a large sum of cash, the church is now in a beautiful building in the Ocala/Candler community of Marion County. The church is small but growing. Their goal is to break out of the usual mode and reach out into the Marion County community with outreach missions.

Brock and Dorothy are deliberately taking it slow, building their base of support for the idea within the congregation.

As for counseling, he uses a method known as Reactverality and/or RAW.

"I let them do all the talking," he said, and he seeks to find out where they are spiritually. "If they are not Christians I see how they see themselves."

At some point, he says, they ask, "What would you do?"

"I tell them, it's not what I would do, but what you're going to do."

Like all good therapy methods, the patient has to admit he or she has a problem before they can begin addressing the issues.

He says he gives them scriptures and encouragement to give them the "vitality" they need to solve their problems.

They have to take responsibility for their actions. He has no patience for the typical comments frequently heard in courtrooms and jails: "It wasn't me. It was the drugs or alcohol that made me do it."

"You can't hide behind that," he says.

Initially, Brock and Dorothy did a lot of alcohol abuse counseling. When the economy bottomed out, the phenomenon brought with it the need for a lot of marriage counseling.

He gives women's sexual abuse cases to Dorothy.

Whatever the issue, however, Dorothy is key.

"She breaks the ice," Brock said, by giving her testimony.

The usual reaction?

"Mine wasn't all that bad."

He has been a chaplain with the Ocala Police Department and has been a member and sometimes official host for the national crime prevention conference.

"My passion is to help get children out of the rut," he said. That "rut," for many, unfortunately, is the criminal justice system. His goal is to keep them from getting in the system in the first place.

"This is directly related to what happened to Dorothy," he said, referring to her attackers both being young.

Another rut, he says, is an education system filled with standardized tests and parents who are failing their children.

"They do not take the time to check on their children, review school work, progress notes, daily teacher notes, or visit the school," he said of the parents. "They believe it is the teacher's responsibility to raise their children," he said.

"Some of the children are very disrespectful to the teachers and this is a reflection of their home life. Children are out of control because the so-called parents have no control."

Because of his interest in children, and because he sees some of the challenges faced by Dorothy in her job, he serves on the board of Early Learning Coalition of Lake County.

Clearly Brock and Dorothy, who still teaches in the public school system, are not just sitting on the sidelines and complaining.

One of their top priorities is operating two group homes: one for troubled children, and the other for people who have disabilities.

The site of one of the homes is in Eustis, in Dorothy's old house. Elsie cooks, cleans and helps look after the youngsters there.

It's an interesting turn of events. The house that once was home to a husband, wife, and two happy little girls, is again the meeting place of love and hope.

CHAPTER 7

Evil on Trial

To the casual eye, courthouses can appear to be a soulless place, no different than any other government building, with people coming and going at a pace consistent with the size of its surroundings. But each one has a distinct personality, matching the judges, the bailiffs and the briefcase-toting lawyers who ply their trade there.

In the early 1990s, the Lake County judicial center, which is so indistinct that it is sometimes mistaken for a hospital, was mostly busy with routine legal grist. County court, with its docket of misdemeanors and small civil cases, seemed busier than circuit court and its felony cases and bigger lawsuits. There might be one major trial each year in the once rural but rapidly growing, ho-hum bedroom community for nearby Orlando—a murder case, usually. That would soon change, however. Within a few short years the dockets would be packed and murder trials would almost become routine.

But in 1994, the Dorothy Lewis case was so shocking it cast a pall over the courthouse.

It's still stunning for those who were associated with the case.

"This is the worst case in my career, in 30 years," Assistant State Attorney Bill Gross said recently. "Sad, so sad," he added.

"I can't think of a worse situation as far as the total innocence of the victims," said Mark Nacke, who was one of Henyard's public defenders and is now a circuit judge.

"Most murder victims at least know each other. This was just a totally random thing. If anybody didn't deserve it—and nobody deserves it—this is it," Nacke said.

"A woman and two children as victims. I can't imagine anything more egregious," said Bill Stone, another defense lawyer in the case. Stone is now the chief assistant public defender in Lake County.

Not only did everyone have a lump in their throat over the slayings of Jasmine and Jamilya, but everyone who came into contact with Dorothy came away with a sense of respect and admiration, if not awe.

The taking of depositions, by design, are contentious affairs, often bringing out the fiercest bullying instincts of lawyers in their efforts to get witnesses and victims to phrase things their way in sworn statements. Because of Dorothy's injuries and her losses, questions directed at her were fairly gentle but still aimed at absolving or convicting Henyard, depending upon which side you were on.

It's not unusual for those who are being grilled to fire back. Not so with Dorothy.

"I don't remember any negative expression, gesture or attitude toward any of us," Stone said. "I deeply respected her," he added.

"She seemed to be a very nice person, religious, a lot of faith in God, and that seemed to be where she drew her strength," Nacke noted.

She would also leave a deep impression on the man who would preside over the case.

"She was always incredibly at peace. That's how strong her faith is. You and I couldn't cope as well," said Circuit Judge Mark Hill. "I always thought that it was a privilege to know her."

Dorothy Is Key

As the clock ticked down toward the May 23 trial date, prosecutors and public defenders stirred the growing pile of paperwork and talked among themselves about how they should handle the case.

Gross would be joined by his boss, State Attorney Brad King, who became the elected prosecutor for the five-county circuit five years earlier when he was only 36. A thin, serious, dry and smart man, his arguments resonate with jurors, in part, probably because they are so straightforward and commonsense. King, who still holds the office today, still tries some cases, including some that have made international headlines. As an administrator he has managed to keep some very good lawyers despite dealing with some very tight budgets. And in spite of all the pressures that come with the job, he looks as if he has not aged at all.

The defense team, led by T. Michael Johnson, was about as solid as it gets. They were all serious, very experienced and smart.

Gross calls Johnson the smartest lawyer he has ever gone up against, which is saying a lot, since one of his regular opponents, Michael Graves, has appeared on many national TV shows and is probably as skillful as anyone in the country in persuading jurors not to impose the death penalty. Johnson, in fact, would end up calling Graves to the stand as an expert to point out that Henyard could be sentenced to a lifetime behind bars, therefore he would no longer be a threat to society.

Johnson, who is now a circuit judge, is a balding, middle-aged man with country roots, a gifted storyteller in the great Southern oral tradition, is folksy, has a great rapport with juries, and is often hilarious when spinning tales in his office between hearings. But he is all business when the chips are down, including his current duties on the bench.

The public defenders knew that they had their work cut out for them.

If they were aghast at the senseless killing of two children, the jury would surely be outraged.

And then there was Dorothy, a respectable young widow who was trying to become a teacher to support her family, a non-hysterical, soft-spoken eyewitness and crime victim, who had a steely resolve that came from her unshakeable faith in God.

There would be a dizzying number of tactical decisions to be made on both sides, but first things first, the lawyers decided.

Some petitions to the court would be "no-brainers," though they would add to the crush of papers that would be heaped on top of squeaky-wheeled carts that were shoved into courtrooms for pretrial hearings.

One issue, for example, would be whether Smalls and Henyard should be tried together.

Since they each blamed the other, Hill had no choice but to grant the motion for separate trials. The Public Defender's office would handle Henyard's case, and the county would pay for Smalls' private practice lawyers to avoid any potential conflict of inter-est that might arise by having the public defenders defend both clients.

"I Raped Somebody"

There was also the issue of what to do with Emanuel Yon, Jr. The 17-year-old boyfriend of Smalls' sister had provided the killers with a change of clothing after the shootings.

Yon told a much different story than the one Henyard first started telling detectives when he conveniently substituted his name for Yon's to try to throw the blame onto his friends.

Yon testified in his deposition that he had gone to the grocery store to buy a birthday cake for his girlfriend and had run into He-nyard and Smalls.

"Ric said he needed money and was going to go across town to rob somebody," Yon said.

When his aunt, Joyce Bradford, drove up, Yon hopped in her car and warned her not to let the others get into the automobile because one of them had a gun.

It wasn't too long after that that Henyard showed up at Smalls' house to see Yon. Smalls was outside in the backseat of the stolen Chrysler. Henyard asked Yon if he wanted to go out that night and when he said yes, he told him that he and Smalls needed a change of clothes.

Henyard still had blood on his hands from the murders. Smalls' mother noticed the blood and asked him about it. Henyard told her he had cut his hand while playing with a pocketknife. He also lied to her about her son, telling her he was out with a girl.

Yon and Henyard left Smalls' house and Yon went to his father's home to get some clothing.

Yon was used to helping his friend. A week before the shootings, he said, Ric had showed up at Smalls' house and asked him to "hold" a gun for him, which he did, for about two days. Smalls was present at the time, Yon said.

Yon figured the car he was riding in was stolen but he said he didn't know the whole story until Henyard turned to him as they were riding down the road and he said, "I shot somebody."

"Yeah, right," Yon replied.

"He said, 'I'm not joking. I shot somebody,' then he told me the gun was on the passenger side in the glove compartment," Yon said in sworn statement.

Yon, who had been arrested in the past on a concealed weapon charge (a large stick in his back pocket), said he opened the glove box, removed the handgun, looked at it and put it back inside.

"And it was quiet, you know. He was telling me, you know, that he ain't had no money. Mostly, mostly he was talking about money, he didn't have no money."

Henyard then said, "I got something else to tell you."

"What's that?"

"He said, 'I raped somebody.'"

Smalls was saying nothing at this point.

Henyard continued, telling how Dorothy kept saying, "Oh God, oh God."

"… and he told me that he said, 'This ain't God, this is the work of the devil,' something like that."

Yon said the three were on their way to Orlando when they stopped at Plymouth, a small community off U.S. Highway 441. He wanted to see some people he knew there. They went to a house where there was a group of people standing in a driveway, including a young man named Bryant Smith, who was attending a birthday party. Smith and Yon knew each other because they had a common connection. Smith was the father of the baby of Smalls' sister, Tamara, the girl that Yon was now staying with.

Yon told Bryant about the story that Henyard had told him. "I said, 'You want to know something?'

"He say, 'What's that?'

"Can you believe that Ric Ric [he didn't know Ric, and I just said,] 'That guy in the passenger seat actually told me that he shot and raped somebody.'"

"And he looked at me and he said, 'You never know what to expect these days.' I said, 'Yeah.'"

One of the reasons the surprised onlookers doubted the wild-sounding story was that when they looked inside the car, they could see that the car was not "chipped," a slang term for an ignition switch that had been broken so that the car could be stolen.

The youths showed off the gun. Yon then opened the trunk, where the group could see a music keyboard and a pair of panties. There were panty hose beneath the seat.

They left after awhile and drove across the highway to see some other people.

"You don't need to be telling everybody," Henyard said.

"I told him, I said, 'Well, you know, I'm just telling it, you know, just in case you really did do that.' And he looked at me and started laughing."

Smith would testify that Yon was even more outrageous than he admitted in his sworn statement, including bragging that Henyard had killed his rape victim.

"He had to burn a bitch," Smith quoted Yon as saying.

But it was Henyard himself who would do the most incriminating damage to himself.

Smith testified: "Ric said, 'Yeah man, we did have us a bitch, man. But I had to burn that bitch. The bitch tried to go for my gun.'"

Yon also bragged about his friends' role in the rape, and was either embellishing the story or was ignorant of the details.

"They had them a white bitch," Yon boasted.

Henyard, of course, told it differently when he was interviewed by detectives.

"Alfonso grabbed the panty hose from under the seat and showed it to them. So all them give each other hand claps like they done did something."

Henyard said one of the "homeboys" picked up the gun, looked at it to see how many bullets were in it, said "nice gun" and gave it back.

The carload of miscreants were in and out of the driveway in 15 minutes. The last thing that Smith and other baffled onlookers would see of the braggarts—until the trial—was the taillights of the Chrysler as it sped down U.S. 441 toward the Orlando area.

Henyard said they stayed at the club in the community of Eatonville, near Orlando, until it closed, at 3:15 a.m. Yon would say in a sworn statement that the three stashed the stolen car in a wooded area behind the middle school in Eustis at 3 a.m. and walked home.

"Did you take the gun into the house?" a questioner asked.

"No, sir."

"How'd it get in your bedroom?"

"I don't know."

Yon said the last time he saw it was in the car, and he said everyone piled down on the couches and on the floor in the living room that night to be close to a space heater.

In addition, he said he did not know what had happened to the blood-stained outfit that Smalls had been wearing.

Yon also denied knowing until later that morning that two children were also slain in the carjacking. He said he is also the one who urged Smalls to tell his mother what happened.

"If you don't tell her, I will," he said, recalling the conversation.

Yon would end up being charged as an adult with accessory after the fact, a felony. That meant he could now be pressured into testifying against Henyard and Smalls and could be given leniency in his sentence if he testified truthfully.

The State Attorney's Office did allow Yon to plead guilty in return for a 22-month prison sentence with three years' probation. But that decision would spark a firestorm of controversy.

"The victim, her family and the arresting officers were not notified of the plea bargain arrangement. They learned of the plea in *The Orlando Sentinel,* said a group called Bereaved Survivors of Homicide, in a letter to the governor demanding an investigation.

Prosecutors are required to keep victims' families abreast of such things and they clearly had not done so in this case. The letter was signed by several people, including Dorothy.

Margaret was particularly upset, Gross recalls. "Rightfully so. I never did that again."

Yon would get into more scrapes with the law over the coming years.

He was arrested and charged with domestic violence in 1995 when his father called 911 to say that his son had pulled a handgun and pointed it at him. It turned out to be a BB or pellet pistol. The charge was dropped.

In 1997, he was charged with aggravated assault with a deadly weapon and was sentenced to 33 months in prison.

And in 2009, he was sentenced to 90 days in jail on a second offense battery.

Battle Over Confessions

A difficult task for the defense teams would be to try and get the confessions thrown out by the judge so that juries would not hear their clients' incriminating statements.

One motion to suppress was fairly standard, but with some specific tailoring. The motion, for example, cited the fact that Henyard was only 18 and "had only completed the ninth grade, he is of low-normal intelligence, with the equivalent social functional intelligence level of a 13-year-old." The motion claimed he didn't have the opportunity to consult with an attorney prior to making the statements and didn't understand that it was within his constitutional rights not to make incriminating statements.

The other motion was a little more unusual. It claimed that because Annie Neal was a frequent confidential informant for the police department, she was acting as an agent for officers and tricked him into making statements when she reportedly told Henyard: "What we got to do is play investigator, because we got some big money on the line."

The motion by Johnson, stated: "The statements given to law enforcement after his arrival at the Eustis Police Station are 'fruits of the poisonous tree.'"

The defense team had been trying to uproot her as a witness during her deposition. Asked if she had ever been a confidential informant, she refused to comment. Asked if she had ever been convicted of a felony, she coyly replied, "Of course."

She wouldn't say how many she had been convicted of, as if it was not public record somehow. Asked if she had been convicted of six, she replied: "No, not six felonies."

Judges, if they don't toss out entire confessions, frequently limit portions of interrogations, sometimes because they reveal unrelated prejudicial information.

Jurors would hear Henyard's first statement—not the portion where he eventually ended up confessing to assaulting Dorothy. Both because of worries about appeal issues and for tactical reasons, prosecutors limited the portions of the confession. Besides, Gross said, "We had DNA, we had Dorothy."

Once the state announced its intention to seek the death penalty, a flood of standard motions descended upon the court clerks. These motions, including some challenging the constitutionality of the death penalty, have already been ruled on by appeal courts but are included in the record in case the courts reverse their earlier rulings.

One motion for Henyard sought more preemptory strikes during jury selection.

Other motions asked that jurors be sequestered, or that selection be done in seclusion, and that the trial be moved to another location because of extensive pretrial publicity. Hill, following established law, either rejected most of the motions or reserved ruling until the trial was set to begin.

There was no argument from anyone that there had been a lot of news coverage, however. Visitors to court archives today can view a phone-book-thick file of newspaper clippings, and the case was covered extensively by the Orlando radio and TV stations. But the law says that merely knowing some facts about the case doesn't disqualify a person for jury duty. It's whether you have formed an immovable opinion that matters.

Some members of the public certainly were upset.

One woman wrote a letter to Judge Hill after she had read about the case in the *St. Petersburg Times.*

"No need to tell you what a heinous crime this was, but I do want to encourage you to show no mercy to the two men (no matter that one is only 15 years of age)!

"I suppose I am like everyone else at this time, that is, that we are letting far too many of these criminals go with just a slap on the wrist. Anyone so cruel as Richard Henyard and Alfonza Smalls should be punished to the fullest extent possible!

"Hopefully, you will remember my letter when you make a judgment in the case."

Hill put it in the court file and sent a copy to Johnson.

Another letter writer was even more adamant, if not articulate, after the conviction of Henyard but before sentencing.

"We've been following the Dorothy Lewis and child case, it is a disgrace!" the writer said, underlining the word in his handwritten note.

"There should be no excuses for Richard Henyard's case, who was found guilty of slaying Jasmina (sic) and Jamilya, plus left Dorothy for dead after rape.

"He should definitely get chair Now no appeals!!

"Rape, murders are the worst kind of crimes, punishment should be castration. Something has to be done on the judicial system right away. It is too lenial (sic), bible (sic) says: 'eye for eye, tooth for tooth.' All these murderers should be punished severely after one, not allowed, to be go free to commit several more crimes, and cost taxpayers for lawyers, appeals & high class lodging of good foods and rewards. Please be fair and inform all judges, to judge immediately, not hold them for years."

It was signed, "A registered taxpayer."

The letter writer went on to also call for severe punishment in two publicized child neglect cases.

Despite the public ire, lawyers were able to pick a jury after careful questioning.

A few years later, on the eve of a sensational murder trial involving a teen vampire cult accused of killing one girl's unsuspecting parents, prosecutors said they were confident they could pick a jury without having to move the trial away from Lake County. "If we could pick a jury for the Dorothy Lewis case, we can pick a jury for this one," one prosecutor told a reporter. And they did.

There were also motions to limit evidence, and there was no question that some things wouldn't even come up as potential evidence, including the fact that Henyard was put into isolation at the jail because of death threats and that he had to be put on suicide watch after he reportedly attempted to strangle himself with a cord.

Sometimes prosecutors themselves decide to streamline cases by limiting information.

Juries can get off track. One Lake County jury, for example, heard the case of a ranch caretaker who murdered the property owners in a cattle rustling scheme and hid their bodies beneath a haystack while preparing to feed their bodies to alligators. The jury got hung up for more than 24 hours in its deliberations—not on the sensational aspects—but on a relatively minor car theft charge.

In Henyard's case, prosecutors decided not to press charges of theft of a firearm and grand theft auto. The owner of the stolen handgun wasn't that interested in pressing charges, Gross said, and it was only a five-year felony sentence anyway. Plus, the theft charge was a lesser charge than armed robbery.

"It would have been overkill" on the charges, Gross said.

"No 'Basket Case'"

Dorothy herself was key to the case. Gross was impressed with her from the start. "When I went to the hospital to talk to her I thought I would see a basket case, a mom who lost her daughters. Instead, she was as calm and composed as was humanly possible."

The defense team, of course, was looking for any possible inconsistencies. She had suffered, after all, not just terrible injuries, but head wounds. In the early hours of her hospitalization, for example, she did tell an assistant medical examiner collecting rape kit evidence that she had been assaulted by only one man.

Lawyers were desperately searching for any gray areas in her statements about the carjacking when she referred to her tormentors as "the older guy" and "the younger guy," since she didn't know their names. Smalls was only 14 but he was big for his age.

When she finally did testify in court, Johnson did his best on cross-examination to try to show she was confused, and to cast doubt in the jurors' minds about who shot her. He asked if she recalled telling Dr. Harold at the hospital that she was wrestling for the gun when she got shot in the leg. She said she did not recall that.

Q: "So if he [Dr. Harold] recalls you telling him that, he perhaps is mistaken?"
A: "I wouldn't say that. I just can't recall telling him that."
Q: "Is that how it happened?"
A: "Is what how it happened?"
Q: "That you were wrestling with the gun and that's how you got shot in the knee?"
A: "I don't recall it happening that way."
Q: "Now, you describe for Mr. Gross that after the first shot you came up and you were like a wildcat, that's how you put it, I believe. Mr. Smalls, the younger guy, was there at the time, wasn't he ma'am?"
A: "Yes."
Q: "Standing right next to the older guy."
A: "Yes."
Q: "And after that you don't remember much of anything that happened to you?"
A: "That's correct."

Dorothy's initial statements, recorded on March 8, 1994 in the State Attorney's Office, didn't end up helping the defense. They did, however, reveal that on some subconscious, heart-breaking level, Dorothy was still thinking about her daughters as being alive.

"And the ... girls were well behaved while you were inside the store?" Gross asked.

"Oh yeah... they know how to act," she replied.

The state, apparently concerned that the defense would try to convince jurors that Dorothy was confused that night about who did the shooting, arranged for her to be taken to the Marion County jail to see if she could pick Smalls and Henyard out of live lineups, rather than depend upon a photo lineup.

Before she viewed the six men in the lineup, she was handed written instructions: "In a moment you will be entering a room where you will observe six subjects lined up behind a one-way mirror. Each subject will be holding a number card in front of them. You may or may not observe the person(s) responsible for the crime now being investigated. Keep in mind certain physical appearance changes can be made such as hairstyles, beards and mustaches, makeup, etc. Look at each subject carefully prior to determining if you can or cannot identify anyone. If you should need any of the subjects to step forward, right or left, or make any statements, please advise the officer of this wish referring to the subjects by the number they are holding. Take as much time as you feel is needed to look at each subject carefully. After you have made up your mind, advise the officer that you have reached a decision. If you are unable to make an identification, advise this, and if you have identified someone, advise the officer [of] that subject number. Due to legal constraints, the officer will be unable to advise you if your decision is correct or incorrect. You are under no obligation to answer any questions asked of you by the defense attorney. Do not discuss the lineup with other witnesses as this will jeopardize any present or future identifications in this investigation."

"That was hard. That was a bad night," Emma, said of having to undergo the process.

But it didn't shake Dorothy's confidence that she had identified number four as Smalls and checked the blank on the form "positively identified."

She was pretty sure when it came to identifying Henyard.

"I wasn't 100 percent sure with Henyard. He was the one who was driving, so he had the back of his head toward me, but Smalls was the one who approached me in the parking lot."

Prosecutors and police were vigilant in making sure Tschida could also identify the ominous figures she saw in the parking lot that night.

After calling police Monday morning to talk about what she had experienced, Detective Hart said he would come out to her house and show her a photo lineup to see if she could identify the two people that she had seen.

She would end up being conscientious about the role she was about to play. She said she walked down the road to pick up the morning paper, "and I realized that they would probably have a bunch of things in the paper, so I didn't read it because I knew that they [investigators] were coming."

She later recalled being shown four or five photos in two rows. She identified the two killers. Later, she was called to go down to the police station where she was shown three groups of photos. She picked out both Henyard and Smalls and Yon. She recognized Yon from his picture in the newspaper, but it was not important to have never been exposed to his picture before, since Yon was not in the parking lot when Dorothy was attacked.

Devastating Evidence

Thanks to science, it wouldn't have mattered if Dorothy could not have identified Henyard.

DNA, or deoxyribonucleic acid, makes up the genetic "fingerprint" that is unique to every person. It's so commonly accepted now it's hard to remember when it was so new it was considered to be exotic and suspect evidence.

Unlike some judges, who let their docket pile up, Hill tries very hard to keep trials on schedule, so he balked at the idea of bringing in genetic evidence.

"Gross, why go to the expense and delay the trial? You've got a ... winner," the prosecutor remembers the judge telling him.

"With all due respect judge, I want to try it my way," said Gross, who has a reputation, right or wrong, of sometimes seemingly wanting to throw in everything but the kitchen sink. In truth, he likes to have a backup.

Gross, for example, was later the prosecutor in a unique murder-rape case with a different judge. For the first time, the Florida

Department of Law Enforcement was able to match DNA found on the victim to a convicted rapist in its computer database.

That should have been a lock right there, but defense counselor Nacke was able to cast enough doubt about it to make jurors wonder.

Fortunately for Gross, he also had called as a witness a bite-mark expert who had helped put away serial killer Ted Bundy. The expert charmed the jury so much that Nacke had to object when jurors wanted to ask questions of the forensic odontologist—as if it was a civil, not a criminal trial. Gross was able to get the conviction but Nacke and his co-counsel were able to keep it to a life sentence.

Hill, well known for being fair and respectful, granted the state's request in the Henyard and Smalls trials. He had already granted many defense motions, which had irked the highly competitive prosecutor.

"It was important to have it," Hill now acknowledges. "That was powerful evidence."

Defense attorneys knew the DNA evidence could be devastating. Seminars were springing up across the nation telling prosecutors to keep it simple, and for defense lawyers to try and to confuse the jury and discredit it any way they could.

In the most famous example, DNA evidence baffled the O.J. Simpson jurors in 1995, with lawyers hinting at contaminated samples and cops planting fake evidence.

Gross was convinced, however, that Lake County jurors would take proper notice of the DNA evidence in the Henyard case.

DNA collected and placed in the rape kit at the hospital was consistent with Henyard's genetic profile, according to an FDLE analysis.

"This profile has a frequency of approximately 1 out of 3 billion whites and 1 out of 809 million blacks," the report stated, indicating that it would be highly unlikely that anyone else would be a match.

Blood stains were identified on eight separate areas of the jean jacket that Henyard was wearing, seven areas on shoes, three locations on socks and four spots on jean shorts.

The DNA profile on the jean jacket matched that of Jamilya. The same was true of the profile found on his shorts. The chance that the profile would be a match to a white person was 1 out of 112 million whites, the FDLE report said, and 2 out of 36 million black people.

Henyard's socks bore the DNA profile of Jasmine. "The frequency of this profile is approximately 1 out of 3 million whites and 1 out of 295,000 blacks," the report stated.

Smalls would not escape this exacting scrutiny. Blood stains on the green shirt and pants he was wearing matched Jamilya, and Dorothy. Dorothy's profile was listed as 1 out of 2 billion whites and 1 out of 1 billion blacks.

Henyard's semen stains also were found on the green clothing worn by Smalls. Henyard's stains were on Smalls' clothing because Henyard assaulted Dorothy first, prosecutors argued. "This profile has a frequency of approximately 1 out of 7 billion whites and 1 out of 1 billion blacks," the report said.

Evidence technicians also found an orange juice can with Henyard's fingerprints that had been in the Chrysler.

But for some reason no semen was found on a condom discovered on the ground near the parked car believed to have been used by Smalls, on a tissue or on jean shorts worn by Henyard.

Even more difficult for prosecutors was the fact that they were still left with the controversy of just who did the shooting.

A crime lab analyst supervisor with the FDLE believed he had the solution, however.

N. Leroy Parker was an expert on blood spatter evidence. There are two types of blood stains, he would testify: cast-off blood, which is flung from a moving object, and splashed blood, which is blood that falls upon itself. Analysis can determine what kind of weapon is used, based on the pattern, the direction the force came from and where people were standing.

Parker's report was clear.

"The blue jean jacket was a target for cast-off bloodstains which were deposited on the lower right front area and spattered blood which were deposited on the lower right front area and spattered blood which were deposited on the right front area and left sleeve," the report stated.

"The front of both legs of the green trousers (pants) were targets for splashed blood," the report added.

"The reconstruction of the pertinent bloodstains as to their origin, direction of travel and location indicated that the individual who was wearing the blue jean jacket was present and in close proximity to forceful bloodshed," Parker reported.

In other words, the wearer of the jacket—Henyard—was the shooter. He was standing within four feet of his victim.

The wearer of the green pants—Smalls—had free falling blood on his trousers, and got the blood on his clothing when he picked up the body of Jamilya.

Henyard had admitted wearing the hooded jacket that night. Also, the suspects wore different sized items of clothing.

Under the law, both Henyard and Smalls could be convicted of first-degree murder, but prosecutors knew that the question of who actually did the shooting would be crucial when it came time to asking for the death penalty.

The state also had a problem, because of Smalls' age. Hill, with an eye toward a recent Florida Supreme Court ruling, would eventually rule that Smalls was not eligible for the death penalty because of his age at the time of the crime. The question was, would it be fair in the eyes of an appeal court to impose the death sentence for one defendant and not the other just because of age? Or would the evidence show that Henyard shot the girls and eliminate that concern?

Both sides presented what they called "statement of facts" before the trial.

The defense motion stated: "At no time was Mr. Henyard 'convinced that Mrs. Lewis was dead.'" The motion referred to Henyard's claim in his confession that he was sure Dorothy was not dead.

Q: "Did you leave her for dead? Did you think you had killed her?"

A: "No, like I said, I just thought I had shot her in the leg."

Q: "Tell me the truth. I mean, did … did you mean to kill her?"

A: "No, I did not."

The state, however, in its motion argued that, "The defendant and his accomplice, convinced that Mrs. Lewis was dead, rolled her body off the road…."

Smalls Gets the Blame

The hospital-looking, seemingly soulless Lake County courthouse took on something of an electric personality when jury selection began for Henyard's trial on Monday, May 23, 1994.

The lengthy process was speeded up thanks to a questionnaire which had been mailed to prospective jurors. By Wednesday, the pool had been whittled from 120 to 12, not including alternates. Many prospective jurors were eliminated because they had formed opinions after reading or hearing about the case in news reports.

As the actual trial began, both sides made their opening statements, laying out the case as they saw it.

Gross set the scene, taking the jurors, in their minds, to that dark, foggy road, starting with the first call to police about seeing a bloody woman in a white dress, until she made her way to the carport of a house more than three hours later, asking for help.

He talked about how police found the stolen car near Eustis Middle School, within walking distance of where the suspects were living. He talked about how authorities found the nine-shot pistol with six spent rounds and three live ones still in the gun.

And he brought up Henyard's remarks when he learned that Dorothy was still alive and wondered if she could identify her attackers.

Bill Stone, like Gross, has a sharp wit, which he sometimes displays for jurors, and like Gross, is very good at what he does.

He once defended a man accused of stabbing a fellow state prison inmate to death. The prosecution's problem was that some of the witnesses were taking medication for psychosis, including one whose nickname was "Dancing Willie."

"So, Willie, are you having any hallucinations right now?" he asked, with just a hint of scorn and amazement that such a person should be testifying against his client.

Stone began his opening arguments in the Henyard trial by apologizing to the jury for the "rigorous" two-and-a-half day jury selection process.

Then, surprisingly, he put Henyard not only in the Winn-Dixie parking lot, but in the car, and in the sexual assault, and shooting Dorothy in the leg. She was also shot three times in the head, he said. "Miraculously, she did not die."

Stone then began hammering away at the only possible defense theory in light of the strong evidence: Smalls shot the children, he insisted. Smalls had the gun in the parking lot and in the car, he pointed out.

Then, he briefly alluded to what would surely come up in both the guilt and penalty phase, and what could be the most disturbing and possibly controversial thing the jurors would hear. He predicted the medical examiner would surmise that the girls, "if they did not die instantly, they were instantly rendered unconscious and more than likely didn't even know what hit them, and then obviously died."

"It's horrible," Stone conceded. "We told you it was horrible. We explained to you when you were being selected just as vividly as we could that there are going to be some rather gruesome aspects of this case, and that's just something that we have to deal with due to the nature of the situation."

He returned to the notion that Smalls killed the girls.

Smalls' clothes were so thoroughly covered in blood that Henyard had to ask a friend, Yon, for a change of clothes for the two of them, he said.

Henyard also turned himself in to police, Stone said, "and he explained to them his involvement in this most horrible episode."

Stone, looking into the faces of the men and women who would judge the guilt or innocence of his client, said: "I want to tell you right now though, that I'm not going to stand here and insult your intelligence, and I don't intend to make a silly charade out of a very important case and a most important aspect of this case and a most important aspect of our justice system. And I don't intend to affront your civil responsibility by trying to delude you into thinking that Mr. Henyard came in here like a stranger to all of us."

He listed Henyard's involvement in all of the crimes except the murders. "...Mr. Henyard denies that he shot Jasmine. He did not shoot Jamilya."

Stone, who urged the jury to listen carefully to every detail, explained the law regarding such cases. Then, he sat down.

There was no mystery now. The defenders, by admitting all but the murder of the children, showed just how strong the state's case was.

"Many nights, weekends and vacation days were spent trying to do something with absolutely nothing," Stone said, years later.

The trial, like so many murder trials, would start with a parade of law enforcement officers, expert witnesses and a few key witnesses who could help the state connect the dots to a guilty verdict.

As the proceedings continued into Thursday, nerves were beginning to wear thin.

Prosecutors usually do everything they can to keep victims' family members out of the courtroom when the medical examiner explains what she found during the autopsy. Prosecutors are afraid that emotional outbursts from family members will result in a mistrial or a successful appeal.

But it was not Dorothy's family who would show signs of breaking under the strain.

Henyard became agitated during the medical examiner's testimony, which dealt with the fatal wounds and the fact that they were delivered at point-blank range. He turned to his lawyers and asked if he could be excused from the courtroom.

Johnson must have immediately become concerned about how this would look to the jury. He once grabbed the leg of a new public defender under the defense table after the young man became visibly upset by a setback. "Don't ever show your emotions like that to a jury," he whispered to the man, who wanted to yelp in pain at the vise-like grip.

The defense team asked for a recess and talked Henyard into staying in his seat.

Because Dorothy was a witness, she wasn't allowed to be in the courtroom until she testified. And while Margaret and other family members understood the need for being in control of themselves, they still bristled under the restriction. It appeared to them that Henyard's family members didn't seem to be so tightly reined in.

Elsie did cry, but the tears came at an unexpected time—during Jackie Turner's testimony, in which she said she did the best she could.

"Momma, why are you crying?" asked Margaret.

"I felt bad for the boy's godmother," Elsie said. "She didn't do it. She didn't raise him that way."

Gross wanted to emphasize that point in his questioning of Turner.

Q: "…while he was staying with you, you treated him like one of your own, didn't you?"
A: "Yes."
Q: "You took him to church?"
A: "Yes."
Q: "You taught him right from wrong?"

A: "Yes."

Q: "Good from evil?"

A: "Yes."

In general, victims' families view the whole process as being loaded in favor of the defendants. Certainly, that is the case in the penalty phase, where defense lawyers hope to get some sympathy for their clients while presenting mitigating evidence, including the testimony of psychological experts.

As for the victims, however, they're practically invisible.

Hill, for example, following the law, granted a defense motion to "exclude evidence or argument designed to create sympathy for the deceased."

The strong prosecution case continued to rain down on Henyard, however, with DNA testimony, the high-speed blood spatter explanation and more.

The jury also heard from Linda Miller about how Henyard incriminated himself by blurting out his concern about Dorothy being able to identify her attacker.

They also heard from Colinda Smalls, Alfonza's sister, who said she had seen Henyard with the gun before the shooting.

Bryant Smith testified about his encounter with the boastful Yon and the other two young men in the stolen Chrysler.

On Friday, jurors heard Luther Reed testify that he was sure Henyard had stolen his gun.

They also heard Henyard's first confession.

On Friday afternoon jurors were dismissed until Tuesday because Monday was Memorial Day.

When Tuesday, May 31, came, it was a day for boiling point emotions.

It is the right of every defendant to face his accuser. It's basic, a cornerstone of the American justice system, but what about the victim, who now must be traumatized all over again at the prospect of having to look at her accuser just a few feet away?

"I didn't know if I could look into the guy's face and say he was the one," Dorothy recalls.

Her church friends and family—50 strong—took their seats in the courtroom to lend their support. Margaret was praying and praying hard.

Dorothy was seeking divine help, too.

"I felt like it was going to be hard. I prayed to God to give me strength," Dorothy said.

Reporter Jill Jordan-Spitz, noting that Dorothy was wearing "a trim black dress with gold designs," recorded the dramatic moment in the June 1 edition (used with permission of *The Orlando Sentinel*, copyright 1994).

"It was the moment Dorothy Lewis has dreaded for 16 months: The instant she would come face to face with one of two teens accused of killing her children and of raping and nearly killing her.

"It came about a half-hour into her testimony Tuesday, when Assistant State Attorney William Gross asked her if either of her attackers was in the courtroom.

"Lewis closed her eyes for several seconds, then turned her head slowly toward the defense table. Her eyes found Richard Henyard, 19, and she recoiled as if she'd been punched in the stomach.

"She paused, then—suddenly and forcefully—raised her right arm toward Henyard and stretched her index finger toward him.

"'He's sitting right there,' she said, her voice slow yet full of determination.

"As he has throughout his first-degree murder trial, Henyard looked down at the defense table and doodled on a legal pad."

Sympathy Tempered

Nacke, who was then a veteran assistant public defender, is a hard-working, no-nonsense lawyer who knows that preparation is absolutely essential for success. He is the "everyman" in the courtroom, a no-frills, plain-speaking person that jurors can identify with.

So when he began making his closing argument, Nacke reminded jurors that they had been warned that it would be an emotional case.

"And I would be less than candid with you if I did not say it would be perfectly honest for anybody to have feelings of sympathy for Dorothy Lewis and her family and her two children. That's absolutely a human feeling and there's nothing wrong with it," he said.

However, he reminded them, they had agreed during jury selection to set aside their feelings and decide the case based on facts and the law.

Henyard was involved, he conceded, and he then went on to predict that the state would say he tried to get himself out of it by going down to the police station and talking to detectives.

But even in the beginning, when he was pretending to have Yon's role in the story, he didn't say that anyone other than Smalls shot the children, he noted. Police, trying to break down his story, intimated that they had found all kinds of physical evidence.

"And still, Richard Henyard said over and over and over again that he didn't shoot those children, Alfonza did."

He asserted it 19 times, Nacke said.

Smalls had the gun at the grocery store, he gave directions in the car, Smalls got out of the car with the gun, Smalls snatched the gun from Dorothy when she made a grab for it, Smalls had Dorothy's blood on his clothing, so much blood that he had to get a change of clothes, Nacke said. Smalls was the one who told Henyard to hurry up with his assault, and the gun was found in Smalls' house, Nacke pointed out.

"When Dorothy said, 'Why don't you just take the car and let us go?' Smalls said, 'No, we can't do that,'" Nacke said.

"Ladies and gentlemen… that 15-year-old is capable of shooting two children and did shoot two children."

Urging the jurors to use "common sense," he attacked the blood pattern evidence. Parker had explained that a bullet wound at close range tends to produce more of a mist than a high volume, dropping action.

Smalls' clothing had more blood on it, and there was no centrally located pattern on Henyard's clothing, Nacke argued.

Nacke, using the best-known defense tactic, attacked the evidence collection procedure. The burden of proof is on the prosecution team. The defense doesn't have to prove anything. All it has to do is cast enough doubt for just one stubborn juror, since the guilt verdict has to be unanimous.

Nacke attacked the evidence collection and the state's key expert witness in one broadside. He cited Parker's testimony in which he said that he did not photograph or make any casts of shoe prints at the crime scene.

"We could have had some more evidence, some proof exactly where everybody was standing, but we don't. He is too busy," he said, referring to Parker.

"They are too overloaded with work. We've got two dead children and a person they want to execute and he is too busy. His workload is too much. But he is not too busy to collect a condom wrapper and a malt liquor can, some feet away, or to measure a trail of blood that they had found out there several hundred feet, which they didn't test. We don't know what that was from or how that was put there," Nacke said.

He then switched back to the idea that Smalls was the killer. Henyard had the gun in the days leading up to the crime but he didn't do anything with it, Nacke said.

"How did the gun end up at Smalls' house? Could it have been that he was afraid his [Smalls'] prints were on that gun last?"

Brad King began his argument to the jury by pointing out that Smalls' sister saw Henyard with the gun.

"This didn't start with Alfonza Smalls saying, 'Hey, let's go jack somebody.' It started in the mind of Richard Henyard," King said.

He also said that it was Henyard who grabbed the gun from Dorothy on the back of the car, while Smalls was assaulting her. Henyard had already abused her, King said.

The Chrysler was recovered in a secluded, wooded area behind the Eustis Middle School. Whoever had abandoned the car had to be a local resident, Anthony Robinson would say years later, because the spot was off the beaten path but within easy walking distance of several houses.

The keys were not in the car. Linda Miller would find the keys in the pocket of the jacket Henyard had been wearing, King said.

Medical examiner testimony showed the slayings were premeditated, based upon the wounds, he said.

He also explained the concept of felony murder.

"If you find the deaths occur in the commission of a kidnapping, you have found first-degree murder. Whether there was any premeditation or not, you have found first-degree murder."

The prosecutor ticked off the possibilities for the jury to consider.

Was it Dorothy's fault, he asked? "That is simply not so."

Was it law enforcement's fault because Parker didn't take footprints, "even though everybody said that they had walked that road countless times looking for those bodies and he made a decision it's not worth it? It's not going to prove to me anything because there have been too many people looking for these children."

He also lashed out at Henyard's 19 statements denying that he had shot the children.

"...does it matter how many times you tell a lie for it to become truth? Because I say it 19 times does it make it so? And we know it doesn't."

King also explained the law involving principals in a crime.

"If two or more people help each other commit a crime, and this defendant is one of them, the defendant, Mr. Henyard, is a principal and must be treated as if he had done all of the things the other person did. If he knew it [kidnapping] was going to happen. At that moment of the plan and the trip to the Winn-Dixie and the getting in the car together, they joined hands as one," he said. Gross had alluded to it earlier. It really didn't matter who pulled the trigger as far as a conviction of first-degree murder was concerned.

King then ridiculed Henyard's account of what happened based on his claim that he was sitting in the car when the girls were shot.

"How would he know that if he was sitting in the car, not wanting to see what happened? Another lie told."

The biggest lie, King said, was when he told Dorothy: "You won't get hurt, I promise you, you won't get hurt."

"She did get hurt. Her children got hurt."

He finished his argument by saying: "You know, ladies and gentlemen, it is true that most of us share within us the innate ability to be merciful. The time for mercy has passed. Today, there is nothing left but justice. That is what we want, ladies and gentlemen. We want justice. And the only way justice can be accomplished in this case is for you to come back in this room and by your verdict say, 'Mr. Henyard, you were wrong. You're guilty as charged, for kidnapping Dorothy Lewis, kidnapping Jasmine, kidnapping Jamilya, for raping Dorothy, for attempting to murder Dorothy, for robbing her of her car, but most of all robbing her of her children. For that, Mr. Henyard, we find you guilty. So say we all.'"

Nacke had the concluding argument and he worked quickly to dispel any possible misunderstanding about what the defense was saying about the way Dorothy was shot when she grabbed for the gun.

"I did not say at any time it was Dorothy Lewis' fault that she was shot. That is absolutely not right. It's not her fault. I didn't insinuate it and I never even thought that that's what anybody would take of what I said."

What he was saying, he told the jurors, was that they had to set their feelings aside while looking at the facts.

Nacke again tossed the blame on the younger teen.

The crime didn't start when Henyard got the gun, the assistant public defender said.

"It started with Alfonza Smalls. He had the guts, he had the nerve to start this whole thing in action."

Merely talking about it "is not enough," he said, referring to Henyard saying he wanted to rob somebody and get a car.

Nacke also denied saying that because Henyard denied shooting the girls 19 times that it meant he did not do it.

"I'm saying there is no proof of who did."

He also tried to dispel the notion that Henyard was the director of the tragedy when he obtained a change of clothes after the shootings.

"It wasn't because he was the leader of anything or because he was controlling Alfonza. It was because Alfonza's clothes were covered in blood and Alfonza didn't want his family to see that."

The judge read the extensive jury instructions and the panel went back to the jury room for deliberations. Three hours later, they returned. The jury foreman handed over a slip of paper. Once Hill had reviewed it, he passed it to the clerk who announced the verdict: Guilty on two counts of premeditated first-degree murder, three counts of kidnapping with a firearm, one count of sexual battery while armed, one count of attempted premeditated first-degree murder and one count of robbery with a firearm.

Dorothy, who had been allowed inside the courtroom for the reading of the verdict, rushed out of the courtroom as soon as the verdict was announced. She was ushered into a small witness conference room.

Dorothy, who had worried and wondered, "why can't I cry?" since the funeral, suddenly felt a mix of overwhelming emotions—joy at the guilty verdict and horror at the realization of what Henyard and Smalls had done. Greta Snitkin, the hard-nosed, soft-hearted victim advocate and a woman of few promises, had predicted: "When the time comes God will let you cry."

Now, the time had come.

"They killed my babies," Dorothy sobbed. "They killed my babies."

Death Penalty Battle

There was nothing left to say at the defense table. The jury found Henyard guilty of every charge, and there was not a single instance in which the panel elected to find him guilty of a lesser charge, like second-degree murder.

The defense team and Henyard may have sagged under the weight of the crushing defeat, but if they did, it was not noticeable to anyone in the courtroom. It certainly was not unexpected but it's never easy for the public defenders, who represent the worst of the worst and still find themselves developing some kind of bond with their client.

How anyone can do such spirit-crushing work is amazing. Everyone has a right to counsel, they say, and they correctly note that everyone is presumed innocent until proven guilty. Some are innocent, too. Even those who aren't can sometimes get a lighter sentence with a negotiated plea.

An investigator for the public defender's office once summed up what it's like after putting in vast, mind-numbing hours of preparation on a hopeless case: "Well, we're ready to go in and take our whuppin.'"

Now, they were preparing to take a "whuppin'" in the penalty phase of the trial.

Johnson understood this, of course. Years earlier, he had been the defense attorney for serial killer Robert Dale Henderson on three of the 12 murder charges he was facing.

Not unlike a lot of public defender clients, Henderson would have no part of any lawyer's strategy trying to help him. For example, if a lawyer suggested he really wasn't trying to shoot everyone he shot, he would reply that there was no doubt once he aimed his gun. "When I aim to kill it, I aim to kill it."

The ultimate sanction should be reserved for the most outrageous of cases, lawyers argue.

Henderson fit the bill for a date with Florida's executioner. Now the question was, would Henyard also be a candidate for the death penalty?

Under Florida law, death penalty cases must be tried in two separate phases of a trial.

The state has strict statutory regulations on the kinds of aggravating circumstances a judge must recognize before he can impose a death sentence. Defense attorneys have some statutory mitigating circumstances they can rely on, but they can also list almost any kind of non-statutory mitigators.

Judges weigh the aggravators against the mitigators. All of this comes only if the jury votes in favor of the death penalty, however. The closer the vote, the more leeway a judge has for imposing a sentence of life without the possibility of parole. Final discretion still goes to the judge, but if he rejects a jury's recommendation, he must have a good reason based on the law, and he must state it in writing.

The defense team, up against the wall on the guilt phase of the case, also had little hope of helping their client in the penalty phase.

"The parade of horrors about his life would turn people off as much as it would be a mitigator," Johnson said years later.

"Drug use, for example. We have a right to be protected from people who use drugs, and Henyard did this," Johnson said, referring to his statement that he "smoked reefer" before the rape and shootings.

"Jackie Turner, she did what she could for him," Johnson said. "Obviously, not everybody that comes out of a situation like this does the things he did."

But during the trial he would emphasize that Henyard was bounced from a boozy, drug-addled mother to a busy dad who found his attitude too troublesome to handle.

"He was kind of slow," Johnson also said of Henyard.

Psychologist Jethro W. Toomer, Ph.D., examined Henyard for the defense and determined that he had an IQ of 85.

Did he understand that he had a right to a lawyer before he made three confessions, his lawyers wanted to know?

Police were trying to intimidate him 85 percent of the time during their interview of him, Toomer testified. Toomer also talked about Henyard suffering a kind of "mental malaise."

If malaise was referring to depression, however, that could have been Henyard's mental state in jail. It would be abnormal not to be depressed in a lockup.

A lot of Henyard's thinking defies description.

Why steal a car, for example, or if you do steal it, why not just take the car and not kill two children and try to kill their mother?

"If he were here today he couldn't explain it," Johnson said.

What about stopping on the way to Orlando to brag about it?

"Some kind of macho thing," Johnson figures.

Could this event have been prevented, say by a tip from someone who had heard Henyard talking about taking a car and putting someone in the trunk and killing them?

Johnson doesn't think so. Not in this crowd.

"It's a lifestyle, they all have guns," he said. "And it's worse now."

The only hopeful sign for civilized society, Johnson believes, was that because these murders were "beyond the pale," everyone seemed to want to come forward and help police after the fact. "It doesn't get any worse than this," he said.

The Pity Witness

Johnson's most important penalty phase witness would be Henyard's mother, Hattie Gamble.

Gamble was brought to the courthouse from St. Petersburg by a public defender investigator. She was in jail for about the twelfth time on shoplifting charges when the shooting took place.

One of the best mitigation factors in a death penalty case is organic brain damage. It frequently comes up, but it is frequently rejected because there is only the suggestion of it and no proof. Such was the case with Henyard.

"...as I was carrying him as a mother, I stayed under the care of a doctor and they were either looking for him not to live long or me. But praise God, we both pulled through.

"...I stayed sickly all the time, if it wasn't one thing it was another."

She testified that when Ric was a baby he was covered with sores so hideous no one wanted to touch him.

She said she had an "ugly" drinking habit while pregnant, and started smoking marijuana when Ric was 3.

Despite swearing she was no longer drinking or taking drugs, it became readily apparent she was under the influence of some kind of substance. Her rambling answers to questions sometimes made no sense.

Asked why, for example, she did not make contact with her son after he left to live with his dad, she said: "I called myself punishing his dad for the things that he didn't do or be around Ric, you know. So to me, as me being as young as I was, I felt like that was the opportunity, to you know, to do for him. I so I felt as if I had to, if I had went in and tried to do anything or say anything maybe that would stop it. I wanted him to see what I was going through. That's the only thing I could say about that. You know, I wanted him to do something for him, you know."

In a more lucid moment, she fielded a question about whether she kept up with Ric when he was staying with his father.

"No, I felt as though that it was his father's time to help him, so I just didn't bother with it, you know."

Gross, on cross-examination, called her on a claim she had made that she was using crack cocaine when Ric was a baby. Crack was not a part of the drug scene until years later.

On redirect, she told Johnson that Ric was 8 or 9 at the time she was using crack.

"Do you love Ric?" Johnson asked.

"I love him very much. I don't agree and I hate all that done happened, but I still love my child," she said.

"I told Johnson later that she was the best mitigation he could have presented," Gross said.

Surely, even the most hard-hearted juror would feel sorry for Henyard after seeing her testify while high on drugs at her son's most desperate hour, the prosecutor concluded.

The Closers

Gross, as he has done so many times over the years, gathered up his notes on a legal pad and walked to a large, heavy podium that, because of its undersized wheels, is balky and tends to make everyone who wrestles with it look awkward, as he or she pushes it to a spot in front of the jury box.

He began his closing statement by dispelling the notion that Henyard had less culpability than he normally would because he was high on drugs.

Before the carjacking, he had shared one marijuana cigarette with two or three other people, Gross said. He said he could not recall if Smalls even took a puff, and there was no evidence of drugs found in the car, certainly not the three that he claimed to have smoked, "the ones that Dorothy Lewis never saw."

Anyway, he said, "... drugs are a convenient and totally bogus excuse."

He talked about the sores on Henyard when he was an infant, and testimony that he had been seen hyperventilating in junior high school, and that his mother had to be rescued from a number of sex partners.

"I don't see the correlation between those events and what happened out on Hicks Ditch Road to two little girls. If you do, then throw them on the scales."

He characterized Henyard's father and his wife as people "who care for him very much."

He also dismissed Toomer's theory that Henyard had been harassed during questioning by police, based on what he had seen in a transcript. Nor is there any evidence of mental malaise, he said.

Henyard was 18 years old, and not a kid, Gross said. It was an army of 18-year-olds, he said, who defeated Hitler in World War II.

He put the responsibility solely on Henyard.

"This young man over here is the one who took this pistol," he said, holding it up, "and fired it until he placed that pistol to the forehead of Dorothy Lewis, until he was convinced that she was dead."

He said Henyard asked Linda Miller if she had seen the news reports that day.

"What do you know about that preacher lady who was killed last night?" he quoted Henyard as saying.

"That's the reason, when he found out later that morning, that she had not died, the first words out of his mouth were: 'You mean she didn't die?' And then, 'Can she ID anybody?'"

He also attacked the notion that Henyard was in fear of Smalls.

"There was no evidence that Henyard was intimidated by Smalls and was magically transformed from buddy, friend, accomplice and witness to four shots into Dorothy Lewis, that he formed himself into some kind of cutthroat killer," Gross said.

"And when he gets to Smalls' house, there is no word of Ric being threatened," Gross said.

Instead, he has blood on his hands, which he explains by saying that he had cut himself playing with a knife.

Gross reminded the jury that Bryant Smith said it wasn't just Yon who was bragging about Henyard's exploits in Plymouth that night.

He quoted Henyard's own words: "Yeah, but I had to burn the bitch, she went for my gun." And when the young men didn't believe him, he opened the glove box and turned a light on so they could see the pistol.

"Smalls said, 'Yeah man, he ain't bull jiving, he's telling the truth,'" Gross said, repeating testimony the jury had heard earlier.

Smalls was not bragging about anything, Gross noted.

Gross then brought up one of the most controversial aspects of the case.

"Even if you decide you just don't know who squeezed the trigger to kill the two kids, it doesn't follow that he should not get the ultimate punishment," he said.

Moving on to Henyard's statements to police, Gross said: "First, Henyard blames Yon. Then, he said he shot Dorothy Lewis one time accidentally, well, three times, but drugs made me do it. Later, well, I did get Jasmine out of the car, but Alfonza made me do it. I did throw Jasmine up and then down into the bushes but Alfonza made me do it. And trust me, guys, I didn't rape her. Trust me on this. I was sitting in the car looking the other way. Trust me," he said.

"I suggest to you the reason all of these people were shot is obvious. Two young men, in good lighting, made no attempt to hide their faces, made no attempt to prevent these people from looking at them." He then argued that the crime fit one of the statutory aggravators for the death penalty—heinous, atrocious and cruel.

He reminded jurors that Dorothy begged Henyard not to assault her in front of the children. His reply, he said was: "Shut up!"

"Is there anybody here who has any doubt that they suffered unnecessary mental torture? Anybody at all?"

The girls saw their mother get shot, and they heard the "Satan remark," he said.

Years later Gross would still be shaking his head at the Satan comment. "Can you imagine anything more terrifying to church-going children than that?"

The defense had urged Hill not to let the jury know about the remark.

"It's highly prejudicial, not relevant to any aggravating circumstance, including heinous atrocious and cruel. There is no evidence that she can prove that her children heard that, and it is simply not relevant," Johnson argued.

Hill said he did not allow it during the guilt phase, though he believed he could have. There is more leeway in the rules governing the penalty phase, he told the lawyers.

Besides, Hill said, the kidnapping charge "specifically mentions the term 'terrorize,' and there certainly is evidence of terrorizing the victims," he said.

"Robbery requires putting people in fear," he continued, "and this is exactly what the attempt was, to put the victims in fear."

He ruled that the jury could hear the statement.

Gross, in his remarks, disparaged Stone's earlier statement that "the defendant's chair is the loneliest place on earth."

Gross then added: "Can you hear Jasmine Lewis crying out for her mommy? Can you hear Jamilya Lewis crying for her mommy? Can you? Because that man over there can," he said.

"Let's talk about outrageously wicked and vile. Let's talk about conscienceless or pitiless. Let's talk about mental torture."

He pointed to a mannequin used in the trial to demonstrate the technique of analyzing high-speed blood spatter.

Henyard made choices to get a gun, steal a car, abduct a young family in darkness and to place his desires over the lives of others, Gross said, explaining that he made another choice, too.

"Eleven to 12 pounds of pressure was placed on the trigger, causing the hammer to fall on the primer, exploding gunpowder, firing a bullet down the barrel into three heads," he said.

He finished by saying: "I ask you to choose death for Richard Henyard because justice requires it. There is no other punishment that fits the crime."

Johnson, who made the penalty phase closing for the defense team, began by saying he was "nervous."

It was an emotional case, he said, punctuated with pictures of a dead 3- and 7-year-old.

"I'm not going to say that anything we brought into the courtroom justifies Ric's participation of what happened on January 30. There is simply no way I can do that."

But he said that things needed to be put into context and he urged the jurors to follow the law when deliberating Henyard's fate.

He said that proof of aggravators must be strong, and he said Gross had shown no evidence to support his argument for it.

He addressed another argument for an aggravator: that Henyard had been convicted of an earlier violent felony. He was a lookout during an armed robbery, not the one holding the weapon, Johnson said.

He also maintained that the state could not use the aggravator that the defendant had enjoyed some kind of financial gain from the crime.

"Nothing was taken from the children," he said.

He also argued against the imposition of the heinous, atrocious and cruel aggravator, pointing out that the medical examiner had testified that in her opinion, the children had not suffered pain because they immediately lost consciousness.

As for his age, "Ric was not a normal 18-year-old," he said, despite Gross' remark that it was an army of 18-year-olds who defeated Hitler. He reminded jurors that Toomer had estimated his age emotionally and mentally at 13 or 14.

"Mr. Gross said, oh, pooh-pooh that."

"Henyard hung out with younger kids. Smalls was 14. He didn't want to go to high school because his friends were in middle or elementary school," he said, referring to earlier testimony.

That's not a justification for what happened, he conceded, but an explanation of how the crime could have occurred. He lacks the reasoning skills of a normal person, he said.

As for drugs consumed during the crime, the state didn't even try to verify or disprove his story, failing, for example, to take a urine sample for a drug test, he noted.

His mother used drugs when she was pregnant. She also drank heavily, and while Toomer could find no symptoms of fetal alcohol syndrome, "we know the kinds of deficits it creates."

She was a "severely damaged person," he said.

"She appeared to me to be high yesterday," he said, referring to her rambling testimony.

Henyard's father was a decent, hardworking man who toiled from 80 to 90 hours a week, but at a young age, a boy needs a dad. His wife didn't even know he was coming to live with them, Johnson said.

"I suggest to you that at age 11, the die is cast ... there is no help for deficits."

He referred to what Gross had called a "tortured set of values."

"Where did he get those values?" he asked.

Gross had suggested Henyard could get as little as 27 years in prison, Johnson said. But he reminded jurors that he had called, as an expert witness, defense attorney Michael Graves, to explain that the minimum-mandatory sentence was 50 years, and the judge could sentence him to six consecutive life sentences.

"That is punishment," Johnson said.

Not surprising—at least to those who knew her—Dorothy was not asking for the death penalty, and she said so in her written victim impact statement to the State Attorney's Office.

"I believe that the men who committed this crime cannot be rehabilitated without Christ being in their lives. Even with the possibility of rehabilitation, however, I believe they should be committed to life in prison without any possibility of parole. I fear that if they are ever paroled, they will commit the same heinous crime against someone else and their children. Other members of my family believe that they should be executed. One member would volunteer to attend the executions," she wrote.

The jurors were reminded that, unlike the guilt phase, they were not required to render a 12-0 sentence recommendation. They were sent to the jury room at 11:10 a.m. At 2:40 p.m., they were ushered back into the courtroom.

They not only recommended death on the two murder counts, but it was unanimous.

It was not an obvious decision for everyone right away. The typewritten jury form reads: "A majority of the jury, by a vote of ...."

and that is followed with a fill-in-the-blank line to record the vote tally. The jury originally had split 10-2, then 11-1, and finally voted 12-0, according to the jury foreman, who put his initials beside the changed numbers and then signed the form.

Scales Tip Toward State

Hill ordered a pre-sentence investigation, dismissed the jury with his thanks and retired to prepare his written sentencing order.

On August 19, Hill, armed with a 24-page order, was ready to impose sentence.

Such orders begin by stating the facts of the case, and much of it is law-ordered and therefore dry. But Hill took note of Henyard's infamous Satan remark on the way to the murder site.

"... Mrs. Lewis was beseeching 'Jesus' for help; which resulted in Henyard's saying, 'this ain't Jesus, this is Satan,' certainly this comment proved to be a harbinger of what was forthcoming," he wrote.

The judge also took note of the blood evidence on Henyard's jacket. Despite denying he shot the girls, evidence "established that Henyard was less than 4 feet from Jamilya Lewis when she was executed." Henyard's co-defendant, Smalls,' clothing was found to have no such "high-speed blood splatter evidence," Hill wrote.

He also took note of Linda Miller's testimony in which she talked about taking Henyard to Smalls' house the morning after the murders, and where he could be seen shaking his finger at Smalls, though the conversation could not be heard. He then went to the police station, "where he, only after intense questioning, begrudgingly confessed his involvement in these murders."

The judge listed five aggravators. He cited the previous violent felony of armed robbery and the convictions for the violent and capital felonies committed during the carjacking. He also sided with Gross in his argument that the murders were heinous, atrocious and cruel. Also cited was the argument that the murders were committed for financial gain, and that the murders took place during the commission of another crime (armed kidnapping).

He listed the mitigators, including the fact that Henyard was only 18. He said he gave it "some weight" in considering the sentence.

He also cited the fact that because of a recent Florida Supreme Court decision, Smalls was too young to be eligible for execution.

"This is a non-statutory mitigating factor; the court considered and gave it some weight."

Hill also accorded "very little weight" to the defense claim that Henyard was acting under an extreme emotional disturbance and his capacity to conform his conduct to the requirements of law was impaired [Florida Supreme Court, Henyard v. Fla., Dec. 19, 1996].

Hill noted that the defense asked him to take into consideration such things as his IQ, his mother's drug and alcohol abuse, unstable upbringing and all of the other factors cited in his young, troubled life.

Hill said he gave little weight to the things mentioned by Toomer.

"The opinions of Dr. Toomer were based in large part upon the self-serving, uncorroborated, lie-filled contradictory statement of the defendant."

Another problem was that many of the psychological tests were machine-scored and Toomer did not take into consideration the machine's warnings that the test results might be inaccurate, Hill noted.

The judge also disagreed with the psychologist's statement that when Henyard was asking for his "Auntie" during questioning by police, he was really asking for a lawyer.

There was no evidence Henyard was an alcoholic or addict, the judge also noted, or that he suffered from any birth defect because of his mother's conduct during her pregnancy, or that infant Henyard's skin condition had any effect on him in his later years.

He also rejected the defense claim that Henyard had no strong father figure. He strongly cares about his son, works hard, doesn't use drugs and is law-abiding, he wrote.

"Unfortunately, the defendant chose to reject his father's strong example."

In addition, his godmother and his father's wife also loved him, the judge noted. This helped offset the objectionable example of his mother, the judge noted.

The poverty in his upbringing was given little weight, he said.

One of the arguments put forward by the defense was that Henyard displayed "no behavioral problems" when surrounded by stable people in a structured environment. "...this was not proven," Hill stated.

Another pitch was that he could adjust to life in prison. Little weight was allowed in this argument, the judge remarked.

Nor was much weight given to the argument that he could serve a minimum-mandatory sentence of 50 years.

In the end, after considering all of the arguments, the aggravating circumstances outweighed the mitigators, the judge concluded.

He sentenced him to six consecutive life sentences for the non-murder charges. As for the murder counts, "Richard Henyard, Jr., a/k/a Rick-Rick Henyard [shall] be sentenced to death by electrocution, or any other manner provided by law," the judge ordered.

Dorothy, who did not call for the death penalty for Henyard, has no misgivings about the need for people taking responsibility for their actions.

"We all have rough times in our lives," Dorothy would say later of Henyard's and Smalls' upbringing. "But that's no excuse to kill my family."

CHAPTER 8

"You're Just Like Job"

During the years of her recovery, many well-intentioned people came up to Dorothy and blurted out: "You're just like Job."

It never ceased to annoy her.

"I don't want to be Job," she said. "I am not Job," she would sometimes reply. "I am not Job's wife," would be another response.

Why did people keep telling her she was like the biblical character in the Book of Job?

Job was described as a "blameless and upright" wealthy man who was minding his own business when Satan showed up to cause trouble.

God knew that it was the devil's intent to separate man from God. But in Job 1:8 God said: "Have you considered my servant Job? There is no one on earth like him; he is blameless and upright, a man who fears God and shuns evil."

Satan, who is arrogant but not a fool, took the challenge, and replies in verses 9-11 (NIV): "Does Job fear God for nothing? Have you not put a hedge around him and his household and everything he has? You have blessed the work of his hands, so that his flocks and herds are spread throughout the land. But stretch out your hand and strike everything he has, and he will surely curse you to your face."

God gives Satan permission to wreak havoc, but says he is not to lay a finger on Job.

Job is not just an interesting story about good vs. evil (that's the gist of virtually every action movie), but a powerful example of the difference between human and divine logic.

We can understand suffering brought on by our own stupidity.

Homer Simpson, the pop icon of drunk and stupid, groaned in a recent TV episode and said, "Oh, why do my actions have consequences?" ("The Simpsons" ["Rednecks and Broomsticks," 2009]).

But why do the righteous suffer? Does God care what happens to us? And if He doesn't cause suffering, why does He allow it? These are the questions that theologians and ordinary people have been asking themselves for centuries. The answers are sometimes very surprising.

Mark A. Copeland suggests in his online outline study of Job that the real question is not why, but "how should the righteous suffer?" (*http://executableoutlines.com/job.htm*)

Another key issue is how we should respond to others who are suffering.

Dorothy's Take on Job

"I didn't suffer like Job," Dorothy says humbly. "I wasn't as bad off as Job.

"He was sick all the time, in pain, lost his family...," she said, also noting that he lost all of his possessions.

That's how she genuinely looks at it, yet her suffering was immeasurable. Mark Hill, the trial judge for both defendants, is absolutely correct when he concludes that few of us would have had the kind of patience and faith that she exhibited.

Like Job, Dorothy was doing nothing wrong when her world suddenly turned upside down.

She wasn't hanging out with someone of questionable character, wasn't going to a nightclub in a bad part of town, wasn't drunk, taking or selling drugs—and not just that night, but every night. She was going to a grocery store to get items for a church luncheon. She had no reason to suspect that she would suffer an unimaginable horror.

Unlike Job, Dorothy was not wealthy but she had some hard-earned material possessions and was working hard to improve her family's future.

Dorothy, like Job, had been hammered by one blow after another, starting with the death of her husband Lewis, even before the carjacking incident.

Job received a series of bad news reports, one right after the other, involving raiders who stole his livestock and killed his servants, then the death of all his children in a fierce blast of wind.

He was grief-stricken, but instead of immediately shouting "woe is me," as most of us would have done, he shaved his head and tore his robe as a sign of sorrow, then fell to the ground in worship, saying in Job 1:21:

"Naked I came from my mother's womb
And naked I will depart.
The Lord gave and the Lord has taken away;
May the name of the Lord be praised" (NIV).

Satan, who is not only crafty but persistent, went back to God, who again says, "Have you considered my servant Job?"

"'Skin for skin!' Satan replied. 'A man will give all he has for his own life. But stretch out your hand and strike his flesh and bones, and he will surely curse you to your face'" (Job 2:4-5).

God again lifts some restrictions but says that Job is not to be killed. Satan then inflicts painful sores on Job from the top of his head to the soles of his feet.

His wife, who is also grief-stricken at the loss of her children and the family's fortune, also lashes out at Job in 2:9.

"Are you still holding on to your integrity? Curse God and die!" she says.

He replies in verse 10: "You are talking like a foolish woman. Shall we accept good from God, and not trouble?"

Mistaken Friends

Soon, his troubles would increase, however, with the arrival of his friends, who had intended to comfort him.

Their first reaction was shock. They could hardly recognize him, and when they realized how much he was suffering they didn't say a word, but sat beside him for seven days and seven nights.

Job cried out that he wished he had never been born. He also began to complain about God, saying he had not sinned, so he didn't deserve to suffer (this is not something that Dorothy did, by the way).

Eliphaz, Bildad and Zophor and a fourth, younger man, Elihu, insist that he must have committed some grievous sin.

It was an example of the retribution principle, which is a belief that the wicked are cursed, says Eric Mitchell, Ph.D., of Southwestern Baptist Theological Seminary. The principle shows up in such places as Proverbs and Deuteronomy.

According to Mitchell, the pragmatic flip side to this principle is that: "If we're acting right, God has to bless me." The problem with that idea, he says, is that it assumes people are capable of manipulating God.

Dorothy's godmother, Emma, couldn't understand why Dorothy was suffering so grievously.

"She was living right. I always thought that nothing bad happens if you were living right. It shouldn't have happened. She was doing something good [preparing for a church luncheon], and she was living right. I just didn't understand it."

"Who can understand?" Ozietta said.

But then, she points out that there are spiritual struggles going on.

"That didn't break her," Ozietta said. "The enemy [Satan] has had it in for Dorothy since day one. He knows how many souls she will win [for God]."

She said her sister "came back greater than ever," and her ministry will become even greater.

"I can't say that what we've gone through has been worth it, but it helps that God is with us," Ozietta said.

"He allowed everything to go away," Denese said, but added that the Lord also allowed Dorothy's life to be rebuilt.

"She now has a larger family, she has regained her strength and raised Joshua with his father."

She had the courage to have another child, Denese said.

Job: What Are the Charges?

Job, still not conceding that he sinned, says in 7:20-21: "If I have sinned, what have I done to you, O watcher of men? Why have you made me your target? Have I become a burden to you? Why do you not pardon my offenses and forgive my sins? For I will soon lie down in the dust; you will search for me, but I will be no more" (NIV).

In verse 10:2, Job says: "I will say to God: Do not condemn me, but tell me what charges you have against me" (NIV).

Earlier, in verses 9:32-33, Job says of God: "He is not a man like me that I might answer him, that we might confront each other in court. If only there were someone to arbitrate between us, to lay his hand upon us both" (NIV).

Today, Christians have the benefit of knowing that Jesus is our arbitrator.

In verses 14:14-17 Job shows his incredible faith in God and an almost unheard-of understanding of heaven for that time when he says: "If a man dies, will he live again? All the days of my hard service I will wait for my renewal to come. You will call and I will answer you; you will long for the creature your hands have made. Surely then you will count my steps but not keep track of my sin. My offenses will be sealed up in a bag; you will cover over my sin" (NIV).

Readers of the Bible today know that Jesus has covered our sins—not by sealing them up in a bag—but with His blood on the cross.

It is in 19:25-26, while Job is still suffering, that he has this amazing revelation: "I know that my Redeemer lives, and that in the end he will stand upon the earth. And after my skin has been destroyed, yet in my flesh I will see God" (NIV).

Job is given an insight into Christ and ultimately the final resurrection, Mitchell says.

Meanwhile, Job's friends are still under the impression that he is being punished for some sin.

Ironically, much of what they say about God is true. Eliphaz in 5:9, for example, says, "He performs wonders that cannot be counted."

In a rhetorical question Bildad in 8:3 asks: "Does God pervert justice? Does the Almighty pervert what is right?" (NIV)

Job and his friends are unaware that it is Satan, not God, who is inflicting his pain and suffering. In fact, they are never told outright.

Finally, when Job can take no more, God shows up in a whirlwind in verse 38:2 and asks the anguished Job: "Who is this that darkens my counsel with words without knowledge?" (NIV)

God then goes on with a series of scathing, unanswerable questions, starting in 38:4: "Where were you when I laid the earth's foundation? Tell me, if you understand."

Job, in 40:4 answers: "I am unworthy—how can I reply to you? I put my hand over my mouth" (NIV).

In 42:3 Job admits, "Surely I spoke of things I do not understand, things too wonderful for me to know."

He repents and God tells Job's friends in 42:7, "You have not spoken of me what is right, as my servant Job has." He orders the friends to make a sacrifice and for Job to pray for them.

At the end of the book, God blesses Job even more than he originally did, with more wealth, seven sons and three daughters in a new, extended family, and a long life.

Lessons Learned

Mitchell believes there are many lessons to be learned from Job. First, God is sovereign. He is in control. Nothing happens without God knowing about it. That is something that Dorothy has recognized and has addressed it in her comments.

Second, Job's trials bring glory to God. They prove the enemy's accusations wrong and they are instructive to Job's friends. "There's some evangelism and instruction going on here," Mitchell says, even though the friends already have a belief in Yahweh. Third, the trials also bring Job into a closer relationship with God.

Jesus also taught the lesson of suffering. He was preparing to heal a blind man in John 9:1-3, when: "As he went along, he saw a man blind from birth. His disciples asked him, 'Rabbi, who sinned, this man or his parents, that he was born blind?' (NIV)

"'Neither this man nor his parents,' said Jesus, 'but this happened so that the work of God might be displayed in his life.'"

Mankind has trouble understanding the origins of evil, Mitchell said. God did not create evil. He created Adam and Eve and Satan. They exercised free will to sin against God. Thankfully, God restrains Satan. "If God let him go unrestrained, Satan would destroy us all," Mitchell said.

What happens when we are tested? Do we pass, like Job, or fail? Do we know ourselves as well as God knows us? And do we know just how strong our faith is until we really need Him?

These questions relate to Dorothy's theory, that despite telling Margaret that she would have to be locked up in a mental institution if something ever happened to the girls, God knew better than she did that she would survive with what Dorothy has correctly described as a "sound mind."

Paul, in 2 Corinthians 12:7-10, wrote that he had been given "a thorn in my flesh, a messenger of Satan, to torment me. Three times I pleaded with the Lord to take it away from me. But he said to me, 'My grace is sufficient for you, for my power is made perfect in weakness'" (NIV).

God knew that Job's—and Dorothy's—faith was sufficient.

Job's story also reveals God's merciful nature through his revelation about the Redeemer, the arbitrator, and his belief that he will not be forgotten and will be called by God after he dies.

Questioning God

Is it OK to question God? Job's friends were certainly appalled at the idea.

"It's not a problem to question God," Mitchell said. "You see it in other places in the Bible, including Psalms, but the psalmist always turns to faith and trust at the end of the song." In Psalm 13:1, for example, the writer asks: "How long will you hide your face from me?" And then, in 13:5: "But I have trusted in Your loving kindness; My heart shall rejoice in Your salvation."

"It is wrong to despair and assume that God is unjust," Mitchell said. That's where Job starts getting off track, he notes.

Often, it's a matter of asking the wrong question.

"It's not right for us to be despairing of God when we become sick or tragedy strikes, asking 'why me?'" Mitchell said.

"We accept life, the grace of life. We accept all the blessings of life on earth. Believers accept the grace and forgiveness Christ offers."

Then, we die.

"If we disagree when tragedy strikes or with the timing or manner of our death, some might say that God is not being fair. There's no such thing as fair. If God were being fair, all sinners deserve hell. However, God is in control. He is holy and righteous, gracious and forgiving through Christ," he said.

"We should trust him...," Mitchell said. He cites Romans 8:28, which reads: "And we know that in all things God works for the good of those who love him, who have been called according to his purpose" (NIV).

"We might not see the good here," Mitchell says. "But if one of my family members dies in an accident, and if they're a believer, they will be with God.

"Would it be better for them to be with God now or to live 80 years and have a lot of grandchildren?" he asks.

It is a matter, of course, of looking at it with the proper perspective, realizing that our understanding of His divine plan is so limited.

"Nothing we can do compares to what God has done," he said.

Coping

Job's suffering had one purpose that is very clear: His faith through his trials provided an example of how we are to face adversity.

Peter also writes about it in 1 Peter 5:8-9, saying: "Be self-controlled and alert. Your enemy the devil prowls around like a roaring lion looking for someone to devour. Resist him, standing firm in the faith, because you know that your brothers throughout the world are undergoing the same kind of sufferings" (NIV).

Then, in verse 10, he tells believers that compared to eternity, suffering is temporary. "And the God of all grace, who called you to his eternal glory in Christ, after you have suffered a little while, will himself restore you and make you strong, firm and steadfast."

Everyone faces his own trials, and it is hard to put ourselves in someone else's shoes.

Harold S. Kushner wrote his best seller, *When Bad Things Happen to Good People,* not as an abstract, theological discourse on Job, but as a way of dealing with his young son's death due to a rare illness.

He would wisely be among the first to advise us not to tell someone in such tragic circumstances, "I know how you feel," unless you have suffered identical circumstances.

The one thing that Job's friends did right (at first) was to listen and say nothing at all. Kushner notes that Job wanted sympathy and his friends didn't deliver.

"Have pity on me, my friends," Job says in 19:21-22, "have pity, for the hand of God has struck me. Why do you pursue me as God does? Will you never get enough of my flesh?"

Kushner, a rabbi, coped with the death of his son by assuming that God cannot change or fix everything.

He said he still believes in God but his perceptions have changed. "He is limited in what He can do by laws of nature and by the evolution of human nature and human moral freedom. I no longer hold God responsible for illnesses, accidents, and natural disasters, because I realize that I gain little and I lose so much when I blame God for those things. I can worship a God who hates suffering but cannot eliminate it, more easily than I can worship a God who chooses to make children sick and die, for whatever exalted reason" (p. 134).

He tells his readers that it is wrong to pray for "the impossible or the unnatural." Yet clearly, both the Old and New Testament are filled with examples of God pulling off both the "impossible" and "unnatural." Elijah, for example, asked God to bring a widow's son back to life. Christians know that Jesus raised the dead. Not only that, but Jesus was resurrected and left us with the Holy Spirit to guide us until His second coming.

Kushner does not tell readers to stop praying. On the contrary, it brings people together in a healing, comforting atmosphere. "Prayer, when it is offered in the right way, redeems people from isolation," he writes (p. 121).

Of course, he is absolutely right in noting that kind of healing power of prayer. He is also correct in noting that God does not answer every prayer with a "yes." Whenever a miracle does occur, acknowledge it as an unexplained blessing and move on, he seems to be saying.

We know God sometimes says "no." That was His answer to Dorothy's prayer for Lewis' recovery. And sometimes He tells believers to wait. We just don't always know why.

Kushner also believes that the meaning of our suffering is what we ascribe to it.

In other words, instead of asking, "Why me?" we should ask, "What am I going to do about it?"

Today, Dorothy can look back and say she had a reason she didn't like to be told that she was like Job. "It didn't help me," she said.

She concedes that she can see the similarities in the way she was restored. Like Job, she got a new, extended family. She married Brock and gave birth to a handsome, intelligent, sensitive son.

"I can see that part," she said.

Others can see that part, too, including Emma, who at the time could see only that Dorothy was "living right."

"Joshua loves his mommy," Emma says. "He's a sweetheart, just a little miracle baby. He loves his mother and makes her happy, and she has a good husband, so she can't ask for more."

Maybe the bottom line is that we just don't understand everything—as unsatisfying as that answer might be. After all, how could the murder of two children and the brutal attack on a young widow possibly make any sense on the human level?

All that we do know is that God doesn't approve of such evil. It was not part of the plan for mankind in His creation. It has never been His desire to inflict suffering on mankind—certainly not for the blameless.

We know this because of Jesus' mission here on earth. He always felt compassion for the lowest, poorest, most helpless people, and He spent his life healing, teaching, loving and saving souls.

The shortest, most poignant verse in the Bible simply says, "Jesus wept" (John 11:35). It refers to the moments leading up to raising His friend, Lazarus, from the dead.

We also know that the Bible is full of texts in which God can take bad things and use them for His glory and the salvation of His people.

Ultimate Goal

Peter John Kreeft, Ph.D., points out in Lee Strobel's excellent book, *The Case for Faith,* that God never answers Job's question about why he has been suffering. Instead, He asks a question of His own: "Who is this who darkens my counsel....?"

Yet, Job is satisfied, Kreeft says, because he meets God face-to-face. That is what Job had asked for while in the depths of his misery. Kreeft calls it a foretaste of heaven, where we are satisfied with just being in the presence of the Creator (p. 50).

That is the very purpose of Jesus' suffering when He dies on the cross—so that we can live with God forever.

It was a steep price to pay for Jesus, and not just in the physical agony He experienced.

Matthew 27:46 states: "About the ninth hour Jesus cried out in a loud voice, 'Eloi, Eloi, lama sabachthani?'—which means, 'My God, my God, why have you forsaken me?'"

Jesus had dreaded that moment because it was when He was taking on the sins of the world and He knew at that moment He was temporarily separated from the Father.

It's an interesting parallel to Job, who also faces not only physical agony, but the pain (he thinks) of losing fellowship with God. In Job 29:1-5 he writes: "How I long for the months gone by, for the days when God watched over me, when his lamp shone upon my head and by his light I walked through darkness! Oh, for the days when I was in my prime, when God's intimate friendship blessed my house, when the Almighty was still with me and my children were around me" (NIV).

Suffering can be a witness for our faith. It was for Job, and Christ's crucifixion certainly was the greatest witness of all.

Peter writes in 1 Peter 4:12-13: "Dear friends, do not be surprised at the painful trial you are suffering, as though something strange were happening to you. But rejoice that you participate in the sufferings of Christ, so that you may be overjoyed when his glory is revealed" (NIV).

There are three truths that absolutely apply to Dorothy: Suffering can bring glory to God when we don't break faith. Suffering can bring us closer to God, and suffering can teach us about God's grace and mercy. Her story has been a witness, a ministry and a blessing to countless people.

Not only are Christians not exempt from suffering, but it can be argued that it is part of their calling. Jesus in Matthew 10:38 says: "...anyone who does not take his cross and follow me is not worthy."

Whatever suffering we endure, it is brief compared to spending eternity with God, where we will be fully restored.

Job didn't have the advantage of being able to read ahead to the New Testament, but we do.

Revelation 21:1-4 reads: "Then I saw a new heaven and a new earth, for the first heaven and the first earth had passed away, and there was no longer any sea. I saw the Holy City, the new Jerusalem, coming down out of heaven from God, prepared as a bride beautifully dressed for her husband. And I heard a loud voice from the throne saying, 'Now the dwelling of God is with men, and he will live with them. They will be his people, and God Himself will be with them and be their God. He will wipe every tear from their eyes. There will be no more death or mourning or crying or pain, for the old order of things has passed away'" (NIV).

CHAPTER 9

Dorothy: "What the Enemy Meant for Evil, God Meant for Good"

"And we know that all things work together for good to those who love God, to those who are the called according to His purpose" (Romans 8:28, NKJV).

I have been asked: "What good could possibly come from such an appalling act of cruelty?"

I wanted to know the same thing.

What good could come from that horrible night?

First, God displayed His miraculous powers.

I couldn't see God's powers being displayed while the bad things were happening that night, but they were being manifested.

God kept me conscious enough to tell the police officers everything they needed to know about me, my girls, the car I was driving and information about my mom. Even though I don't remember giving them all of those facts, I know I did because I didn't have any type of identification with me.

I had been shot in the head, and I have been told that my head was so big that you couldn't even see my shoulders.

When I had surgery on my head (which I had at first stubbornly referred to as, "If it ain't broke don't fix it"), there was a hole in the dura layer, that protects the brain, that was about the size of a quarter.

There were bullet fragments floating all around that hole. The doctors said that if just one fragment had gone through that hole, I would have dropped dead on the spot.

I'm talking about the miraculous powers of God.

I thought about all the time I spent ducking and dodging car headlights. A bullet fragment could have easily gone through that hole. I could have bled to death, but God allowed the outside temperature that night to be low enough to keep my blood from flowing rapidly.

The tragedy resulted in other miracles, too.

It brought a community together. It didn't matter if you were black or white, love was shown in a way that I had never witnessed before.

There were numerous people praying for me, people from many parts of the world.

I received so many letters from people that I didn't even know, telling me how much they were praying for me and that they were inspired by the amount of faith I had.

People just wanted to show their love and concern toward me in any way they could.

I received a beautiful painted portrait of the girls and me from artist Anne Bell and an angel-themed needlepoint from Jill Jordan-Spitz, the reporter who covered the trials.

John T. Murrell, DMD, gave me free dental work.

He gave me a beautiful smile, and I no longer had to put my hand over my mouth to hide my missing teeth. That was the first time I felt happiness since the tragedy.

I even received letters from inmates in prison telling me how sorry they were for my loss. Almost all of the letters were encouraging, but I do remember receiving one letter suggesting that I must have done something that was really bad in another lifetime, therefore, the tragedy that I experienced was a way to pay me back for my wrongdoing.

Needless to say, I didn't dwell on that much. It was "too deep" for me.

The experience brought about other miracles.

Some doubters became believers, some unsaved people became saved, the outpouring of love helped the hopeless become hopeful and some with little faith would end up with great faith.

My own family members began to have a closer walk with the Lord and turned their lives around.

I drew closer to the Lord, too.

After I made up my mind that I wasn't going to let fear over-rule my life, I moved back home to Eustis with my brother Arthur Gene.

That was a giant step to take, moving back into the house without the girls, but I knew it had to be done in order for me to complete my college degree in elementary education.

I also knew that God didn't spare my life for me to sit around and do nothing. Knowing that God was with me, along with Arthur Gene, I felt safe, and it was time for me to move on.

Arthur Gene was one of the family members who began to have a close walk with the Lord. He would be the first to admit that for him to give his life to the Lord was a miracle in and of itself. Today, he serves as a deacon in his church.

Having Brock come into my life was a blessing, first as a counselor, then a friend, and finally my husband.

He assured me that I could not have done anything differently to save the girls.

He also reassured me that God was still with me and that I was never alone. He read Psalm 139:1-9 to me. It says: "1 For the Chief Musician. A Psalm of David. O Lord, You have searched me and known me. 2 You know my sitting down and my rising up;

You understand my thought afar off. 3 You comprehend my path and my lying down, And are acquainted with all my ways. 4 For there is not a word on my tongue, But behold, O Lord, You know it altogether. 5 You have hedged me behind and before, And laid Your hand upon me. 6 Such knowledge is too wonderful for me; It is high, I cannot attain it. 7 Where can I go from Your Spirit? Or where can I flee from Your presence? 8 If I ascend into heaven, You are there; If I make my bed in hell, behold, You are there. 9 If I take the wings of the morning, And dwell in the uttermost parts of the sea, 10 Even there Your hand shall lead me, And Your right hand shall hold me" (NKJV).

Those words confirmed God's assurance and presence in my life. The Word of God became alive in my spirit; reiterating that there was no place I could go to avoid God's spirit. For me, that was something good.

After about a couple of counseling sessions, Brock and I became friends. Even though he had the title of Christian counselor, I believe I helped him just as much as he helped me.

About one year and three months later, Brock and I became husband and wife on July 3, 1994.

I chose that date because of the numbers seven and three; the ages of my daughters.

Brock was very understanding of everything that I wanted to do. When we got married, he didn't demand that I change my name to Brockington.

Brock understood that I wanted to keep Lewis as my last name because it is the last name of my daughters.

There were countless blessings but among the best was my first full-time teaching assignment after I got my degree in 1995.

Jamilya had been a student at Eustis Heights Elementary School. The school put up a plaque on the school's playground, honoring her memory and Jasmine's. Another plaque on the playground also memorializes a little boy who had attended the school when he passed away.

I wanted to work there. I applied but didn't get a call back right away. Eventually, the principal called, set up an interview, had me meet with some of the teachers and finally called me into the office to say that I would be teaching first grade.

That was what I wanted. I said, "Lord, God, you do love me don't you?"

Later, I heard about a teacher who wondered why I would want to teach at the school. "Wouldn't it just bring up bad memories all the time?" she asked.

I felt like it was an honor.

Jamilya's teachers reached out to me, telling me what a joy she had been.

Jamilya was a very outgoing, smart little girl.

A sharp dresser, thanks to godmother Emma, she made quite an impression.

She was supposed to be in kindergarten but because she was working on a first-grade level, they put her in an advanced class.

She liked to do everything, including reading.

Due to Brock's previous marriage, I became an instant stepmother.

Before I met Brock, I didn't know if I would ever consider having another child. I thought that I would be overprotective. I thought something bad might happen.

I had all kinds of negative thoughts. After helping nurture Hugh and Kristopher, my feelings of becoming a mother were restored.

I still had some issues in my life. There were some disturbing side effects from the gunshot wounds, for example.

I had experienced some seizures because of the head wounds. Brock said he came home and found me on the floor. Later, I had a grand mal seizure. Brock witnessed that.

A doctor prescribed strong medicine, with strong side effects, including a swollen face.

I said: "I'm not taking this medicine, it's killing me."

Brock insisted.

"I don't want to take any medicine," I said.

"Promise me if you have another seizure you'll take it again," he said.

"I promise."

I had to get back on it. But one day I felt light-headed and I felt like God was telling me, "You are healed. You are healed."

Brock was wary.

I tried to make Brock happy.

I was conflicted. Mom was telling me to be patient, that a transition was taking place.

Mom said, "Dorothy, you taking the medicine doesn't mean you're not trusting God. God is healing you of the medicine."

The medicine made me feel like a zombie. I thought, "This is so not me."

Then, a strange thing happened at a church service.

We were singing a song called "Thank You." Its lyrics include:

"I could've been dead, sleeping in my grave

But you made death stand back and behave.

I've got to say, thank you Lord."

As we were singing I felt like there was a transformation taking place within me.

Mom then began singing a different version of "Jesus loves me."

"Oh yes he does," the song says.

I said, "I'm not taking any medicine. I am healed."

That was in February. On December 8, 1997, at the age of 40, I gave birth to a healthy baby boy, Joshua Caleb Brockington.

You see how God works? If I had not stopped taking that medicine when I did...?

He's my miracle baby.

I refused tests to see if the baby was going to be OK, and I didn't care if it was a boy or a girl. I just prayed. We talked to the baby and played classical music.

He's a good boy. He's bright and intelligent. He gets straight A's. He can be anything he wants to be. He has a gift for music. He hears something, he can play it. He takes karate, too.

He's very sensitive. I'm praying that one day he will have a wife like him.

Joshua is an anointed boy who has a calling on his life to be a leader for his generation. He is such a blessing in my life.

There were other miracles, too.

I had lost my sense of taste and smell after being shot in the head. But while I was still pregnant, one morning I could smell bacon being fried in my sister's kitchen. And I can again taste food.

Why Did God Allow It to Happen?

As I have mentioned earlier, I have been asked why I wanted to tell my story. I know there are aspects that make it a hard story to hear.

But I wanted to tell my story so that it can be used as a tool to glorify God, and help others recognize that there is hope when facing situations that seem hopeless.

Once you've read about my nightmare that wasn't a dream, I hope you will say, like many others: "After hearing all that you have been through, I don't have anything to complain about."

Countless times I was asked, "Why did God do this to you?"

Countless times I would say, "God didn't do this to me, however, He does allow things to happen in our lives."

Please understand that God is not the author of confusion, and He is not evil. God has given us all a free will to make our own choices—good or evil.

There may be various reasons why God did not prevent these hideous crimes from occurring.

Perhaps God was sparing my daughters from something that was even more gruesome in the days ahead. Maybe the trauma they experienced that night would have affected them very adversely in the future. Or maybe God was ready for my daughters to begin their eternal lives with Him.

Some things are beyond our human understanding. This is one of the key lessons of Job in the Bible.

Over and over again, and even today, people have told me: "You're like Job!"

I kept saying: "I'm not Job," and "I don't want to be Job."

However, like Job, I may have been "considered" for this trial.

God may have allowed tragedy to happen in my life because He saw something in me that I didn't see in myself. He knew what I could bear.

I know that I rejected the comparison many times, but after reflecting upon Job's character, I count it an honor to be compared to Job.

I, too, lost everything—my daughters—who are still very much a part of me.

And like Job, I never stopped trusting God.

As we were being carjacked, I kept praying and calling on the name of Jesus out loud.

Henyard said, "Well, you can stop calling Jesus, 'cause this ain't Jesus, this is Satan."

I didn't stop calling Jesus because I didn't know what else to do.

Even though I was faced with a crisis that I had never experienced before, God carried me through it.

Yes, God is faithful, He is real and He is love.

God has proven Himself in my life so many times. God's miracles and mercies never come to an end.

I want to tell my story to facilitate a change in the lives of many people, and for that I say, "To God be the glory!"

CHAPTER 10

Justice

With Henyard pondering his fate on death row, lawyers turned their attention to Smalls and his October 17, 1994 trial date.

Since the Public Defender's office was now off the case, private attorneys Jeffery M. Pfister and Charles A. Fantl were appointed to handle Smalls' defense.

Pfister, a former prosecutor, is a genial, big man. He has won many battles over the scales of justice but is candid about losing battles with the bathroom scales.

Pfister would later defend a man in a case that sparked national headlines. Ricky Adams led an army of volunteers and law enforcement officers on a three-day wild-goose chase in search of his missing young daughter, Kayla McKean, only to later confess that he had stomped her to death while in a rage, and buried her in the Ocala National Forest. Pfister, who is surprisingly light on his feet, paced off a short space on the courtroom floor, "about the size of a bathroom," as he put it, and indicated it would be the prison cell space where Adams would spend the rest of his life. "That's punishment," he told the jurors.

He also produced a cigar box filled with intricate carvings that Adams had carved out of bars of soap to demonstrate that he had some value to society. It was a stretch, but Pfister still shows the box to young lawyers to demonstrate that you can use almost anything in death penalty mitigation.

The jury, which had a hard time believing any father could kill his own child, imposed a life sentence instead of the death penalty.

An avid reader of history books and a literate man, Pfister teased reporters in one murder trial by indicating his client could not have shot his victims. It was similar to the defendant in *To Kill A Mockingbird,* he said. In the classic novel by Harper Lee, the defendant could not have struck the alleged victim with the hand that would have matched the injury because his arm on that side of his body was paralyzed. Pfister argued that his client was innocent because he couldn't have shot his victim with the hand he normally used because of where he was sitting in the backseat of a car. He even set up chairs and used a co-counsel to demonstrate where people were sitting in the car. Unfortunately for Pfister, the demonstration didn't convince the medical examiner who was asked to comment on the demonstration, or the jurors. It didn't work for Gregory Peck's character in the movie, either.

Pfister doesn't try to impress jurors with his education or with literature and movie references, however. He likes to try and convince them that the State Attorney's evidence is like an Irish stew. If there is even the tiniest piece of rancid meat in the mix, then the whole batch needs to be thrown out, he argues.

Fantl, a longtime attorney, has a sharp sense of humor, is smart, effective, and like all skilled lawyers, knows when to be the nice guy and when to go for the jugular. Among his many victories was a mess of a state's case against a preacher, who was charged with lewd and lascivious behavior with foster children. Charges were either dropped, dismissed, pled down, reduced, adjudication withheld or charges rejected by not-guilty verdicts.

There was the usual blizzard of legal papers for Smalls, especially at first, with at least the possibility that the state might seek the death penalty for Smalls.

Of course the defense was concerned about pretrial publicity. Now that Henyard had been convicted, there had been even more press coverage. The defense team sought a change of venue.

They also wanted a jury questionnaire like the one used in Henyard's case.

Many of the questions seemed standard enough, including whether the prospective juror had formed any opinions about the case, what their views of the death penalty were, and what they had heard about the case. But there were also questions about political party affiliation, how often they attended church, marital status and question 35, which read: "Are the people you usually run into in your neighborhood: All White, All Black, Both Black & White?"

There was also the usual defense concern over the possibility of "highly prejudicial and inflammatory" evidentiary pictures being shown to the jury. The showing of the pictures would violate Smalls' constitutional protection against "cruel and unusual punishment as guaranteed by the Eighth and Fourteenth Amendments," the motion declared.

Judges are typically very careful about this kind of evidence and agree to screen out the goriest photos.

There was also a motion to suppress Smalls' confession. He was only 14 at the time of the crime, the motion stated. He only had an IQ of 72, was suspended from the seventh grade and was in a special education program.

King was worried about how the jury would treat Smalls if they thought he was mentally challenged.

There is no diminished capacity defense in the state of Florida, he pointed out in his arguments.

Pfister replied that he was not trying to prove diminished capacity, but was only trying to show that Smalls was a follower, subject to coercion. The only thing he would talk about, Pfister said, was that he was in the seventh grade and was a slow learner. "We're not going to say anything further than that."

Judge Hill said he would allow it, but said he would not allow anything to be argued about "threshold of duress." That is a term that shows up sometimes in contract law, in which the court decides that a pact is so unconscionable that it cannot be enforced. The person entering into the contract would have had to have been misled, was not aware of the whole story or entered into the contract under duress.

The motion also claimed that Smalls' mother, Annette, was "a frequent user of crack cocaine."

Law enforcement violated state laws regarding parental notification of children taken into custody and that his right to counsel was infringed upon, the motion also stated.

"Alfonza Smalls' mother, Annette Smalls, was at the Eustis Police Department, waiting to see her son, as members of law enforcement were interrogating Alfonza Smalls," the motion read.

Pfister was not surprised that his client had talked. About 80 percent of the people hauled into the police station talk without counsel, he said.

"My grandmother used to say, 'You never get in trouble for what you don't say.'"

Another truism, he says, is "you never talk your way out of trouble but you can talk yourself into it."

Sure enough, Smalls tried to talk himself out of trouble with FDLE Agent David West and others at the Eustis Police Department by portraying himself as an innocent bystander.

He said he was at a popular barbecue stand in town when Henyard walked up and asked him to go with him to the Winn-Dixie.

"...he told me that he wasn't going to walk back home, he was going to find a ride. He told me he was gonna wait until that black lady come out of the store and ask for a ride because he say he knew her."

He claimed she willingly gave the two a ride, and while going to Jackie Turner's house "the back way," on the rural road, Henyard pulled a gun on her.

"What you gonna do to me?" Smalls said, quoting Dorothy.

"He [Henyard] told her, 'Don't worry about it,' and he called her a B, the B-I-T-C-H word. And then after she got out of the car, he sexually abused her and then made her walk over in the bushes and that's when he shot her. Then he got back in the car, rode down the road some more, and made her two little girls get out and he shot them. And that's when we turnt around and went back towards my house."

"I ain't know he had no gun," he claimed.

Smalls quoted Dorothy as saying, "Don't kill me. Just take... let me and my daughter[s] go and you can take the car."

"He told her no."

Smalls said one of the girls said, "You gonna kill us, too? Like you did my mama?"

"And he told them, 'Don't worry about that.'"

"He made them lay on the ground and shot them."

Henyard then picked up their bodies and threw them across the barbed wire fence near where they had been standing, Smalls said.

A written transcript of the interrogation listed an "unidentified speaker" asking Smalls: "There was nothing occurred at the Winn-Dixie parking lot, is that what you are saying, right?"

"Huh-uh."

Smalls said Henyard never told him Dorothy's name, saying only that she was from "Ocala."

"Why would he want to kill her?" the questioner asked.

"Because earlier that day, earlier that day, he was talking about he got some unfinished business to do and this other kind of stuff. And before night fell, I guess he got the gun back and that's when he did it."

Law enforcement agents were puzzled by that remark, and asked if the "unfinished business" was between Henyard and Dorothy.

Smalls then said he didn't think Henyard even knew her.

Smalls, continuing to downplay his role, said he told the crying children to be quiet in the car and promised nothing was going to happen to their mother. He also claimed he was in the backseat with the children, said Dorothy was driving, then said he stayed in the car while Dorothy was being assaulted and shot, and while the children were shot.

He also quoted Henyard's Satan remark.

He said Henyard shot Dorothy in the back, dragged her into the bushes and shot her in the head. He said he walked off, went back and shot her again in the head, for a total of four shots.

He said Henyard was shaking and in a state of panic after he shot Dorothy. He said Henyard cursed while telling the crying children to "shut up."

"I just told him to take me home. He told me no. He say, 'We fixin' to ride.'

"Then he said, 'Hold up.' And he stopped the car and he backed up and turnt around and went back down there towards the mother and he shot the kids and put them out of the car."

He said the two of them went back to Eustis to pick up Yon, who got them a change of clothing from his house, and the trio headed off toward the Orlando area.

The transcript shows the officers and Smalls taking a brief break. When the questioning resumes, there is a big change.

Investigators had allowed Annette to talk with her son during the break.

West says on the tape: "Alfonza's mother and he just had a brief conversation in which Alfonza described having had sex with the victim.

"He cried and said that, 'Ric-Ric made me do it, made me have sex with the lady,' and that's sort of generic but I didn't … I didn't take any notes," West said in his deposition.

West described Annette Smalls as supportive, urged him to tell the truth, then she left.

Back on tape, Smalls repeated his claim that Henyard threatened him.

"You have sex with her or I'm gonna do something to you, you won't like," Smalls said, quoting Henyard.

Smalls insisted that he had been making truthful statements under oath, saying, "that's what happened."

"That's... that story about how the thing happened didn't include you having sex with the woman at all," West said.

"It didn't include you helping him throw the girls in the bushes or any of that, didn't include you having any blood on your clothes, it didn't include a lot of details about what really happened. We want you to tell the truth this time."

Smalls apparently was reduced to a soft-spoken mumbler after this exchange.

Q: "Did he ever give you any reason for why he killed the kids?"

A: (Inaudible).

Q: "Did you ever ask?"

A: (Inaudible).

Q: "Why did he kill her?"

A: "I don't know."

Q: "Y'all never did discuss that?"

A: (Inaudible).

Q: "Then everybody that says that y'all had been talking about it in front of them, they're all lying, is that it? That you had made plans earlier to do something like this and that you knew what you were doing when you went over there, is that all a fairy tale?"

A: "I didn't know he was gonna do it until we got to Winn-Dixie."

Q: "You knew he was gonna jack somebody that day, right?"

A: "Yeah, he say he was gonna jack somebody, but he didn't say when he was gonna do it."

Q: "And you wanted to ride with him, too, didn't you?"

A: "He didn't tell me, he didn't tell me we were gonna do it 'til we got to Winn-Dixie."

Smalls also told officers that Henyard had told him that he had killed someone in the past.

When officers asked who he had killed, Smalls said: "I don't know. Only thing I know about Ric is his name. I don't know who he is, I don't know where he from. All I know is he stay with Ms. Jackie (inaudible), that's it."

Smalls was asked if he had talked to Henyard that morning.

He admitted that he had. Henyard wanted to know if the stolen car had been recovered by police. He said that it had.

"Did he ever threaten you about what you should or shouldn't tell the police?"

"Yep. He told me, he told me this should be a secret between me and him. I shouldn't tell nobody."

Smalls had, in fact, by this time already talked to Yon.

"He called me out, he called me outside," Smalls said of Henyard.

"Is that when your mother got upset and knew something was really going on?"

"Yep."

Annette Smalls had heard her son's version of the truth before he was taken to the police station, and one of the reasons she went to the station apparently, was to get him to tell the police about his claim that Henyard forced him into raping Dorothy.

She laid out her version of the story in her sworn statement in a series of questions by Henyard's attorney, Johnson.

She had been looking for Alfonza all evening. At one point, she sent Yon to look for him. Yon didn't come back with her son, but did come back between 9 and 9:30 with the birthday cake he had purchased at Winn-Dixie.

"… I asked him where was he, and he said he didn't see him, said he was gone across town to some girl (sic) house."

Henyard showed up at her house around 11:30 p.m., she said.

"He knocked at the door and I asked him where was Alfonza. He said Alfonza was across town to a girl (sic) house."

Asked where exactly, Henyard replied that he did not know.

He asked Yon to step outside, she said.

Q: "And then you saw Emanuel coming back inside?"

A: "Yeah, looking very strange."

Q: "Define that for me, please, ma'am, can you be more specific?"

A: "He had a different look on his face. OK, when he came back in, he had an awkward look, like something was wrong."

She said after Henyard and Yon left, Tamara remarked that she had seen blood on Henyard's clothing.

Q: "You didn't see it?"

A: "I didn't see it."

Q: "Did you see blood anywhere on him?"

A: "On his hand and I asked what happened to his hand and he said he cut himself."

Henyard then apparently made a show of returning a six-inch knife to Yon that he had borrowed.

"They said they was going to get Alfonza and they were coming back."

She said she was the one who woke up around 3 a.m. and unlocked the door so Alfonza and Yon could come in the house.

"He had on different clothes from what he had on when he left, had on a light pair of green pants and a striped-like green shirt, but when he left, he had a solid suit made out of satin, satin-like green."

She wanted some answers.

"I asked Alfonza where he had been and he said he was across town to a girl, to one of his friend (sic) house helping a brother fix on a truck.

"So I asked him where was his clothes, he said they had got greasy."

Alfonza claimed the girl would wash the clothes for him and return them later.

"Well, this girl might have been mighty important for you to be over there helping fixing a truck this time of morning," she told him.

"I told him to go to sleep, when he wake up the next morning me and him was going to discuss why he went without telling me and why he went to this girl house without telling me."

She went to sleep but was awakened at 4:30 a.m. "... he was jumping in his sleep and I thought somebody was trying to come in. I heard, you know, like a bump. So when I got up, he was jumping in his sleep and his foot was hitting the sofa. I woke him up and asked him what was wrong with him. He said he had a bad dream."

She said at 10:30 a.m. Sunday, she went down the street to visit a neighbor and saw several police cars and a lot of activity in the neighborhood. While drinking a few beers, she learned of the girls' murders and that police had recovered the stolen car behind the nearby middle school.

"Alfonza, they found a car around there," she commented to her son a short time later. "You all know anything about a car?"

"He say, 'No ma'am.'"

Not much later, she saw Henyard approach Alfonza, and while she could not hear what they were saying, "I noticed the way he was pointing his finger in Alfonza (sic) face."

She called him aside and asked him what was going on.

"He looked... at first he said nothing. I said, 'Junior, something happened that you're not telling me.'

"I said, 'You better tell me what's going on and tell me now.' I said, 'Otherwise I find out later.'

"So he broke down and he started crying and that's when he started telling me Ric made him...That's when he said Ric made, forced him to have sex with the lady. Then he turned and he shot the lady."

"Who shot the lady?" Johnson asked.

"Ric-Ric shot the lady," she replied.

"Said Ric shot the lady and said he tried to run, said Ric told him if he run, he was going to shoot his ass and made him lay down beside the lady. So he turned and he went back."

She said her son also told her that Henyard forced him to get the girls out of the car and that Henyard shot them.

"I don't know what happened out there because I wasn't there," she said, in a curious statement, suggesting that perhaps she didn't believe him.

"And I said, 'Well, why didn't you tell me this when you came home?'

"He said, 'I was scared. Because Ric Ric threatened me that if I tell anybody, he was going to do the same thing to you all.'

"So that's why he didn't tell me. So I sent for the police."

Judge Hill would eventually rule that there were no grounds to suppress the confession, but for tactical purposes the prosecution did not play the tape for the jury.

But the biggest bone of contention in pretrial hearings was whether the state would be allowed to seek the death penalty for Smalls. On that issue, Hill had to wait on the Florida Supreme Court.

Justices were grappling with the case of a youth who was convicted of armed robbery and murder at a gas station in Titusville. He was 15 at the time of the crime.

The justices noted on March 24, 1994 that, "more than a half century has elapsed since Florida last executed anyone who was less than sixteen years of age at the time of committing an offense. In the intervening years, only two death penalties have been imposed on such persons, and both of these later were overturned."

Also, with an eye toward an earlier U.S. Supreme Court ruling, the justices said the death penalty in such a case would either be cruel or unusual.

"We cannot countenance a rule that would result in some young juveniles being executed while the vast majority of others are not, even where the crimes are similar," the opinion read.

Hill and the trial lawyers now had their answer. The trial would now be less complicated and go more quickly if Smalls was convicted in a non-death penalty case, court officials noted—not to mention a less cumbersome appeal process.

Not everyone was happy about the legal decision, however. A seething Margaret told reporters that if you're old enough to terrorize and kill, you're old enough for the ultimate penalty.

Brock agrees.

"Age should not be a determining factor when it comes to the death sentence because every child knows the difference between right and wrong with no excuse. The children under the age of 18 commit these crimes knowing that nothing will happen to them because of the law of injustice," he said.

Dorothy's family members were not the only ones who felt that way. Hill, again, received mail on the issue.

"I am a concerned citizen writing to you about the case of Alfonza Smalls, Jr. I read in the newspaper that his attorney, Jeffery Pfister, has filed a motion asking you to rule that death is an inappropriate penalty for his client," she wrote.

"Two of his reasons for this motion are as follows:

"The Supreme Court has ruled that 15 years old is too young to be executed and that sentencing children to death is cruel and unusual punishment. 'Inexperience, less education and less intelligence makes the teen-ager less able to evaluate the consequences of his or her conduct.'

"'A fourteen-year-old such as Alfonza Smalls cannot serve on a jury, purchase alcoholic beverages, wager or bet, enter into a contract, hold judicial office, marry or divorce... One whose maturity is expressly deemed legislatively and legally insufficient in all these settings... cannot be considered mature enough to suffer society's ultimate punishment.'

"Your honor, when I read this I felt sick to my stomach. The fact that he is 15 years old and should not be executed is ridiculous. We all know that if he is sentenced to death, he will not be executed until he is at least 20 years old. At 15, I knew and understood what murder was. Jasmine and Jamilya Lewis will never reach 15, but they realized what a horrifying thing murder is at ages 3 and 7. They saw their mother attacked and shot twice in the head. Can you imagine what those two little girls were thinking as they witnessed this? At their young ages, Jasmine and Jamilya did not fully understand the concept of death, but they were sentenced to it by Alfonza Smalls. If he is mature enough to hold a gun to the heads of little children and willfully pull the trigger, then he is certainly mature enough to die for what he has done.

"It is undisputed that the rate of teen-age crime has increased over the years. One of the main reasons for this is because they are underage and can get away with anything. Look at the case of one of the suspects in the murder of the British tourist near Tallahassee. He is 13 years old and has a record of over 50 arrests. This person obviously has no concern for human life or the rules of society, much like Alfonza Small, (sic) Jr.

"I have a 22-month-old son and to lose him would be worse than losing my own life. I couldn't begin to imagine the tragic loss that Dorothy Lewis faces every day knowing that she will never see her precious children again.

"If you allow Alfonza Smalls to live after committing such a gruesome crime, that is only sending a message to other teen-agers that they, too, can get away with murder. Please consider Dorothy Lewis' loss and the effect your judgment will have."

Dorothy Key—Again

Picking a jury took some time because there were many prospective jurors who had heard of the case, including a number who said they already had their minds made up.

Pfister, who later acknowledged that he didn't have much to work with, laid out the defense's case in his opening statement.

Smalls was 25 pounds lighter when the crimes were committed and was a "follower," he told the jury. He was "submissive." Henyard was four years older.

Pfister noted that it was Henyard who went and got a change of clothes for the two.

"It was an absolute brilliant move, showing his criminalistic skills and his criminal aforethought in this case."

Smalls was so unsophisticated he ditched his bloody clothes near the spot where the stolen car was abandoned, he said. And Smalls was slumped in the backseat on the joy ride to Orlando. [He] "possibly didn't fully know what happened," Pfister argued. Or Yon, for that matter, he added.

Once they returned to Eustis, it was Yon who went into the back bedroom where the gun was later discovered. Smalls slept in the living room.

As for who shot Dorothy, he said: "How much can [she] really know? Dorothy Lewis suffered grievous, grievous wounds."

He also mentioned Yon getting into his aunt's car at Winn-Dixie and warning her not to give Henyard a ride. "Ric has a gun," he said.

Smalls' sister, Colinda, also testified that she saw Henyard with the gun at her house—not her brother. And Smalls' sister, Tammy, saw blood on Henyard after the shooting.

A box of bullets and the holster were found in the jacket Henyard had been wearing, he added.

Assistant State Attorney Bill Gross, as he had done in Henyard's case, set the stage for the jurors, taking them back to that foggy night on desolate Hicks Ditch Road.

After telling how the case initially unfolded, the prosecutor made a point of trying to paint a more realistic picture regarding Pfister's remarks about Smalls being younger and a follower.

Smalls, who was 14½ years old, was 5-foot-11 and weighed 175 pounds when he was arrested. Henyard, who was 18½ was 6-foot-2 and weighed 160 pounds, Gross said.

Blood found on Smalls' clothing came from the bullet wounds of Dorothy and Jamilya, Gross said.

It was Smalls who approached Dorothy's car in the parking lot, Gross said. It was Smalls who showed the gun, and it was Smalls who said to Henyard, "Come on, man, this is the one."

It was Smalls who used profanity in the car and told the crying girls to "shut up."

And it was Smalls who put a condom on when it was his turn to assault Dorothy, Gross said.

Gross explained the concept of felony murder to the jurors, saying it made no difference who pulled the trigger.

"There will be no doubt in your mind that this young man over here engaged willingly and voluntarily in a kidnapping, that either he or his accomplice caused two small children to die and almost caused the death of their mother," he said.

Many of the same witnesses, of course, testified in Smalls' trial. There was the usual parade of law enforcement officers, doctors and FDLE crime lab technicians. Anyone expecting to hear Smalls' confession tape would be disappointed, however. Prosecutors decided not to play any of it. However, it was not so surprising in retrospect, since Smalls spent so much time heaping the blame on Henyard during his statements to police.

One of the witnesses was Dr. Julia Martin, the forensic pathologist who collected rape evidence at the hospital. Dorothy told her she had been attacked by one man, she testified. Robert Tippett, a special agent with the FDLE, interviewed Dorothy twice. He testified that she told him that two men had assaulted her.

Another expert witness who testified was Leroy Parker, the blood spatter expert.

Dorothy's testimony was again key. Of Smalls, she said: "He pulled up his shirt and showed me the gun and said to get in the car and don't say a word."

She said that it was after she was assaulted and was about to be shot when she told her attackers: "You said if I did what you told me to do, that we wouldn't get hurt."

Gross, who stays up nights trying to think of things he might forget to present to a jury, frequently turns to the prosecutor's desk in the courtroom before sitting down and whispers to whoever is sitting there, "Can you think of anything else?" This is especially true when it comes to trying to turn away every point that might be scored by the defense.

To make sure he refuted Pfister's claim that Smalls was a follower, Gross asked Dorothy: "During the entire episode, beginning at the time that you first saw these gentlemen resting on that bench [at the grocery store] until you lost consciousness, did the younger of the two at any time appear to be scared or nervous or afraid or intimidated?"

"No he did not," she replied.

When asked if she could identify her abductor she pointed to Smalls sitting at the defense table.

"Any doubt?" the prosecutor asked.

"There's no doubt," she said.

"Don't Take Me"

Brad King's closing was piercing.

"Richard Henyard got in to drive, they drove out of the parking lot, and as they drove out she gave them a choice. 'Don't take me, just take the car and go.' Alfonza Smalls says, 'We can't do that, we can't do that.' Two young men who didn't bother to conceal their looks, didn't bother to hide who they were, had her in the car and they started out and they refused to let her go and just take the car."

The crime, which began shortly after 10 was over around 11 p.m., and Henyard went to Smalls' house to see Yon.

"They were changing Alfonza's clothes for him so they could go out and party while Dorothy Lewis is laying unconscious on the side of the road," King said.

Fantl, in his closing, attacked what he said was a lack of evidence, while also acknowledging that "we're probably talking about the most horrible crime in Lake County history."

He went on to say, in part: "There are two dead children. There is a woman who is disfigured and internally maimed for life."

He stipulated that Smalls was with Henyard but maintained that it was Henyard who raped and shot Dorothy.

Dorothy was unconscious when the children were slain.

"What the state has failed to prove is that Alfonza intended to commit any of these crimes or that he did, in fact, commit these crimes," Fantl argued.

"I don't think that she's certain about anything from that night and that's very understandable, that somebody in her condition wouldn't be certain of a lot of things. But the state has to prove its case against Alfonza Smalls. You can't use your sympathy for Dorothy and say we feel bad for her, she's in a horrible situation and somebody has got to pay and that man is sitting there so let's just do it. That's not the way it works, the state has to prove its case."

He insisted that Henyard had the gun that night and that Alfonza did not enter the bedroom where Yon was sleeping where the gun was later found.

He also said, "I'm not saying that Alfonza didn't pick up the child after she was shot. Contact blood proves it. But he wasn't anywhere near where the gun was shot. He was there, picked up one child. Now, that may be an accessory after the fact, it may not be, depending upon the circumstances, but he's not charged with being an accessory after the fact."

Blood spatter evidence showed he was not within three or four feet of the gunshot wounds when they occurred, Fantl said.

Fantl also jumped on the fact that no semen was found on the discarded condom.

"Because it didn't happen, that's why."

He attacked the credibility of the lineup where Dorothy identified Smalls and what he called "wrong evidence" on clothing.

He attacked the testimony of Lynnette Tschida, who jumped in her car, locked the doors and drove off just before Dorothy and the girls came out of the grocery store. It was dark, Fantl said, trying to plant the seeds of reasonable doubt as to who she identified as a bad guy that night.

Tschida, the would-be victim that night, confused even the lawyers a bit when she gave her description of the two in the parking lot that night.

Pfister asked her in her deposition if there were any distinguishing characteristics between the two.

"The man in front of me, hair was funny. I mean, it sounds stupid, but remember the Gumby doll, where the head pointed up on one side? The person in front of me, his hair did that and that's what I remember about it."

Pfister would point out in photos that it was Henyard, not Smalls, who had the "Gumby" hairdo.

Despite the confusion over who stood where, Tschida was able to pick out both men in a photo lineup and Yon.

Fantl tried to paint the investigation by FDLE Agent David West and others as a rush to judgment.

"…police wanted suspects, they wanted people arrested and charged with it. He was motivated."

He described Dorothy as "semi-conscious" when she made it to the lighted carport and banged on the door looking for help.

She didn't remember her trip to Orlando Regional Medical Center, he said. Nor did she remember talking to the forensic pathologist who collected rape evidence at the hospital, he said.

He also pointed out what he said were contradictions in her descriptions of the suspects' clothing.

He also tried to plant seeds of doubt about who shot her when the first bullet struck her in the leg.

When you are flailing about, he said, "You don't know who you're struggling with on the ground."

Then, he told the jury that Smalls had to have the intent to kidnap that night, for that charge to stick.

King began his final presentation first by attacking the notion that Smalls had no intent to kidnap anyone that night.

"Folks, this is not a situation when, as Mr. Fantl tried to put it, that poor Alfonza Smalls was standing in the Winn-Dixie parking lot one minute and was on the ride of his life, being terrorized as these crimes were being committed, along with Mrs. Lewis, the next. That's simply not what happened. You can go back and look at the evidence and determine the facts."

Starting with the clothing, King said Smalls' own family identified the clothing he was wearing that night, the same clothing he told West he later ditched in front of the car.

Not only that, but the clothing had blood on it from both Dorothy and Jamilya, and body fluids from Henyard.

King then explained the law regarding principals in a crime.

If the jury finds that both men did the kidnapping together, "from that moment onward it doesn't matter who did what. They stand right there together before the judgment of the law...."

The same holds true for whoever did the shooting, he said. "...we don't care and neither does the law of the state of Florida care who pulled the trigger. It doesn't matter. It's as simple as that. Once they started acting together they became responsible for what they did."

He asked jurors to remember Dorothy's testimony, and reminded them that she swore an oath to tell the truth.

"...you get to evaluate her as a person and her credibility and her demeanor. I want you to stop and think and recall not just what she said, but her honesty and forthrightness with which she said it. When she didn't remember something, she flat said I don't remember that. When she remembered something she told you when she remembered."

He also asked them to remember her reaction when she identified Smalls as one of her attackers.

"...she sat here and she looked straight out and she steeled herself for what she was going to have to do. She closed her eyes and she looked and she said, 'That's him right there, that's the man.'"

"Think of the Pain"

It was a solemn jury foreman who handed a slip of paper to the bailiff with the jury's findings.

Tension in the courtroom was palpable. Dorothy and Brock held hands. The family, and Smalls' family, sitting across the aisle just a few feet away, held their collective breaths.

After looking at the slip of paper, Hill passed it over to the clerk who read the results: guilty on all counts, two of first-degree murder, three counts of armed kidnapping, one count of armed sexual battery, armed robbery and attempted murder.

Smalls was fingerprinted in the courtroom and led away. The judge ordered a pre-sentence investigation.

At a sentencing hearing, Margaret, speaking for the family, was given the opportunity to read the victim impact statement.

"I am Margaret Reid-Lewis," she said. "Dorothy Lewis is my sister. Jamilya and Jasmine were/are my nieces. The jury rendered guilty verdicts for all eight charges against Smalls. I am standing before you for Dorothy, Jamilya, Jasmine and my entire family urging you to uphold the jury's verdict and let justice prevail.

"For me, justice would prevail only if Smalls died for his horrendous acts. But the Florida Supreme Court took that decision out of your hands." She then speculated about various sentences that might be imposed, and said that "justice would be served if Smalls spends the rest of his life in jail."

She continued: "I am hoping that you will not let this animal's age sway your decision. I am hoping that you will show him the same mercy he showed Dorothy, Jamilya and Jasmine. He does not deserve mercy. Smalls initiated and carried out a chain of events that proved to be a living nightmare for Dorothy and the end of life for Jamilya and Jasmine.

"My life will never be the same. My little girl, Aljahra, was born one month before Jasmine. Aljahra has dreams about bad men hurting her the way Jamilya and Jasmine were hurt. When she prays, she prays for her cousins in heaven and prays that she doesn't go to heaven yet. I hurt every time I look at my daughter because there are times she looks so much like Jamilya. At least once a week she asks me when will she see Jasmine and Jamilya. It is not right that I should have to explain death to my baby. It's not right that Dorothy and I can't talk about what our girls did today. My daughter has asked me why did the bad men hurt Jasmine and Jamilya? Your honor, I have no answer. That's what my entire family would like to know. Why? How could Henyard and Smalls kill our babies and leave their mother for dead? What kind of monsters could commit such horrible acts?

"After Dorothy's husband died, I called her every day and I would always end the conversation with, 'Kiss the babies for me.' I can no longer say that. I will never hear them say, 'It's Aunt,' and see them run to my car. I can't begin to describe the pain I suffer every day. A senseless pain that none of us should be enduring. We love Jamilya and Jasmine. We miss them so much.

"Sir, when you pass sentencing I want you to think of the horror the family felt and endured as we received the news of this horrible night. Think of the horror and fear Jamilya and Jasmine felt when their mother did not come back to the car and the fear they felt as Henyard and Smalls took them out of the car and aimed that gun at their little heads.

"Think of the hours Dorothy spent walking around ducking in the bushes at the sight of car lights.

"Think of the pain Dorothy felt when she asked me about the girls and I had to tell her that the girls did not make it. Think of the pain Dorothy suffered as she buried her babies. I made the funeral arrangements. I had to go to the babies' closet and pick out the clothes they would be buried in. I gave them dresses alike for Christmas. Never in my wildest dreams did I imagine that I would never see them in those dresses again.

"Think of the pain Dorothy endures every day as she walks in her house and goes to her babies' room and they are not there.

"Think of the pain she endured from four gunshot wounds. She has four metal plates in her forehead, along with 24 screws. She can't see out of her right eye. She can't smell or taste anything.

"Let your sentence reflect the fact that when she closes her eyes she can still see Henyard and Smalls' faces.

"It would be a cruel and unjust act for my family and any community at large if Smalls ever spends one day outside of jail. Please, your honor, throw the key away. Say that Smalls will spend the rest of his life in jail. This, your honor, would be justice."

Gross, too, argued for the stiffest sentence possible. The range is 27 years to life, the prosecutor said of the sentencing guidelines. "The state recommends a departure—eight consecutive life sentences."

The state had offered a deal before the trial of two life sentences, Pfister would later reveal. "He listened to an uncle. We went to trial."

Gross also read a portion of Dorothy's victim impact statement, quoting her comment, "residual effects of my life and my family's life has been forever changed by this barbarism."

Pfister cited Smalls' low IQ and the fact that he was in the seventh grade as mitigating factors.

One month later, everyone again met in the courtroom, this time for sentencing, and Hill didn't pull any punches.

He began by citing the Florida Supreme Court's recent decision not to impose the death penalty on any defendant younger than 16.

"The Supreme Court of Florida, unfortunately, has spared Smalls from facing the same fate as Henyard, in spite of their being equally guilty of the same acts," Hill said.

"Smalls has asked this court for even more of a leniency at this sentencing hearing, with which this court will not abide."

Hill, continuing with the theme of Smalls being equally guilty, cited a Florida Supreme Court ruling on the legal definition of heinous, atrocious and cruel.

"Extreme cruelty is by no means confined to physical violence," he said quoting from the decision.

It could include "continuous and intense mental pain and suffering," Hill noted. "Certainly the definition of cruelty is applicable to Mrs. Lewis' situation. This case is impregnated from one end to the other with the most foul and obscene set of circumstances I can imagine and each set of circumstances are additional reasons for the sentences which shall be imposed in this case."

He imposed six consecutive life sentences all together, three for the kidnapping, then one each for sexual battery, attempted murder and armed robbery. He then imposed consecutive life sentences, with minimum-mandatory sentences of 25 years for each of the murder charges, and ordered that they be served consecutively to the other life sentences.

Margaret got her wish. The judge ordered the key to be thrown away.

Days in Court—Again

Even when someone is convicted, the wheels of justice can turn very slowly because of an avalanche of appeals. This is especially true in a death penalty case.

First, there is an automatic appeal. Then, there is a Florida Supreme Court review and ruling, plus there can be pleas for stays, writs and other appeals before the federal district and the U.S.

Supreme Court. There are also state motions for post-conviction relief, asking the courts to reduce a sentence or order a new trial.

Henyard raised 11 claims in his appeal to the Florida Supreme Court. Among the claims was that law enforcement officers violated his right against self-incrimination. He had implied he wanted a lawyer when he asked for his aunt and asked how long he would be at the police station, his appeal lawyers said.

Here is the record of Henyard's conversation with the FBI:

FBI AGENT: "I can't—I can't talk you into this, OK? This is your own decision. You're saying what you're telling us is the truth."

FBI AGENT: "You just stay here a minute—you know, we can't force you stay here (inaudible)."

A: "Take me to my auntie's house."

FBI AGENT: "We're going to have your aunt come down here."

A: "I can tell you something. I ain't going to say that I don't care them two children got killed, but I ain't did it, so why worry about it? I ain't killed them children so I ain't got nothing to worry about."

FBI AGENT: "OK."

A: "Something told me not to come down here."

The Florida high court, citing case law, said unlike some cases, the confession in Henyard's case was not the essential part of the state's case, so it really didn't matter. Prosecutors had witnesses who testified about events leading up to the shooting, there was also Dorothy's sworn statements, DNA evidence, blood spatter evidence, the gun, a motive, intent and witnesses who said he implicated himself after the crime.

"Moreover, Henyard consistently denied any role in killing the Lewis girls, and, at trial, Henyard's trial strategy was, in essence, to concede his participation in the crimes except as to the killing of the children. Hence, his statements were consistent with this strategy."

Besides, prosecutors didn't even play the second or third statement he made that day, the justices noted.

The court didn't buy his statements about wanting to see his "auntie" as assertions that he wanted police to stop questioning him and to get him a lawyer.

Justices also rejected Henyard's claim of jurors being prejudiced by pretrial publicity, and his claim that the state was allowed to challenge a juror who said he could follow the law on death penalty recommendations, despite concerns that Henyard was only 18 years old. The juror said he could NOT follow the law, the justices noted.

The court also rejected his assertion that FDLE lab tests should not be allowed because the lab did not meet national DNA lab standards.

He also said the jury pool was prejudiced by the prosecutor when he said that jurors must recommend the death penalty if the aggravators outweigh the mitigators. "...a jury is neither compelled nor required to recommend death where aggravating factors outweigh mitigating factors," the court noted.

But the error was repeated only three times during the lengthy jury selection process, justices said, and the law was quoted correctly during the trial.

"...we do not find that he was prejudiced by this error," the court ruled.

He also quibbled over the prosecutor's closing statement, in which he implied that he never owned up to raping Dorothy. That confession was made, but it was in the third and final confession which was not played for the jury.

"When the prosecutor's closing argument is read in its entirety and fairly considered, it is clear that the prosecutor was referring to Henyard's lack of candor and failure to be completely forthcoming about his involvement in the offense when he initially confessed," the court ruled.

Henyard also contended that the hearsay rule was violated when the judge allowed a police officer to testify about how, when he first came up on Dorothy, she gave him a description of her two attackers, a description that matched Henyard and Smalls.

"...we find that Ms. Lewis was still experiencing the trauma of the events she had just survived when she spoke to the officer and her statements were properly admitted under the excited utterance exception to the hearsay rule," the court said.

Even if allowing the statements had been improper, "we find the error harmless," the justices noted.

He also claimed that his juvenile felony record should not have been allowed to become an aggravator in his sentence. The court also rejected that argument.

"... the testimony concerning Henyard's juvenile adjudication was modest [describing him as a lookout] and served to minimize his role in the prior offense," the court said.

Court records actually show a long list of referrals by the Department of Health and Rehabilitative Services, Children, Youth and Families.

He faced a shoplifting charge in Lake County on January 1989 but the charge was dropped. Later that year, he faced charges of armed robbery, burglary, larceny and burglary again. He was adjudicated as a delinquent in those cases. He faced another burglary charge in 1990, and also faced sanctions for that crime. Over the next two years, in Palm Bay County, where he stayed with his father, he was charged with shoplifting, burglary, petty theft, contempt of court and escape. The contempt and shoplifting charges were dropped.

The juvenile record turned out to be a moot point because under Florida law, the court can count "contemporaneous convictions." There were six of those for Henyard in this case: armed robbery, armed sexual battery and three counts of armed kidnapping. But the juvenile record did seem to lend credence to the letter writer's point about teen criminals' frequent disregard for the law or for anyone else, not that Hill could have taken her point into consideration, even if he wanted to.

Henyard also objected to the blood stain evidence being used "because it was not relevant to prove the existence of any aggravating circumstance."

The court, however, noted that, "Henyard offered evidence that he was not the triggerman in these murders and argued that lingering doubt as to whether he actually shot the Lewis girls should be considered in mitigation. Consequently, the testimony of the state's witness concerning blood-spatter evidence was proper to rebut Henyard's continued assertion that he did not actually kill the Lewis girls. Moreover, testimony concerning the close proximity of the defendant to the victim was relevant to show the 'nature of the crime.'"

He argued that his death sentence was disproportionate since Smalls was ineligible because he was younger than 16.

The court rejected that claim, too, citing their own decision earlier not to execute juveniles.

"Under the law, death was never a valid punishment option for Smalls, and Henyard's death sentences are not disproportionate ...." the opinion stated.

He argued against the application of the pecuniary gain aggravator, but the justices quoted Henyard as saying "he was going to get himself a car" a week before the shootings.

He also insisted that the girls were each killed with a single bullet, and said the court would not have applied the heinous atrocious and cruel aggravator if the girls had been adults.

The justices rejected that argument, too, quoting case law that says, "fear and emotional strain may be considered as contributing to the heinous nature of the murder, even where the victim's death was almost instantaneous."

The court said the heinous, atrocious and cruel standards were met, based upon "the entire sequence of events, including the fear and emotional trauma the children suffered...."

And, the court added, "contrary to Henyard's assertion, not merely because they were young children."

Henyard was especially adamant, it seems, in his argument that Dorothy should not have been allowed to testify during the penalty phase about him saying, "You might as well stop calling Jesus, this ain't Jesus, this is Satan."

The justices said the heinous, atrocious and cruel standard can be proven "in part by evidence of the infliction of 'mental anguish' which the victim suffered prior to the fatal shot.

"In this case, Ms. Lewis testified that she was sitting in the back-seat between her daughters, that the girls were quiet at the time Henyard made the statement at issue, and that Henyard spoke loudly enough for all to hear."

Every single argument was rejected.

"Accordingly, we affirm Henyard's convictions and the imposition of the sentences of death in this case."

"It is so ordered."

The date was December 19, 1996, almost four years after the slayings.

Five years after his conviction, in October 1999, Henyard was again back in a Lake County courtroom for a post-conviction re-lief hearing, claiming his attorneys didn't do a thorough job at his trial.

First, however, the appellate lawyers filed a motion seeking to have Hill disqualify himself as the judge.

Because the motion for relief included an ineffective counsel claim, and Johnson was by this time a circuit judge in the same cir-cuit, "Judge Hill's personal and professional relationship with Judge Johnson presents a conflict because Judge Johnson may be a wit-ness…." the motion stated.

The lawyers went so far as to ask that no other judge in the five-county circuit should preside over the proceedings either.

The motion continued, saying that "clearly" Hill would have to step down.

"Mr. Henyard reasonably fears that he will be denied the cold neutrality of an impartial judge."

Hill, after reviewing the request, denied the motion, saying it was legally insufficient.

The appeal lawyers claimed that Henyard's defense team failed to find crucial witnesses, didn't look into whether he had brain damage from his mother's drug and alcohol abuse, and did not tell jurors that he had been sexually abused as a child.

Gross argued that Henyard had filled out a form before the trial saying that he had not been sexually abused. Anyway, saying it doesn't make it so, he noted, though he could have also added, "especially with this man's record of lying."

Henyard was now claiming that he had been raped. Another time he said it was fondling. One time he was supposedly 16, another time he said he was 7, Gross pointed out.

"There's a big difference between allegations and proof," Gross said.

Nacke said he was not aware of the childhood sexual abuse claim. If he had been aware of it, he might have used it as a mitigator, he said.

Henyard made other ineffective counsel claims, including what he viewed as a failure on their part to question them about why the jury changed its recommendation of death, from the original 10-2 to 12-0.

Johnson testified that the case had been "a grim case to defend."

He added: "We didn't give up on the guilt phase, but we agreed we needed to spend the bulk of our efforts on the penalty phase."

There was also testimony during the post-conviction hearing about Henyard's mother's reckless behavior as a drug addict and prostitute. Hattie Gamble had died of AIDS after Henyard's trial.

Jackie Turner testified that her friend looked like "walking death."

Neighbor Rosalee Adams testified that Henyard was raised "door-to-door."

Hill rejected all of Henyard's arguments but did grant his state-appointed appeal lawyers' permission to see if they could find evidence of fetal alcohol syndrome. That would prove to be a lost cause, however.

Johnson perhaps summed it up best.

"There were two dead children in this case," Johnson said. "What else can I say?"

"Killa" Appeal

In October of 2007, Henyard claimed to have new evidence. A prisoner sharing lock-up space with Smalls in 1993, Jason Nawara, said Smalls was calling himself a "killa." It proves Smalls was the one who shot the girls, Henyard said.

Nawara, who was 14, was awaiting trial on charges that he had raped and murdered his 10-year-old stepsister.

The justices, in a September 10, 2008 ruling, were not impressed.

"Even if Nawara's hearsay statement was somehow deemed admissible at trial, we conclude Nawara's statement does not cast doubt on his culpability or death sentence for the murders."

Henyard's appeal, along with claiming the state's death penalty is unconstitutional, did not fly, according to the state's highest court on September 10, 2008.

Even if Henyard could prove Smalls' statements to Nawara, "it would not alter the end result," justices said.

Henyard planned the carjacking, raped and shot Dorothy and "was in the immediate proximity when Jasmine and Jamilya were shot," the justices said.

"...the overwhelming evidence of Henyard's dominant role makes his current assertion that he was a 'relatively minor participant' both unbelievable and without credibility."

The appeals process, which takes on a life of its own, included state-appeal lawyers demanding every disc, recording and each scrap of paper generated by the case, which in turn produced more and more pounds of paper in the file. On July 9, 2008, Gov. Charlie Crist signed the death warrant.

Finally, the day of reckoning had come. The time of execution was set for 6 p.m., on Tuesday, September 23, 2008.

Florida had effectively retired its electric chair, "Old Sparky," after a condemned man's head was set on fire in 1997. The state could execute a prisoner in the chair only if the condemned man or woman chose that method. Now it was death by lethal injection, which had generated its own controversy.

Opponents of the death penalty and many news reports referred to the lethal injection execution of Angel Diaz in 2006 as a "botched execution" because it took longer than it should have for the toxic cocktail to kill him. It raised questions about whether the sentence violated the constitutional ban on cruel and unusual punishment. The flap led to new training and other procedures, but Henyard raised the issue anyway.

That wasn't the only controversy. In June of 2000 condemned prisoner Bennie Demps used his opportunity to utter some of his last words by turning to his attorney and saying, "they butchered me back there. This is a low-tech lynching by poison."

Demps was convicted in what became known locally as the 1971 "Trunk Murders" case. A Lake County jury found that he and another man forced a married couple and a real estate agent into the trunk of a car and riddled the car with bullets from a .22 and an AK-47 assault rifle. The trio had stumbled upon Demps and his accomplice trying to open a stolen safe that had been taken to an orange grove, ironically, not far from Hicks Ditch Road. Unfortunately for Demps and his companion, one of the three intended victims survived to tell the story.

It was one of the most notorious crimes in the history of the county, which was even more sleepy and rural in 1971 than it was in 1993. Then-State Attorney Gordon Oldham displayed the AK-47 in his office for a long time afterward as a kind of trophy.

Demps and his partner, along with Charles Manson in California and a host of other killers, had their death sentences overturned the next year when the U.S. Supreme Court ordered all states to redo their death penalty laws. But the ex-Marine, Vietnam veteran would later be convicted of killing another prisoner in 1976.

So, when Demps claimed he was innocent of the 1976 crime that eventually led him to the execution chamber, and that he had been "butchered" by the execution team trying to find a viable vein for the lethal injection intravenous line, prison officials were at once skeptical, defensive and dismissive.

Then came Diaz six years later, and more appeals, changes in procedures and additional controversy.

On April 21, 2008, Walter A. McNeil, secretary of the Florida Department of Corrections, wrote to Gov. Crist assuring him that there would be no problems for the upcoming executions of Henyard and another man.

"The procedure has been reviewed and is compatible with evolving standards of decency that mark the progress of a maturing society, the concepts of the dignity of man, and advances in science, research, pharmacology, and technology. The process is not going to involve unnecessary lingering or the unnecessary or wanton infliction of pain and suffering. The foremost objective of the lethal injection process is a humane and dignified death. Additional guiding principles of the lethal injection process are that it should not be of long duration, and that while the entire process of execution should be transparent, the concerns and emotions of all those involved must be addressed."

When one reads these words it's hard almost to grasp the big picture. On the one hand, one almost has to remind himself that he is talking about killing a man, right?

There is, apparently, just something kind of surreal about the idea of ceremonially taking someone's life. After all, life is so precious, yet we take it for granted. One is reminded of the time that famed *1984* novelist George Orwell witnessed a hanging and watched as the condemned man walked around a mud puddle on his way to the gallows. Here was a man doing a very normal thing, but what difference would a few minutes of comfort have made in his life, Orwell wondered?

The second major realization, of course, is that Jasmine, Jamilya and Dorothy certainly were not treated with dignity or compassion. Nor were they free from "unnecessary lingering," or "unnecessary or wanton infliction of pain and suffering."

The idea, of course, is the state is on a higher moral plane than thoughtless, vicious killers like Henyard.

Execution procedures, for example, state that, "The inmate will be offered and, if accepted, will be administered an intramuscular injection of diazepam, in an appropriate dosage relative to weight, to ease anxiety."

Another procedure calls for the prisoner to be unconscious about halfway through the procedure before continuing the release of more toxic chemicals. The net effect is that the witnesses are viewing what looks like a person falling asleep.

Of course, no one wants to see a man's head set on fire in a 76-year-old oak chair.

Then, there is the "transparent" process of execution that McNeil mentioned in his letter.

In the early days of the lethal injection controversy, state officials insisted on secrecy concerning what chemicals were used in the toxic cocktail. That veil has been lifted. As it is, the names of the executioner and the back-up executioner are still kept secret, both for traditional and security reasons. The executioner is paid a $150 fee.

The chemicals used are Sodium Pentothal, pancuronium bromide, potassium chloride and saline solution. Sodium Pentothal, a barbiturate, has been celebrated as the so-called "truth serum," because in small doses it relaxes people and makes them talkative.

It would be interesting if the execution team could use the drug in low doses to test the prisoner's claims of innocence. Demps, who refused to talk about the Trunk Murders, maintained right up to the end that he was not guilty of killing a fellow prisoner.

Despite the assurances that McNeil mentioned in his letter, the execution process is still not totally transparent. There are steps in the process, for example, where the team must close the curtains if the procedure is not working properly, then open them again when the problem is fixed.

Controversy will no doubt continue. Polls show public support for executions, while the courts and legislatures continue to get more and more squeamish. The one exception may be when it comes to terrorists, including Oklahoma City bomber Timothy McVeigh.

On the day of the execution, the condemned prisoner can pick out his own last meal as long as it costs $40 or less, the food is available at the prison and the food director approves.

Prison officials told reporters that Henyard had eaten most of his last meal: two fried chicken breasts, turkey sausage, fried rice, chocolate chip cookies and a Coke, though it is hard to imagine.

The prisoner also gets to take a shower. Normally, death row inmates can shower on the unair-conditioned row only every other day.

Once the governor signs a death warrant, the prisoner is moved from his 6-by-9-foot cell, with 9.5-foot ceiling, to a death watch cell, which is 12-by-7, with an 8.5-foot-high ceiling.

Henyard was supposed to get a visit on his last day from godmother Jackie Turner but she didn't show. Prison officials said he had only one visitor in 15 years on death row, and that was Turner. Officials concede he may have had other visitors in the days before computer records were used to keep track of visitors, but as far as they know she was the only visitor. She visited for the first time on the Friday before the execution, according to prison officials.

His only visitor on the day of execution was his Muslim spiritual advisor.

After an execution, the prisoner's body is taken by hearse to the Medical Examiner's Office in Gainesville for an autopsy. It has become a ritual among news photographers to take a picture of the hearse leaving the prison, although the picture shows virtually nothing. No doubt, it is because there is virtually nothing else to photograph. They are not allowed in the death chamber or in the witness section.

Henyard would return to Turner one last time—after his autopsy and cremation.

Outside the prison fences, on a large grassy plain, protestors and supporters of the death penalty routinely show up with their handmade signs. Over the years, demonstrations have become more subdued—certainly quieter than the raucous mob that shouted and cheered when serial killer Ted Bundy was executed in 1989.

Florida's Catholic bishops wrote a letter to Crist saying although the "untimely deaths of the two young victims and serious injury to their mother cry out for justice, we are reminded that executions diminish us as a civil society and perpetuate a culture of death," (Dec. 11, 2008, www.American *catholic.org/news/news2print/news report.aspx?id=489).*

On the night of Henyard's execution, almost all of Dorothy's family came to her house. Arthur Gene and Brock were absent because they were witnessing the execution.

Like the Catholic bishops, Brock had grown up opposing and had been trained in seminary to oppose the death penalty. But Henyard's "cold heart," as he put it, forced him to go back to the scriptures and to do some soul-searching.

"When we break God's law 'thou shalt not kill' we then subject ourselves to civil law," Brock said. The civil law was very specific in Henyard's case, he said. "For murder the jury's recommendation was for execution and therefore it is approved by God when His law is violated. This individual will also be held accountable by God," he said.

Even Jesus was subject to civil law, though He had the power to be able to defy it if He had chosen to do so, and He was without sin, Brock said.

He disagrees with the Catholic bishops' argument that "executions diminish us as a civil society and perpetuate a culture of death."

"Executions hold people accountable and would reduce the number of murders," Brock said.

Dorothy has had a different view regarding Henyard's execution.

"I was sad. I had mixed emotions," Dorothy said. "Taking his life was not going to bring my girls back," she added.

"I didn't go because it was not going to bring me any satisfaction seeing someone die," she said.

There was another reason, too.

"I didn't want to see anything like that. I don't want to see anyone die."

She issued two press statements, which were released by prison officials. Both were essentially the same. One of them read: "The question that I would like Mr. Henyard to answer is, 'Why did you kill my babies? You shot them down like they were wild animals. Why?'

"I want to thank God for His love, His grace, and for His miraculous power that is being displayed in my life. I also want to thank all of you who have had me in your prayers.

"I am sure that many of you are wondering if this day will bring some closure in my life. Well, let's define closure. Closure is defined as 'a feeling of finality or resolution, especially after a traumatic experience.'

"When my daughters, Jamilya and Jasmine, were murdered about 15 years ago, that was definitely a traumatic experience for my family and me. Today, Mr. Henyard's life was taken; and I do not have a feeling of resolution. Therefore, this day has not brought any closure in my life. Taking the life of Mr. Henyard is not going to revive my daughters. I do not consider this event as a joyous occasion, and I am sorry that this execution had to take place; but Romans 6:23 clearly states, 'The wages of sin is death, but the gift of God is eternal life through Jesus Christ our Lord.'

"I pray that Mr. Henyard has sense enough to ask God to forgive him of his sins."

It was quiet, mostly, at Dorothy' house that night. There was a lot of individual praying.

"We were praying for strength," Dorothy said.

"Henyard had some loved ones, and they were losing him. His family needed strength to go through that. My family needed strength because a life was being taken," she said.

"I was in my bedroom most of the time, trying to rest. My family was in the living room. They would come back and see if I was OK."

The TV was on, the channel set on an Orlando station in case there was a news update about the execution.

There were 25 people on the execution witness list and five alternates. Some were officials. Ten were reporters. No one from Henyard's family was present. Besides Brock and Arthur Gene, Greta Snitkin was on the list, and so was Dr. Owen Fraser and law enforcement officers Robert O'Connor, Bud Hart and Anthony Robinson.

Robinson met one witness who was the daughter of one of the jurors. Her father had passed away, but because she had heard so much about the case, she wanted to witness the execution, Robinson said.

James Reid had intended to go.

"I wanted to see that," he said. "I would've pulled the switch myself. I think they waited too long to do it."

Ozietta said she had "mixed emotions."

"It didn't erase what happened. We're still without Jasmine and Jamilya and Dorothy still has reminders of what happened to her," she said.

"In the beginning I wanted both of them dead. I wanted them to die a slow death."

Over time, her opinion softened.

Snitkin had not seen Dorothy's statement on closure, or the lack of closure, on this day. She has her own thoughts on the matter, however.

"Closure is when the neighbor kid steals your lawn mower and gets caught and has to write a letter of apology. Nobody is hurt. That's closure. When there's a homicide there's never closure," Snitkin said.

"Jasmine and Jamilya are still alive in her [Dorothy's] heart and in the memory of everyone—and should be," Snitkin said.

Yet, on this night, Snitkin was at Florida State Prison near Starke, if not exploring the issue of "closure," then at least she was standing in for her friend, Dorothy, as the state prepared to extract its retribution.

Large prisons are like cities, not exactly the gated communities of the rich, but very secure in their own way. Lawn areas are neatly clipped with old-fashioned, non-powered push lawn mowers. Barbed hedges around administrative buildings are squared off perfectly. They couldn't be more precisely trimmed than the animal-shaped shrubs at Disney World.

The surrounding area outside the prison fences is beautiful in its own way. The area in North Central Florida is flat, green and marked by long stretches of farmland and piney woods. Besides Starke, with its turn-of-the-20th-Century courthouse, there is Raiford, which is little more than an open crossroads. Besides Florida State Prison, there is also Union Correctional, which also houses death row prisoners. Nearby is the prison department's Lake Butler processing center, a camp and barbed wire bus terminal to human warehouses across the state. Virtually everyone in the county, it seems, has either a direct or family tie to the prison system, either through employment or some other economic benefit.

On any given day, prisoners are usually busy running errands or going from place to place on prison grounds. There is constant movement, a restless spirit that can be seen in the exercise yard, in prisoners pulling weeds and in performing thousands of other chores.

But in the hours leading up to an execution, it is strangely quiet. Prisoners at the facility are locked down. There is no hustle and bustle inside the gleaming rolls of razor wire. The only sound is that of some loud banter drifting over from the windows of nearby cell blocks, which would not be heard if the cells were air-conditioned and the windows closed.

Witnesses sit in a small, white room minutes before the execution. They are required to remain silent. The only sound is the hum of an air conditioner. They stare at a large window, but there is nothing to see because a large heavy drape on the other side of the window blocks their view of the preparations on the other side.

Finally, when it is time, someone from the execution team pulls the curtain back for the deadliest show on earth.

A speaker switch is flipped on and the execution team makes a call to the governor's office to make sure there are no last-minute stays. There is also a fully-charged cell phone in the chamber in case the phone service is interrupted for some reason. If there are no last-minute stays, the condemned man or woman is given the opportunity to make a statement. The warden then announces that the execution is underway. When it's over, he tells the governor on the open phone line that the execution has been carried out.

It was scheduled to go off at 6 p.m., the normal time for executions in Florida, but Arthur Gene called to say there was a two-hour delay. The delay was caused by a last-minute plea to the U.S. Supreme Court.

When Arthur Gene called again he simply said, "It's over."

Brock would tell her later that when asked if he had anything to say, Henyard simply shook his head no.

"I really didn't know what to expect," Dorothy said. "It would've been nice if he had said he was sorry."

Brock described it as "disappointing and disheartening."

"Not one time did he utter the words, 'I'm sorry' or ask for forgiveness. I was advised by the staff that they very seldom hear the inmates say these words.

"I wanted to be able to say maybe he did change and turn to God. If you're under [God's] conviction you will see a change and you won't go out with your eyes closed. It was just like he couldn't face anyone," he said.

Ozietta described it as a "bittersweet" moment.

"My hope was that this boy made peace with God, realized what he had done and asked for forgiveness. I was not happy that a life was taken. I hope he got it right," she said.

Asked if she thought Henyard did "make it right" with the Lord, she replied: "I really don't know."

Christians, in general, find it disheartening when people turn to the Muslim faith for their salvation. Christians take the Bible, and specifically John 14:6, seriously when Jesus says: "I am the way and the truth and the life. No one comes to the Father except through me."

Was there relief for Dorothy when the execution was over?

"It's not a big help at all. There is no closure. You accept things and go on," she said.

To this day, she remains consistent in her feelings about the death penalty.

"I didn't want that guy to get out of jail. I know some people say that if we had more of it [executions] it would reduce those kinds of crimes." She made her desires known, then left it up to the justice system.

"The law is going to do what the law does. I wasn't going to make that decision."

Unfortunately, because of all the appeals, the process can drag on for years, with each step becoming a painful reminder for victims' families.

"I do believe that when someone has been found guilty for murder without a shadow of doubt the system should be reformed for swift justice instead of victims and their families having to waiting for 14 years for the death sentence to be carried out," Brock said.

"This is an injustice to the families as well as the taxpayers who waste millions of dollars on inmate upkeep," he said. "Many of the inmates live better in the prison system than on the streets," he said, and get free health care and other benefits that the average citizen does not.

For one thing, lawmakers should limit appeals to three years, Brock said.

Yet, for all the frustrating delays in Henyard's case, today, judges and lawyers in the Lake County courthouse have a feeling that because of the heinous nature of the crime, Henyard was put on a "fast track" for execution.

Circuit Judge G. Richard Singletary of Lake County recalls going with his old boss, former State Attorney Gordon Oldham, to the Attorney General's office in Tallahassee one day. There on the wall were pictures of every death row inmate and a description of their crimes.

Singletary studied the pictures, at first deciding that the heinous facts from Lake County's Freddie Lee Hall's case made him the most eligible for execution.

Karol Lea Hurst, 21, was seven months pregnant when she was carjacked from a Lake County grocery store parking lot in broad daylight. Like Dorothy, she had been assured by her two captors that she would not be harmed.

After pleading for the life of her unborn child, she even wrote them a check after they promised to leave her alone, but the two assaulted and killed her and the unborn baby girl. Later, they would kill a sheriff's deputy before they would be caught.

Yet, when Singletary looked at Henyard's profile, he remembers thinking, "No, this is the one."

There must be a system, lawyers speculate, where the governor calls up the AG's office and says, "which is the worst one?" He then signs a death warrant for that person.

The Florida Department of Corrections states that the average stay on death row is about 14 years, which is about what Henyard's was. Many, like Hall, whose case is complicated by the fact that he is arguably retarded and mentally ill, have been on death row a lot longer. He has been on death row off and on since 1968, making him one of the longest-term residents. There are almost 400 people on death row in Florida.

Delays can be torture for the victims' families.

"I felt some kind of pressure that was stressful," Dorothy said of the news reports that came up every time there was an appeal and when the execution date finally loomed.

It also affected Joshua.

He became angry when "they started bringing everything up," he said of the reporters and their stories.

"I got mad because I'd see her crying. That hurt, watching her cry every day. That hurt," he said.

"I would hug her .... Most of the time I couldn't say anything. I was speechless. She had always been so strong. Seeing her cry was different," he said.

"I dodged reporters," Dorothy said, not just those who called but some who showed up at her school.

"I really wanted to be left alone," she said.

"When something was in the news it would kind of rehash that feeling of loss again, and bring everything back up," she said.

"I prayed my way through that."

CHAPTER 11

Forgiveness

Tucked in among the many lessons of Job—including the fact that suffering can teach us so much about God's grace and mercy—is the lesson of forgiveness. The theme not only is prevalent in Job, but it runs throughout the Bible. In fact, it could be argued that it is THE theme.

Yet, forgiveness is one of the least understood, hardest to do and most resisted acts in Christianity.

Looking from the outside in, for example, one asks: How can Dorothy and her family possibly forgive those who committed these monstrous crimes against her and her children?

The crimes are the most ruthless, self-centered, outrageous and compassionless acts imaginable—and neither man asked for forgiveness or showed any remorse. Yet, Dorothy and her family not only say that they forgive Henyard and Smalls, they mean it.

"As Christians we have to forgive individuals and love the person but we don't condone the behavior," Brock points out—an important distinction.

"You don't forget. To do what they did leaves a mark that is not forgotten—not only on her [Dorothy] but on everyone associated with the case."

Law enforcement officers were among those affected the most.

Bud Hart still thinks about Dorothy every day.

"I still keep a picture of Dorothy and her two girls in my office, wherever my office is," he said.

"I wanted to change the road name, put up a memorial or a park. I started to put up a sign a year later but I was afraid I would get in trouble," he said.

Hart's captain, Carmine Aurigemma, for years kept a small wooden model of Florida's "Old Sparky" electric chair in his office next to a picture of Henyard. He is now retired from the Eustis Police Department.

Dr. Harold noted in his deposition that he and Margaret had been co-workers for 11 years.

"I had a nephew murdered a couple of weeks after that, I think, February 12, or something like that. So we cry on each other's shoulders and talk about the investigations and the trials," Harold said.

Of course, the family is the hardest hit.

Rosalyn Lewis was still mourning the loss of her son to meningitis three years earlier, when suddenly she lost her two granddaughters.

Dorothy and the girls had just visited her in New Jersey a few months earlier, a memory she cherishes to this day.

"I forgave them," she said of Henyard and Smalls, "but I don't forget." The retired seamstress couldn't forget, even if she wanted to. Years after the slayings, people who have forgotten or who don't make the connection somehow still ask about her grandchildren in Florida.

She calmly tells them that her former daughter-in-law is still alive but that the girls passed away.

Despite the hurt, she chooses not to be bitter.

"I don't let it upset my world. I still have other children to be concerned about," she said. She still talks on the phone to Dorothy and visits her in Florida. "Mama Lewis," as she is known, has embraced Dorothy's new family. After all, she says, Dorothy has always been like a daughter to her.

But the loss of Jamilya and Jasmine has been hard to take.

"We don't have many girls in our family," she said. She has two surviving sons and one daughter. She had six grandchildren but Jasmine and Jamilya were the only girls.

Two of Rosalyn's sisters have died in recent years, and last year she lost a niece to cancer. She has three great-grandchildren, however, and two of them are girls.

"I try to keep my family close. I reach out to them," she said.

And while she has managed to forgive her granddaughters' killers, she acknowledged that, "it was really hard."

"It's been a year since the older boy was executed. I'm just happy that he paid the price."

But she is unhappy that Smalls will never pay the ultimate penalty. It could have been a kind of finality to the tragedy that has eluded her, and always will. It would have made the forgiving easier, she said.

"I'm not trying to be mean or anything, but if you take a life, you should pay the price."

Mrs. Lewis also attended both trials.

"It wasn't good," she said of the stress, especially when they showed pictures of her granddaughters tossed over the high shrubs. But she was determined to stand in the gap for her grandchildren.

"But I placed myself on the right-hand side [of the courtroom] so I could see right into his face," she said of both Henyard and Smalls.

Dorothy's godmother, Emma, was furious at Smalls and Henyard during their trials.

"I wanted to get up and kill them," she said. "They were trying to act like they were good."

She also wasn't buying into the idea that they committed the crimes, at least in part, because they didn't have strong father figures in their lives.

"You do what you do because you want to do it," she said.

But she also acknowledged that at some point you have to relieve yourself of the anger.

"You can't go around with bitterness in your heart. They needed to ask God to forgive them and I pray that they did," she said. "If God can forgive them, who can hold on to it?"

Some people can hold on to it, however, but to their detriment.

A man whose girlfriend was shot to death during a bank robbery in Lake County a few years ago could be seen seething with rage in the courtroom where the defendant was on trial. Anger was etched on his face. He seemed to live for the chance at revenge, which, of course, would never happen, not at his hands, anyway. At one point, he stormed out of the courtroom when the killer tried to show he was a God-fearing Christian by breaking into song while on the witness stand, singing a hymn about mercy.

The man's anger was understandable. It was one of the most over-the-top performances by a defendant in any courtroom, anywhere.

But a man at a courtroom defense table could care less if people are angry or not. He is not being harmed, or affected at all. They rarely show true remorse, other than the fact that they regret getting caught. If a family member's guts are boiling with rage, it only hurts the person who is angry.

The stress on family members sitting in a courtroom and watching the wheels of justice turn slow takes its toll on the human body even if a person is not angry. It's not like a TV show, with dark mahogany paneling and a wisdom-of-Solomon judge on the bench in good lighting. You can hear empty stomachs churning with acid, see people rush to restrooms during breaks and see chain smokers puffing away outside over growing mounds of cigarette butts. Courthouses could probably supplement their costs by selling tissues to dry up all the tears.

"The trial was like reliving everything all over again," said Ozietta. "And you're seeing one individual and not being able to go up there and hurt him. To hear the testimony, some of the things I couldn't hear. I got up and left quite a bit."

It is stressful. That's why armed bailiffs are in the courtroom, not just to keep an eye on the defendant, but to patrol the narrow aisle dividing the families of defendants and the victim's family.

Sometimes the powder keg explodes. In the Kayla McKean murder trial, spectators and jurors were terrified when a man who had wanted to adopt the child took a running leap at the courtroom door from the hallway. He nearly broke down the locked, heavy, wooden doors after hearing his wife break down in tears after testifying on the witness stand. Had he been able to reach the killer, there would have been another murder trial. As it was, bailiffs tried to calm him but ended up having to handcuff him and place him under arrest.

Sometimes corrosive anger lingers for years, threatening the very fabric of the soul.

In 1998, Karol Lea Hurst's family observed the twentieth anniversary of her death, and were still waiting for the execution of her killer, Freddie Lee Hall. The appellate courts did everything possible to keep him alive, it seemed. An interview in *The Orlando Sentinel* showed that the delayed justice had taken its toll on family.

One brother of the slain woman said it was as if the family had been punished for 20 years—not the killer, who is still on death row (his accomplice had his sentence commuted to life). One of the victim's sisters confessed that she could not take communion at her church because she was bitter and could not forgive him.

They are understandable feelings and a justifiable slam of the criminal justice system, but it was especially tragic for the family. That was over a decade ago. One can only pray that the family has found the peace of God that comes from asking Christ to help you forgive. We can't do it on our own. It is so against human nature that we have to ask God for His help. He understands that, however. That's why He has left us with the Holy Spirit to guide us.

And it is another example of why we cannot rely on the state to provide swift justice. Apparently, Hall will die of natural causes in prison—perhaps years for now.

Margaret, like Emma, was also seething during the trials.

"Dorothy is the epitome of a Christian," Margaret said. "[But] I was angry. I wanted all three (Yon included) dead."

She was also angry at having to adhere to the prosecutors' orders for the family to keep emotions in check.

"It was so unfair to us," she said, but she and others went along with it because they did not want to do anything to jeopardize the state's chance for conviction or risk a mistrial and having to start all over again.

"She couldn't have taken that," Margaret said.

"But I wanted to choke that boy," she added. "I've come a long way. I have put it behind me," she said, referring specifically to Smalls. As for Henyard, she jokes grimly and says: "He's dead. I might as well forgive him."

Arthur Gene also knows that forgiveness is the only way.

"I was always taught not to hold a grudge against anyone," he said, but in a soft, deep, brooding voice adds: "I would have liked to have driven up at that time in the parking lot and asked them what they thought they were doing."

James Reid takes it a step farther.

"It was a heart-breaker. If I had run up on them they wouldn't have had to have a trial."

Reid, who says he believes in God and goes to church, though not as regularly as other family members, has not been able to forgive like Dorothy, Arthur Gene and others.

"I couldn't forgive them. I don't have no forgiveness in my heart now. They took those two babies' lives and hurt my sister."

Maybe one day, he says, "something will turn my heart around." Yet, he recognizes the power of what Dorothy calls "spiritual surgery" in her life.

"She grew stronger. For somebody to be able to do that, it makes my problems look minor," he said.

"For her not to curse God, to still believe in her faith. She's a very strong young lady. I couldn't say I wouldn't lose my mind."

Ozietta has come to terms with it.

"I've forgiven them at this point in my life. It didn't come easy. Even after I gave my life back to the Lord," she said.

"Dorothy did it right off. She forgave them and prayed for them. It probably took me at least five years to forgive them," Ozietta said.

"This kind of thing stays at the forefront of your mind. Sometimes it's still like that."

Ozietta prayed that she would be able to forgive.

"Just take this anger away," she prayed. "I knew I couldn't be the kind of woman of God I needed to be [without forgiveness]."

Dorothy and her family also learned that, like Job, sometimes you have to forgive those who are supposedly showing up to comfort you.

Of course, you have to wonder what the real motivation was for the prison inmate who wrote to suggest that she was suffering because she had bad karma, that she had done something really bad in a past life. There is no part of Christianity that recognizes such a concept.

Then there was the man who asked Greta why Dorothy got into the car, when her children were already in the car.

Call it blaming the victim, but it is almost an example of the kind of thing that Job's friends did, the implication being that she had done something wrong and deserved to be punished with horrible suffering.

Dorothy and her family know that they are commanded to forgive in such scripture as Colossians 3:13, which reads: "Bear with each other and forgive whatever grievances you may have against one another. Forgive as the Lord forgave you" (NIV).

The commandment was important enough that Christ felt it should be included in His "Lord's Prayer," saying in Matthew 6:12: "Forgive us our debts, as we also have forgiven our debtors."

He was even more blunt in verses 14-15, adding: "For if you forgive men when they sin against you, your heavenly Father will also forgive you. But if you do not forgive men their sins, your Father will not forgive your sins" (NIV).

Jesus drives home the point very clearly, as only He could do, in Matthew 18:21-35 (NIV), in The Parable of the Unmerciful Servant:

> 21 Then Peter came to Jesus and asked, "Lord, how many times shall I forgive my brother when he sins against me? Up to seven times?" 22 Jesus answered, "I tell you, not seven times, but seventy-seven times. 23 "Therefore, the kingdom of heaven is like a king who wanted to settle accounts with his servants. 24 As he began the settlement, a man who owed him ten thousand talents was brought to him. 25 Since he was not able to pay, the master ordered that he and his wife and his children and all that he had be sold to repay the debt. 26 "The servant fell on his knees before him. 'Be patient with me,' he begged, 'and I will pay back everything.' 27 The servant's master took pity on him, canceled the debt and let him go. 28 "But when that servant went out, he found one of his fellow servants who owed him a hundred denarii. He grabbed him and began to choke him. 'Pay back what you owe me!' he

demanded. 29 His fellow servant fell to his knees and begged him, 'Be patient with me, and I will pay you back.' 30 "But he refused. Instead, he went off and had the man thrown into prison until he could pay the debt. 31 When the other servants saw what had happened, they were greatly distressed and went and told their master everything that had happened. 32 "Then the master called the servant in. 'You wicked servant,' he said, 'I canceled all that debt of yours because you begged me to. 33 Shouldn't you have had mercy on your fellow servant just as I had on you?' 34 In anger his master turned him over to the jailers to be tortured, until he should pay back all he owed. 35 "This is how my heavenly Father will treat each of you unless you forgive your brother from your heart."

Dorothy first learned the lessons of forgiveness from her mother's kitchen table lessons. One of Elsie's favorite Bible verses was Ephesians 4:32, which in the NIV reads: "Be kind and compassionate to one another, forgiving each other, just as in Christ God forgave you."

Dorothy cites the Lord's Prayer as one of the key reasons that she forgives.

"I had to. Jesus taught his disciples to forgive…" she said. "I knew that I had to give forgiveness to go onto the next level. If my heart was full of hate how could I witness?"

And what a witness she has been.

"It was the worst case I was ever involved in," said Pat Kicklighter, the 30-year lawman who was the investigator with the State Attorney's Office.

Like most real investigators, he probably wouldn't make the casting call for a bruising movie detective. Pat, with his glasses, dry, gentle teasing wit and ready smile, looks more like a high school math teacher, which is fitting in a way, since he has spent his professional life trying to be as exacting and precise as possible. But he also has a big heart, and because he lives near Dorothy's mother and

746743

would frequently drive by on his way home, he said, "I would think about that entire situation again."

At the crime scene on that terrible day, a reporter asked Kicklighter and Gross why it took Dorothy several hours to walk from the spot where she was shot to the house where she asked for help. Gross said Kicklighter didn't say anything to the reporter, but after he left, Kicklighter showed an unusual flash of anger and said under his breath, "It would take you a long time, too, if you'd been shot four times."

Kicklighter wondered how he and his family would react if struck by a similar tragedy.

"They had just the most unbelievable strength. It made me so proud to help work on the case," he said.

He knew that their strength came from God.

"It was not new to me to go to church," Kicklighter said. He had grown up in the First Baptist Church of Umatilla. As a child, sometimes he and all five of his siblings would sing in the choir.

Kicklighter's daughter, Cindy Brown, also grew up in the church, but notes that sometimes it was more important for the children to go to church and Sunday school than it was for her father. Sometimes Dad's job interfered with his attendance. Or if it was a difference between doing a chore or going to church, the chore might take precedence, she said.

But the murder of the two young children, and the many trips to the hospital to see Dorothy affected him in ways he could not have predicted.

"My dad is not a talkative person, so when he says something you listen," Brown said. But he talked even less while the case was still under investigation.

"You could tell when he got home, it was quiet," she said.

Years later he studiously followed the progress of Henyard's appeals until they finally ran out, then he watched and read news accounts of the execution.

Dorothy's willingness to forgive helped Kicklighter and others develop a deeper faith. He became ordained as a deacon and was a regular in the choir.

His faith has also deepened his compassion for others.

"I always wanted to help people," Kicklighter said.

Ironically, Cindy had never met Dorothy until recently. Doubtful that it was the same Dorothy, she said, "My dad knew a Dorothy Lewis and he adored her."

"Who's your dad?" Dorothy asked.

Once Cindy realized it was the woman she had heard so much about so long ago, Cindy hugged her and said, "You've really inspired me."

"My father was dealing with the worst case of his life," Brown said. "She inspired people to do the best they can and to seek the guidance of God."

If Jesus is our role model—and He is for Dorothy; if we are truly Christians, for us too—how can we not forgive?

The alternative is unacceptable: bitterness and cynicism, hallmarks of police squad cars, newsrooms and courthouses. Even worse is revenge, and the world's and eternal judgment that that brings.

Sometimes non-Christians can even shame us into forgiving by their example.

Benny Demps, the condemned killer who claimed he was innocent in the killing of a fellow prisoner, had criticized Florida Gov. Jeb Bush for signing his death warrant. But the converted Muslim believer used some of his last words to refer to Bush, saying: "I forgive you. I leave this world hating no man. I have no malice to anyone. I leave in peace."

Paul said it in a way that would turn the world upside down if Christians acted on what he said in Romans 12:17-21: "Do not repay anyone evil for evil. Be careful to do what is right in the eyes of everybody. If it is possible, as far as it depends on you, live at peace with everyone. Do not take revenge, my friends, but leave room for

God's wrath, for it is written: 'It is mine to avenge; I will repay,' says the Lord. On the contrary: 'If your enemy is hungry, feed him; if he is thirsty, give him something to drink. In doing this, you will heap burning coals on his head.' Do not be overcome by evil, but overcome evil with good" (NIV).

Chester Wood, in his excellent workbook on anger management, *Hurt People Hurt People,* notes: "Forgiving the offender does not mean what was done is OK. It does not mean the offender should not be held accountable. It does not mean you will allow repeated offenses to occur. It does not mean you are wrong to be angry about what has occurred. It does not mean you have to pretend it never happened, that your life was not affected; the consequences resulting from the incident have to be dealt with" (p. 61). He also writes: "Without forgiveness the offender may continue to control the life of the offended one" (p. 62). The responsibility has to be shifted to the one who is causing the hurt, he said.

It also does not mean that the offender should not be punished. Karla Faye Tucker, who died in 1998, was the first woman executed in Texas since the Civil War. Petite and attractive, her execution created a storm of controversy because she had become a born-again Christian after killing two people with a pickax during a break-in in 1983.

Sure, the state was exacting its retribution, but what about forgiveness and redemption, some members of the public wondered?

In an interview with Larry King on CNN, King noted with surprise that with the clock ticking down, she remained upbeat.

"You have to explain that to me a little more. It can't just be God?" he said.

"Yes, it can. It's called the joy of the Lord," she said. "I don't—when you have done something that I have done, like what I have done, and you have been forgiven for it, and you're loved, that has a way of so changing you. I mean, I have experienced real love. I know what real love is. I know what forgiveness is, even when I did something so horrible. I know that because God forgave me and I accepted what Jesus did on the cross. When I leave here, I am going to go be with Him" (*http//:edition.cnn.com/2007/larry.king.tucker/index.htm*).

Again, if our role model, Jesus Christ, can forgive, we can too, if we rely on the Holy Spirit to help guide us. After all, it was Jesus in His last moments on earth who said, "Father forgive them, for they do not know what they are doing" (Luke 23:34 NIV).

He said this, not during a theological debate or during some minor crisis, but while His executioners were hanging Him on a cross.

It was because of this sacrifice that we can spend eternal life with Him. Can we, then, be less forgiving?

Jamilya and Jasmine at 3 years and 3 months.

Jasmine, Dorothy, and Jamilya on Easter 1992.

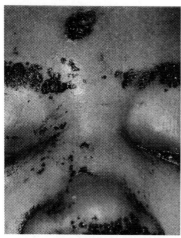

Dorothy was shot four times, including a bullet in her forehead.

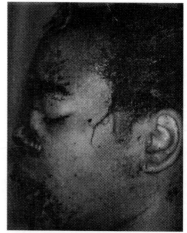

Dorothy Lewis after the brutal murder attempt.

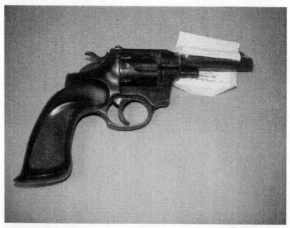

The murder weapon was a nine-shot .22 revolver, which was found in Smalls' house under a chair.

When a detective noticed blood on Henyard's shoes, he replied, "How you know that ain't no ketchup stain?"

Prosecutors used a large aerial map to show the location of sites in the crime. The top marker shows where Dorothy walked for help.

Prosecutor Brad King prays with Dorothy, her sister, and their mother after the hearing. Used with permission of the *Orlando Sentinel*.

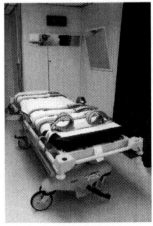

Gurney at Florida State Prison in Starke where Henyard was killed by lethal injection.

Dorothy and husband Hugh celebrating life with their son Joshua on his 5th birthday.

CHAPTER 12

Dorothy: On Peace

I have heard the word *peace* described as the absence of mental stress or anxiety.

But how do we get that kind of peace?

The Bible says that if we keep our minds focused on the Lord, He will keep us in perfect peace.

Isaiah 26:3 from the Message Bible says: "People with their minds set on you, you keep completely whole, steady on their feet, because they keep at it and don't quit."

I have been able to have a mind of peace because I continue to stay focused on the goodness of the Lord.

Jesus said in John 14:27, "Peace I leave with you. My peace I give to you; not as the world gives do I give to you. Let not your heart be troubled, neither let it be afraid" (NKJV).

In John 16:33, He said: "I have told you these things, so that in me you may have peace. In this world you will have trouble. But take heart! I have overcome the world" (NIV).

If you have suffered in a terrible crisis, it doesn't mean that life has to come to an end. It's natural to think that you can't go on, or that there's no longer any purpose in your life, but that's the time you need to use all of your willpower to take action, in order to keep from having a nervous breakdown.

Your purpose is not just to fight to keep from having a nervous breakdown, of course. Your purpose is to live during these difficult, painful times, and to let the God in you be glorified.

You might think, "I don't know God, and how can God live in me?" The Bible lets us know that God is spirit, God is love, God is omnipotent, and He is all-powerful. It also teaches us that man was created in the image of God (John 4:24, 1 John 4:8, Revelation 19:6, Genesis 1:26). Therefore, man is a spiritual being. Man inhabits a body, but he has a soul. Because he is equipped with the spirit, he has the power within him to live through any crisis.

Think about how powerful God is, then know that the same power is within you and you begin to be alive.

After knowing who God is, and knowing that the spirit and power of God is within you, begin to speak encouraging words to yourself, to your spirit. Words such as, "I can do everything through him who gives me strength" (Philippians 4:13, NIV).

Also, "I've got the power! I can continue to live, to exist, despite this emotional and traumatic change that has happened in my life."

Romans 8:37 reads, "Yet in all these things we are more than conquerors through Him who loved us" (NKJV).

The Greek word for conqueror is *hupernikao* (hoop-er-nik-ah-oh). It's from *huper,* "over and above," and *nikao,* "to conquer" (*Strong's Concordance,* No. 5245). The word describes one who is super victorious, who wins more than an ordinary victory, who is overpowering in achieving abundant victory. This is not the language of conceit, but of confidence. Christ's love conquered death, and because of His love, we are *hupernikao.*

So, tell yourself that you're not just victorious, but you're super victorious, and you're overpowering in achieving abundant victory. Tell yourself that you're not going to let your crisis defeat you, but you will defeat your crisis. Tell yourself that you will live and not die during these difficult times. Speaking words of this magnitude will motivate and encourage you to believe in yourself, and to trust in the power that the Almighty God has given unto you. To God be the glory for the things he has done!

No one is exempt from trials and tribulations, but we can choose how we will deal with the traumatic changes.

I'm sure you have heard the saying, "When given a lemon, make lemonade." When you feel as though life has given you a lemon, you have the choice to remain bitter, or the choice to make lemonade. Your attitude will determine whether anything good can come from the challenges you face. You can decide if you want to be hateful or loving, fearful or faithful, depressed or hopeful. It's your choice.

Because God is love, I recommend love over hate. Having hatred in your heart will just make matters worse for you and those who are around you. Choose faith over fear because God didn't give you the spirit of fear. He gave you the spirit of love, power, a sound mind, and He gave you a measure of faith. Choose hope over being depressed. As long as God is alive—which is forever—there is always hope to overcome your situation.

The Word of God says, "We often suffer, but we are never crushed. Even when we don't know what to do, we never give up. In times of trouble, God is with us, and when we are knocked down, we get up again" (2 Corinthians 4:8-9 CEV).

God is the only one who can give me the peace that I need to guard my heart from being troubled or afraid. I found out the more I study God's Word, the more I become transformed by the renewing of my mind. It was the Word of God that helped me to be free from hostility and obtain peace.

I had to guard my heart from evil thoughts and to keep thinking about the goodness of Jesus. Being able to keep your mind on the Lord will allow Him to keep you in His perfect peace (Isaiah 26:3).

It is so important not to continue to feel sorry for yourself, but to think about ways your story could help someone else.

It gave me great joy to know that my testimony was helping so many others.

The peace of God is within you.

My mind continues to be changed and restored to think differently, to consider the attributes of Jesus.

Being transformed helps me to understand that I have to forgive my trespassers in order for God to forgive me.

Having this kind of peace makes it less complicated to forgive those who have wronged you.

This kind of peace will help you pray for your enemies like Jesus did in Luke 23:34 when He said: "… Father forgive them for they know not what they do" (NKJV).

This kind of peace is beyond the nonbelievers' way of thinking; they just can't understand how you can forgive someone who has hurt you so badly.

But God's peace goes beyond anything we can imagine. The peace of God will guard our hearts and emotions. I try to keep my mind focused on Jesus as much as possible so that His peace will stand guard over me.

Our emotions begin in our hearts then filter into our minds. Once our minds become cluttered with negative thoughts, we become double-minded and unstable.

That's how the enemy wants us to be, but I refuse to let Satan use my mind for his battlefield. I will not dwell on things that are not good. If we would allow ourselves to have the same mind in us that was in Christ Jesus, we would be able to operate more like our Heavenly Father.

Colossians 3:15-17 in the Message Bible perhaps says it best: "Let the peace of Christ keep you in tune with each other, in step with each other. None of this going off and doing your own thing. And cultivate thankfulness. Let the Word of Christ—the Message—have the run of the house. Give it plenty of room in your lives. Instruct and direct one another using good common sense. And sing, sing your hearts out to God! Let every detail in your lives—words, actions, whatever—be done in the name of the Master, Jesus, thanking God the Father every step of the way."

I can truly say that the love and peace of God has protected me. Our trials and tribulations come to make us strong. Because I was considered, like Job, I am stronger, and wiser.

January 30, 1993 was a horrible night. It was a shocking night, but there were a lot of good things that happened as a result of that one bad night.

The power of God was being exalted, and souls were saved.

When people look at me, they see a living miracle and God is being glorified.

I have a wonderful husband.

I gave natural birth to an amazing son.

I'm the stepmother of three children.

I assist my husband in pastoring our church, New Directions Family Worship Center. I am a much stronger, bolder, and wiser servant for the Lord.

Any way that you look at it; the good outweighs the bad. The evil that the devil thought that he would use to kill, God used instead, with my testimony, to display His grace.

And that's something really good!

There's not a day that goes by that I don't think of my girls. I love them and I will always love them. I celebrate their lives. I rejoice over the life they had here on earth and the eternal life they now have with the Lord God Almighty.

It feels as though my internal organs are being ripped out whenever I think about how Jamilya and Jasmine must have been terrified with fear that night.

No doubt, they saw everything. I had two helpless girls crying for their mommy to help them, and where was I? In the bushes, shot and left for dead.

Here I was thinking that I did the right thing to try to protect my babies, by doing what I was told to do.

That mistake cost me dearly. I did put up a fight, but I waited too late.

I hate the way Jamilya and Jasmine died. I hate that I couldn't save them. The only good thing about their physical death is that they will never, ever suffer gain.

I have to continue to dwell on the good and not the bad.

Philippians 4:8 says: "Finally, brethren, whatever things are true, whatever things are noble, whatever things are just, whatever things are pure, whatever things are lovely, whatever things are of good report, if there is any virtue and if there is anything praiseworthy— meditate on these things" (NKJV).

Amen.

Citations

Copeland, Mark A. (*http://executableoutlines.com/job.htm*).

Jordan-Spitz, Jill. "Lewis recounts night of attack in an emotion-packed courtroom." *The Orlando Sentinel* (June 1, 1994).

Kushner, Harold S. "When Bad Things Happen to Good People" (New York: Schocken Books, 1981).

Life Application Study Bible, New International Version (Grand Rapids, MI: Zondervan, 1991).

Peterson, Eugene. *The Message Bible,* Numbered Edition (Colorado Springs: NavPress Publishing Group, 2005).

"The Simpsons." "Rednecks and Broomsticks" (Fox Broadcasting Co., 2009).

Strobel, Lee. "The Case for Faith: A Journalist Investigates the Toughest Objections to Christianity" (Grand Rapids, MI: Zondervan, 2000).

Wood, Chester W. "Hurt People Hurt People" (Longwood, FL: Xulon Press, 2008).